The Vixen Manual

The Vixen Manual

HOW TO FIND, SEDUCE, & KEEP THE MAN YOU WANT

Karrine Steffans

GRAND CENTRAL
PUBLISHING

NEW YORK   BOSTON

Grand Central Publishing
Hachette Book Group
237 Park Avenue
New York, NY 10017

Visit our Web site at www.HachetteBookGroup.com.

Printed in the United States of America

First Edition: July 2009
10 9 8 7 6 5 4 3 2 1

Grand Central Publishing is a division of Hachette Book Group, Inc.
The Grand Central Publishing name and logo is a trademark of Hachette Book Group, Inc.

Library of Congress Cataloging-in-Publication Data

Steffans, Karrine
The vixen manual/Karrine Steffans. – 1st Ed.
  p. cm.
ISBN 978-0-446-58227-8
1. Man-woman relationships – Handbooks, manuals, etc. I. Title.

HQ801.S7944 2009
646.7'7082–dc22

2008030402

Book Design & Composition by Mada Design, Inc.
Illustrations by Giorgetta Bell McRee

This book is dedicated to

My Husband.

It takes one hell of a man to tame a vixen

and one hell of a vixen to let him.

Acknowledgments

What a ride it's been, and even though this journey began with the help of a multitude of individuals by my side, it has continued with far more less company than during its origin.

Lolita, thank you for helping *The Vixen Manual* become exactly what I imagined it to be.

Karen and Jamie, thank you for your support and confidence in me. I only hope I have made Grand Central proud.

Jeff, you're a pit bull of an attorney. One day, I'll let you go crazy, I swear. Thanks for pulling it all together.

Naiim, thanks for being the best kid ever who lets Mommy work and for making me sandwiches when I was too busy to feed myself. It's all for you.

Contents

Preface

Who Died and Made You an Expert?

Before there was *The Vixen Diaries*, even before *Confessions of a Video Vixen*, there was *The Vixen Manual*. I began writing this book in late 2004 and over time continued adding to its pages. I would have to continuously reread my chapters over the years and change most everything I'd written. My chapters kept changing because I kept changing. My, how I have grown since penning that first chapter way back then, and I am astounded at how much more of a metamorphosis there is left. Still, along the way, between all my torrid affairs and boomerang boyfriends, I have been given undeniably relevant and accurate advice and examples pertaining to the relationships between men and women.

Ironically, a lot of the information in this book comes from my very own trial and error. It is rare that we learn from people's perfect achievements and more common that we learn from one another's mistakes. In putting together the sections in *The Vixen Manual*, I often referred back to my own misgivings, misjudgments, and ill-fated maneuvers. I thought of all the advice I'd heard but not listened to from my elders, women and men who knew more of life and love than I, and in the midst of organizing the book's pages I took heed to it all and finally applied it to my life.

As I continued penning this manual, however, I could imagine the sneers and snickers of those who have read my previous works, countless interviews, and Internet blogs. Some people would be well within their rights to question my ability or qualifications to give advice of any kind, much less that which pertains to the improvement of female behavior and the guidelines of healthy male-female relationships. Who the hell do I think I am?

I am most certainly no expert, nor am I a saint. Millions of readers know I have never been a woman to walk the straight and narrow, for I am always searching for my own path and reasoning. But that very refusal to fall into what is seen as society's definition of the norm is exactly what qualifies me to, at the very least, share with you what I have learned thus far.

None of us is all-knowing nor immune, not even those who have dedicated their lives to the study of human behavior and relationships and have been honored with degrees for their years of collegiate commitment. They too suffer from esteem and relationship woes. The truth, however, is that we are all experts about *our* own lives, and we all have stories to share and advice to pass along. Sadly, we rarely follow our own counsel but give it freely in hopes that someone will make proper use of it. You can say this is my advice to you, but, mostly, this manual is just a conversation between us girls—and even you, fellas! It is a compilation of things I have learned combined with experienced direction from those much older and much wiser than I am. I have followed some of the advice within these pages, and some I am still trying to learn and adhere to. Trust me, I too am reading along with you.

One old adage comes to mind: "Do as I say and not as I do." I never understood what it meant when adults hurled it toward me as a child, but now it all makes sense to me. Making mistakes is a natural part of the human experience. It's not unusual for all those clever little sayings that never made much sense when we were young to make a world of difference as we grow older and, hopefully, a bit wiser. Life isn't about who's coming to the party but who will be there to help you pick up the pieces when all the guests are gone. There is so much promise in all of us and, as I entered my third decade of life, I yearned for more in some areas and for less in others. More than anything, I yearned to live up to my promise. After all the wild nights and endless days, after all the people, places, and things I'd encountered and experienced, I wanted to fall in love and I wanted to fall for someone who would fall for me. Most pertinent, I wanted to be worthy of it all. You see, ladies, it doesn't matter where you've been, but it does matter what you've learned while you were there. There's nothing wrong with going to the party, but there is something very wrong with staying too long. Somewhere in my twenties, I realized I had overstayed my welcome.

At some point in our lives, we have to get serious about our futures and about our relationships. Being young and reckless is never attractive, though we've convinced ourselves that it is. Being available to and sexually irresponsible with miscellaneous males is definitely undesirable, to say the least. Somehow, we've been duped into believing that just because we can have whomever we choose that we have to exercise that right. Women, I implore you—do not do as I have done in the past. In this instance, please consider what I have to say now that the party is over. Laurel Thatcher Ulrich contributed an empowering slogan in a 1976 printing of *American Quarterly*: "Well-behaved women seldom make history." Well, like my memoirs, *The Vixen Manual* is a piece of my history—the history of a woman maybe less well-behaved than some but also maybe more learned in life and love's faux pas. Contrary to what some of you may have expected, *The Vixen Manual* isn't about how to please every man, but how to be worthy of just one—the right one—by way of finding peace and pleasure in ourselves. Aside from that, it's just plain, good old-fashioned girl talk. I hope you enjoy.

Section 1

Being Single

This is how you start, as a single woman looking for a life

and, eventually, a life mate. At first it is exhilarating, and then

one day it becomes exhausting and you long for more.

But until that day, there is a lot to consider.

Chapter One

Single vs. Singular

So you're a single girl. You're Mary Tyler Moore, throwing your hat up into the air, thinking you're gonna make it after all. Maybe you're Laverne (or Shirley), skipping down the sidewalk, determined to make your dreams come true…doing it your way. Hell, maybe you're even Samantha Jones, the outspoken PR maven and sexual libertine from *Sex and the City*, sleeping with every available man, and occasional woman, who crosses your path. Whatever the case, honey, you're *single*, and no matter what your theme song is, it has the potential to suck.

Odds are you're also *singular*, which is pretty easy to be when you're not in a relationship. You define yourself by setting your own boundaries, doing what you want whenever you want, mistress of all you survey within your domain. There's no one to answer to, no feelings to consider. When a relationship enters the picture, however, it has the potential to change everything, including the singular dynamic. It becomes much more difficult—at times, nearly impossible—to focus only on yourself, but that doesn't mean you have to give up your identity. One of the primary keys to a healthy relationship is for both of you, though no longer single, to remain singular. There's a fine line between being *in* a relationship and being *absorbed* by one, and that's what will happen if you're not sure of yourself as an individual first.

As a nurturer, I have the tendency to covet and consume my mates. For most of my life, I have believed in the now-comical mantra, *You complete me*. So there I was, looking for a man to complete me, giving him all of me in the hopes he would return the favor and make his every waking breath my own. With each boyfriend, I wanted to go where he went and do what he did, and I would make myself available day and night, without compromise. In one of my more intense relationships, I even canceled sections of my first book tour to follow my lover as he traveled the country. I was a no-show at Temple University and several other prestigious higher learning establishments, skipping speaking engagements just to be "completed" by him. He was a nocturnal creature and, though I cherished my sleep, I would force myself to stay awake in the wee hours of the morning to be with him, forsaking rest and comfort. I would hop atop his kitchen counter at four in the morning as he juiced fresh, organic vegetables and fruits and would never share in the nectar. I'd watch him drink. I just wanted to be near him. I just wanted to be "completed."

I lost myself in him and, ironically, began to resent him because he had his own life and I didn't! He didn't complete me after all! We even made a funny little saying that wound up not being the slightest bit funny: "You deplete me." That, ladies, is the sum of all parts when you cease being a singular individual before, and especially after, you are no longer single.

Vixen Tip

For me, it's always been difficult to not become absorbed by my relationship. It takes an enormous amount of effort to stay on track and to live my life as if there weren't this hunky piece of man flesh laying in my bed just begging to be ravished. The only way to keep on track is to write out a schedule and stick to it every day, no matter how difficult it may be to leave his side. Make certain things rituals; wake up, make the bed, take the kids to school, go for a walk, shower, and head to the office. For those of us who work at home, it is twice as difficult to concentrate, which makes having a schedule even more important. What has worked for me is to save most of the personal time for after business hours, after I have completed everything on my list for the day, everything from tidying the house to running an office. Take care of yourself first and, trust me, he'll be there when you're done. But, to ensure this, make sure you don't become so *self*-absorbed that you forget to schedule lots of time for him, as well.

Of course, being a single woman can be fun, especially when it's done on your own terms. There's something very fulfilling about not needing a man to buy your drinks, take you shopping, and show you a good time. Still, even in your singleness, you can find yourself not being your own person, a singular woman. You may look for others to validate you by making you feel pretty, worthy, smart, or desirable. These are the feelings that should come from within. There's an old saying along the lines of "If you don't go within, you go without." Giving others the ability to define how you view yourself means you've surrendered your power. By expecting others to give you what you need—dignity, pride, self-esteem, confidence—you become a hostage, subject to their whims and insecurities. You must learn to mine your own strengths, which you already possess in great abundance.

> **Vixen Say What?**
> Too many cooks spoil the pot. (Thanks Grandma!)

If you're the type of woman who can't bear the idea of leaving the house without being in the company of a gaggle of girlfriends, you're not a singular individual. Men are attracted to a woman's independence and strength. There's nothing more magnetic to a man than seeing a woman confidently strutting by with a sense of purpose, not checking for who's checking her out, because she's apparently got somewhere to be, something to do—something that matters. It's hard for a potential mate to see who you are when you're lost in a cacophony of women, all of you laughing and huddling and talking over each other. This may seem communal and fun, even necessary at certain times, but make no mistake—it is not attractive, especially when your objective is to be viewed as an individual.

Eventually, most of us women tire of being single, always hanging out with the girls, meeting up for margaritas and club crawling, only to have to slink back home to an empty bed. We begin to long for the fulfillment of a relationship. This doesn't have to mean we're lonely, unable to be in the company of just ourselves. It simply means we no longer want to operate alone. Romantic companionship can be tremendously enriching, enhancing all areas of our lives, under the best circumstances. There's something uniquely beautiful about Blockbuster nights under a fluffy duvet with someone special, our feet touching, our bodies entwined as we steal each other's warmth. If only for a season, we all experience a very visceral need to couple, to be touched, and to at least *feel* loved. If it happens with enough repetition and mutuality, you may soon find that you're no longer single. The trick, however, is to still be you. Even though you've found Mr. Wonderful, or just Mr. Seasonal, it's important to remain singular and not get so lost in this wonderful (possibly seasonal) bliss that you disappear as an individual.

Make sure you have a strong understanding of who you are and what you stand for before you set out to be in a relationship. Know your singular self. The more you know about you, the better equipped you'll be to participate in a healthy relationship, and you'll be much less likely to tolerate what you don't deserve.

Recap

- One of the primary keys to a healthy relationship is for both of you, though no longer single, to remain singular.
- If you don't go within, you go without.
- It's hard for a potential mate to see who you are when you're lost in a cacophony of women.
- Romantic companionship can be tremendously enriching, enhancing all areas of our lives.
- Know your singular self.

Chapter Two

The New Dating Game

This is where things start to get fun, ladies, but it may require a bit of thinking outside of the box on your part. Feminism was supposed to liberate us, to broaden our options and level the playing fields. For some reason, however, in the postfeminism era, things have gone terribly awry for us on the dating front. Contrary to the ways of our grandmothers, we've relegated ourselves to dating one man at a time. *One* man? How absurd! Many of you consider this the only way, the wholesome way (as if!), but here's why this is not such a good idea: dating one man at a time can be not only a setup for severe disappointment but also a waste of precious child-bearing years, quarter- and midlife crisis time, even your retirement. None of us have time to waste, even in our youth. We should always be learning, growing, exploring, and expanding. So why do we insist on seeing just one man at a time, putting all our figurative (and sometimes literal) eggs in a proverbial basket that might end up being a monumental disaster?

> **Vixen Say What?**
> Too many cooks may spoil the pot, but not if there's more than one pot cooking.

I'd be lying, however, if I said I didn't understand why some of you date in increments of one. Something very interesting happens when a woman—a confident woman—elects to broaden her options by dating in multiples. Words like *whore, strumpet, tramp, trollop, tart*, and *harlot* have existed for as long as those sorts of women have been around. Once upon a time, these terms were reserved strictly for their literal use, applied to women who earned them and, quite frankly,

> **Vixen Say What?**
> Opinions are like assholes—everyone's got one and they're all full of shit.

may not have minded that sort of branding. Whores have been business owners and entrepreneurs, evolving into *madams* with their own successful brothels. These terms exist because these types of women exist, but why must these terms be carelessly and cruelly applied to a woman who has simply chosen to weigh her options? Do not let the fear of being labeled keep you from making the best decisions for yourself. If that includes dating multiple partners, then do so with confidence, unmoved by the unwarranted scrutiny that may come your way.

Today, in certain social circles, if a young woman danced with ten different men during the course of an evening in a nightclub, onlookers are likely to turn up their noses. Some of those noses may be attached to the faces of jealous women or to men on the prowl for easy prey. The young woman may be called any number of derogatory terms, but why—for filling her dance card? Some of you might ask, "What the hell is a dance card?" and that, I say, is where my theory begins.

From as early as the eighteenth century, when an unmarried woman attended a social affair, such as a formal ball or cotillion, she carried what was known as a dance card—an elaborate booklet attached to the wrist by a decorative cord. This booklet listed the title of each dance and the name of the composer, along with a blank space to enter the name of the man with whom the woman had agreed to dance for that particular song. The men a woman danced with were typically suitors, those who were most interested in her. Dance cards were a big deal, especially in the nineteenth century and well into the first part of the twentieth century. In some instances, it was the rule that a woman (who, by the way, was always referred to as a "lady," not a "strumpet" or a "whore") should not dance with the same partner too often. Variety was encouraged. If a lady danced with the same man more than twice, it was assumed he was her fiancé. Once a lady's dance card was full, that was it. Whether it was five men or fifteen, it was a simple courting ritual that was both recognized and respected. Having a full and varied dance card indicated a woman's desirability.

This ritual continued beyond the ballroom. It was the norm for an unmarried woman to see several suitors while in search of her one true love. It was also standard, even required, for a man to ask permission of the woman's family, particularly her father, in order to visit. If permission was granted, the suitor would perhaps come over for dinner, participating with the entire family and never left alone with the object of his affection. Eventually, permission would be given for the man to take the woman on a date, and even then a chaperone might accompany them. This was required of each suitor so that the family, and the woman, could determine his suitability. Sure, times have changed, but if it was okay back then for a woman to be courted by several men, why not now, when we're so much more progressive?

I'm all for bringing courtship back, and the only way to do that is to create competition. Men love a challenge. They are hunters and gladiators. They love the thrill of winning and being proven better than any other man. Give them the chance to bring out their inner hunter. Make them fight for you—figuratively, of course. You don't want your suitors to come to blows. Requiring a man to compete for your affections will allow you to assess who he is and the way he may strategize, implement, and achieve—or, conversely, fail to do so. It lets you see just how much you mean to him and how far he is willing to outmatch and outwit his peers to gain your love. Creating competition amongst your suitors is easy. Let's begin with what I like to call the *Starting Five,* as detailed in the Vixen Tip on the following page:

Your first—and therefore, faulty—assumption was probably that I was recommending that you have five men whom you juggle sexually, which is far from what I would ever suggest. When men don't have to work for something, they don't. If you had five men who could access your bed

Vixen Tip

In a notebook or on a sheet of paper tacked to your refrigerator, write the numbers one through five in ink and fill each slot with names—in pencil. For a more manageable list, try using just three names. These should be men you like and enjoy spending time with.

- Your *number one* should be the man who captures your attention like no other and who pays the most attention to you. He is sincere, thoughtful, and caring, a real gentleman. For this man, you will answer the phone any time of the day or night, even though he knows better than to call at disrespectful hours. You will join him on trips out of town and lay around with him for days, talking about anything and everything. You will leave another man at the drop of a dime if he calls, but only because he has earned it, not because you are slavishly at his beck and command.

- Your *number two* is a close runner-up but is missing that certain flair that keeps you up at night, replaying the events of the last time you saw one another. Still, he is fun to be with and gives you something number one does not. Usually, these two men are polar opposites.

- *Numbers three though five* are mostly for emotional support, chitchatting and the like. These men are not of any romantic interest to you, per se, but are great to talk to or just hang out with. I prefer to keep these people at bay. Feed them with the proverbial long-handled spoon.
  Give them rules and limitations: no calling after nine, limited or no personal contact—that sort of thing.

To remind these fellows that they're in a competition, let each one know about the other and reveal to them their ranking and that their current ranking is always subject to change. When each one calls, address them by number instead of their names once in a while, just for sport. This ups the ante. Number one will be flattered. The rest will wonder why they're not him. They will ask what number one has or does that they don't. Most important, they'll want to know what *he* gets that they don't. Let them know. Don't be shy. Then sit back and watch the games begin.

without restriction, you would see no more of them than they wanted you to. Sex, ideally with someone with whom you share a mutually strong emotional, spiritual, and physical connection, is reserved for the top dog, and maybe number two, if he is a close contender and you want to explore his potential to be more. By having options, you allow yourself the freedom to change your mind, the latitude to get to know other men who, in the process of competing for you, reveal aspects of themselves that you may ultimately find more endearing, attractive, and commitment-worthy as you get to know them. Moreover, if your top candidate unravels at some point,

> **Vixen Say What?**
> A man who hasn't worked for you will only play with you.

as men sometimes do, you still have others with whom you've been cultivating friendships, men who are excited about you. And what woman in her right mind doesn't love that?

Now, for me, this method is tried and true. After years of putting my heart and soul and life on hold for nearly every man I'd been involved with, I was exhausted! It's funny how one man can leave you spent, but when you have many, your energy can be reserved. Hmmm. How is this so? I suddenly found myself more in control because I gave the men in my life their positions of relevance. When I was dissatisfied with one, I would quickly demote him and place another, more deserving suitor in his slot. I was in dating heaven! Just as I explained above, it was so empowering to finally be in control of my emotions and the way I related to the men in my life. My courting ritual was my own and not dependent upon the fleeting fancies of any man.

But wait! Before you go rounding up your Starting Five, be sure you're ready to play this new dating game. There is so much for you to know and practice before you go cavorting with different types of men. Heaven knows what you're going to encounter out there among these gladiators and hunters. You, your self-worth, your self-esteem, and your overall self-image need to be fortified. The vicious flip side of this dating strategy is that you can easily become a pawn in the game and be played, moved all over the board, and jumped by any random rook. Learn yourself first. Be assured of your power, as well as your freedom, and become proficient in utilizing them both effortlessly. Doing so will take time and loads of practice. In the chapters to come, we'll talk about how to accomplish these things in more and in greater detail, so for now, hold tight. Trust me, the men aren't going anywhere.

Recap

- Dating one man at a time cannot only be a setup for severe disappointment but a waste of precious child-bearing years, quarter- and midlife crisis time, even your retirement.

- Do not let the fear of being labeled keep you from making the best decisions for yourself.

- Having a full and varied dance card indicated a woman's desirability in years past.

- Create competition among your suitors.

- By having options, you allow yourself the freedom to change your mind.

Chapter Three

Falling in Love, Part Two

So you've mastered the new dating game and you're being courted left and right. Great! *But hold on, Vixen*, you say. *Not so fast. I've hit a snafu.* Both your number one and your number two have stolen your heart and you don't know whom to choose. You can't. You *won't*, damn it! Each of these choice men brings something so unique to your life and you love them both so differently but so completely that you couldn't bear to let one of them go. We all know that this will not end well. At least two hearts stand to be broken in this scenario: yours and one of theirs. (If things go really badly, all three of you lose.)

Vixen Say What? Two rights can sometimes make a wrong.

Eventually, after all that dating and numbering and ranking and carrying on has reached its saturation level, you will have to decide which suitor fits you best. Determining which one is good for a lifetime versus which one is only good for, well, a good time, may not be such an easy decision to make. How will you ever decide?

From my experience, the decision, though not an easy one to make, is really quite cut-and-dried. After dating several men for an extended period of time, the man you choose to share your life with should be the one who loves you and cares for and about you, not regardless of who you are and have been, but *because* of it. The man for you brings you chicken soup when you're sick, throws your used tissues away without flinching, and curls up next to you at night, unconcerned with his own health. He is the man who loves the children that are not biologically his. He loves whoever you love and defends your honor, no matter the consequence. Your dogs, your bird, your mother, and your quirky drunk uncle—if you love them, he loves them and makes them his own.

In traditional marriage vows, we promise to love and support one another, whether rich or poor, in sickness or in health, but most of us never take the time to imagine the "poor and sickly" part of that promise. Those days are just as possible as the "rich and healthy" ones. The man you choose should be able to imagine those days and, even further, imagine sharing them with you, being a pillar and a source of strength and resolve; and you should be able to do the same. Substantial, long-term relationships are built on times of trouble and lean, not just of flourish.

Any couple can flourish when they are unchallenged. Any guy can be expected to stay when times are always good. Not every man listed on your dance card will be able to supply that need—*the stick-to-it-iveness*—that's required of a long-term, trusting relationship. You may have to go through several versions of your dance card before finding the right man who can.

Once you have made this decision and are sure you've chosen the right man, you may still find your heart attached to another. Maybe it's the funny guy who made you laugh until your stomach hurt, or the spontaneous guy who swept you off your feet with surprise picnics at the beach. Every man has something to offer, and each relationship has the potential to teach you something about life, love, and yourself. Enjoy these experiences, but at the end of the day, really put into perspective which one will love you at your worst and celebrate you at your best. Love alone cannot be all there is. Love as an emotion, no matter how genuine, is incomplete without love as an action. There may be days when you wonder if you've made the right decision, and moments when you'll swear you're ready to walk out the door and go back to an ex. There may be days when you actually do. Before you make your final decision, however, ask yourself these questions, listed in the Vixen Tip below.

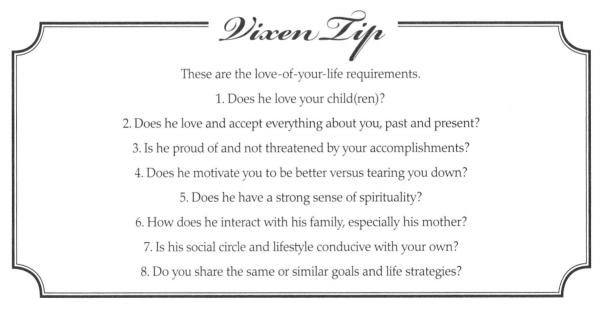

Vixen Tip

These are the love-of-your-life requirements.

1. Does he love your child(ren)?

2. Does he love and accept everything about you, past and present?

3. Is he proud of and not threatened by your accomplishments?

4. Does he motivate you to be better versus tearing you down?

5. Does he have a strong sense of spirituality?

6. How does he interact with his family, especially his mother?

7. Is his social circle and lifestyle conducive with your own?

8. Do you share the same or similar goals and life strategies?

It's always easy to imagine smooth sailing when thinking about an ex. You'll only remember the good times, not the reason an ex *is* your ex. Trust me, there's a reason he's your ex, and the moment you get back with him, if you dare to go that far, you'll remember it. If you've found a man who loves and cares for you in every way, it's unrealistic to expect that there won't be challenges. Work through them. That's the only way you and he will build a strong foundation on which you'll be able to withstand future issues as they arise. It's easy to run into the arms of someone from your past, but you'll never grow if you indulge in this practice. Trust that you have chosen the right man for you and then commit to that decision. If he is willing to be there for you, you should be there for him.

No man wants to be in constant dread that the woman he loves will run back into the arms of another suitor, a suitor he once competed against for your affections. You owe your man more than that. You owe it to yourself to learn how to weather the realistic challenges of love. That, ladies, is a mistake I know all too well. Once, through my own misjudgments and insecurities, I almost lost one of the most enduring and fulfilling relationships in my life. I was so afraid to make a commitment and move forward *in* that commitment that I continuously found myself reaching back to my past, and to one lover in particular. There I was, juggling them both, calling this one, calling that one, professing love for one and love for the other. What a mess I had gotten myself into, sneaking off to see one, lying to them both. One was a superstar, with all the perks that come with being a high-profile celebrity. There were many tangible goods at my disposal, but very little comfort and emotional security. It's not as if my other choice was a pauper or any less than a man, but what he lacked in monetary currency he more than made up for in emotional wealth. I had to make a choice and it had to be the right one.

You have to weigh your options, and the best man won't always be the one the rest of the world would expect or approve of. He's the one who loves you unconditionally and, at times, more than himself.

Recap

- You will have to decide which suitor fits you best.
- You may have to go through several versions of your dance card before finding the right man.
- Love as an emotion, no matter how genuine, is incomplete without love as an action.
- Trust that you have chosen the right man for you, then commit to that decision.

Chapter Four

Casual Sex

One day several years ago, I was on my way home from a long night out. As the sun rose over the city, I anxiously waited for what felt like the longest red light in the world to turn green. While waiting, I noticed something unusual out of the corner of my eye—it was a cardboard box, rocking back and forth. Upon closer inspection, I could see four feet sticking out from the box (which apparently once housed a refrigerator). Two shopping carts filled with cans were in the "driveway" alongside the cardboard house. It took me a few minutes to realize it, but I was looking at two homeless people having sex in a cardboard box on one of the busiest street corners in Los Angeles. That dawn, I learned a very important lesson: sex is the easiest thing in the world to get. You don't even have to have a home, a bed, or a place to shower. Anyone can have it anytime, anywhere.

Vixen Say What?
There is nothing casual about sex. Easy, yes, but not casual.

From that day forward, I thought differently about sex, especially that of the casual variety. Nothing that easy can be worth having! As human beings, we tend to value that which requires a certain level of investment, whether it be sweat equity, our time, emotions, or our hard-earned money. Things easily had are often easily discarded, as we feel we can effortlessly attain them again. I like a challenge and typically enjoy doing things most people aren't doing. After my epiphany that morning at the traffic light, I knew, without question, that I didn't want to be a member of the "bums in a box" club.

I began to think about everything that comes with sex without commitment. I pondered how things have changed between the sexes. How, not only can today's liberated women supposedly do anything the boys can do, but do it better and with just as much emotional disconnect. I thought about it long and hard—and came to the conclusion that the theory of us handling sex as casually as men is all a bunch of crap.

Casual sex comes with an enormous amount of baggage, and I don't mean the adorable vintage Louis Vuitton trunk-set type. It's more the free-duffel-bag-with-purchase they burden you with at department stores just because you bought a lipstick. You end up stuck with an unstylish piece of luggage that makes you look bad and, pretty soon, is full of holes. Being a woman who has had more than my share of casual sex and all the subsequent pitfalls, headaches, and ridiculously negative consequences, I am a believer that casual sex requires too much energy for so little return. Every time I found myself with a homie-lover-friend, I found myself alone at the end and the emotional toll was never worth the physical ecstasy. Never. I began to look around during holidays and birthdays, good times and bad, and there I would be—alone—unless I was being the good-time girl, the casual sex recipient, the jump-off, the homegirl. No matter what name we gave it, no matter how close the friendships, the sex was always meaningless and the consequences were always dire. I was never a life partner, never a wife. I needed more. Damn it, I *deserved* more!

Sometimes we feel we have to have sex like men in order to be perceived as sexually astute. We pretend as if having a man crawl on top of us and shoving himself inside our bodies, panting and sweating without much focus on any further intimacy other than our bodies connecting, is no big deal. It is. The sexual act is an invasive process. Our bodies don't just touch a man's when we copulate. We actually take them in. Everything about men becomes a part of us as they move around inside our most private personal space. It's a huge deal, ladies, and if we acted as if it *were* a huge deal, there would be no talk of "having sex like a man." There would just be sex, pure and simple, between two conscious, consenting human beings.

Vixen Tip

Don't be afraid to be a lady and to take an old-fashioned approach to dating and sex. If no one has ever taught you old-fashioned ways, talk to an elder woman about the way things used to be. Ask questions of your grandmothers and even of your grandfathers. Watch old movies such as *An Affair to Remember* (1957), *Breakfast at Tiffany's* (1961), *How to Marry a Millionaire* (1953), *Carmen Jones* (1954), and *Gone with the Wind* (1939). Learn from women with grace and dignity, like Jacqueline Kennedy-Onassis and Coretta Scott King. These films and people are studies of the way ladies represented themselves and were treated. Don't be intimidated by today's diminished standards, and don't start believing you can't be as refined as women in earlier generations. Proper posturing, appropriate language, coyness, and restraint are traits we could all stand to inherit. Then, allow these old but new, gentler habits to seep into your ideas about sex. When you present yourself as a lady, you will be treated as such, and ladies don't go around just giving it up. A lady makes a man work, and work damn hard, for every morsel of affection.

Anyone who has ever taken Anatomy 101, or knows how men and women are physically constructed, understands that the act of copulation is internal for women and external for men. Think of it like this: it's impossible for a woman to be emotionally disengaged once she has sex with a man for the simple reason that he enters her body and, literally, lays among her organs—the very instruments that keep her alive and give her the gift of life. This is personal, extremely personal. There's no disconnecting from something this intrusive, no matter how much you try to convince yourself you can.

When a woman's internal organs are injured from something that goes horribly awry during, or as a result of, sex, her ability to procreate can be ruined altogether. The primary male sexual organ—the penis—is on the outside of his body. And while it may endure its share of bumps and bruises, a reckless swatting of the penis doesn't have to mean a man can't father children anymore. Ladies, this sex thing is serious business!

Once you've been someone's casual sex partner for an extended period of time, one of you inevitably begins to crave more. It's a natural progression that occurs when the two same bodies repeatedly intermingle with each other. But let's say that you've already set your standards and demands extremely low. Suppose you began a relationship on a sexual basis only, agreeing with someone that sex, and sex alone, would be enough and you wouldn't require more than just a physical connection, but now things have changed for you. You've become emotionally invested. You actually like this guy…maybe even love him. To tell you to expect things will now change in your favor would be lying. We all know it doesn't work like this. It's difficult to talk a man into being your life partner after months or years of noncommittal sex. You'll be accused of trying to change the game in the ninth inning and men generally do not respond well to this.

There is a way to prevent this. If we were just more honest with ourselves from the very beginning and not so adamant on playing by the man's rules, things could be different. We should choose to introduce our own rules, instead of bending to those that don't come natural to us. You shouldn't be afraid of what it means to be a woman, and part of that means understanding that we are wired to feel an emotional connection with a sexual partner, especially one who makes a repeat appearance. If more of us were up front about this basic sexual truth, we'd stand a much better chance of finding more long-term, meaningful relationships.

Men seem to be more effective at compartmentalizing than women. They generally have more success than we do at putting things and people in priority and in perspective. When a woman settles for casual sex, she places herself very low on a man's list of priorities, and he will treat her accordingly. He won't understand her ranting about needing more of his time. He will become confused about where such intense feelings are coming from, especially if both parties agreed from the beginning that their relationship was just about sex and nothing more. You can't blame the man for this. Once the terms were set, the terms were set. This is why you shouldn't accept this kind of situation at all, not if you're actively seeking a fulfilling relationship. There's no tricking the man down the road, no winning him over to your side of things. A situation like this usually ends badly, with the woman feeling demoralized and hurt because the man wanted nothing more than the use of her body, and with him resenting her for having tried to switch what he believed was an honest, straightforward situation. Don't settle, ladies. It will only work against you. When a woman ups the ante and demands more of herself and of a potential partner, the odds of getting what she wants increases exponentially.

Aside from the emotional baggage a woman can carry around with her for life, there can be serious physical repercussions related to casual sex. Aside from the inconvenient and embarrassing itch of crabs, the blistering discomfort of genital warts, or a lifelong relationship with herpes, you can flat-out die after contracting AIDS. There's no Airborne—that over-the-counter product developed by a schoolteacher for staving off the flu—that you can take to ward off these things. The ideal way to protect yourself is to employ good judgment, doing what is best for you in the long run.

Let's be even more blunt about this, just to make sure you get it. Having too much casual sex can result in a woman becoming worn out, and I'm talking literally, in this particular instance. Have you ever seen a woman you can tell has just been physically run through? Everything about her appears to be spent. Her face seems beaten and weathered, and her body has begun to give in to gravity, because that's what happens when it's subjected to too much wear and tear without sufficient preventative maintenance. And let's not even talk about what sex does to your nether regions. Don't lie, ladies. We all know what "porn pussy" looks like. The lips are practically hanging out of the panties on these women. The labia majora are now labia gigantica. You don't want that, do you? Because the more casual, uncommitted, random, sex-for-sex's-sake sex you have, the more beleaguered you and your genitalia will become. Why do you think the very

Vixen Tip

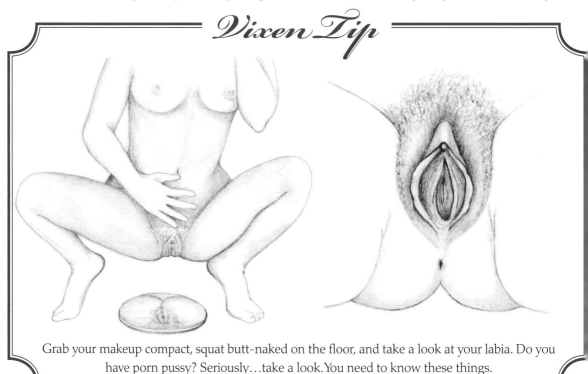

Grab your makeup compact, squat butt-naked on the floor, and take a look at your labia. Do you have porn pussy? Seriously…take a look. You need to know these things.

lucrative market for vaginal rejuvenation has emerged? Way too many women have been having way too much casual sex.

Additionally, there's the possibility of gaining a reputation that can follow you your entire life. This doesn't mean just among men, but among women. No one wants to be the person in the room that people fall into hushed whispers about. It doesn't feel good. And yes, girls will always talk about girls. That's our nature, and we can sometimes be very vicious and heartless in the way we do it. Men can be even worse, however, with their locker-room mentality, when they high-five each other for having been with certain women, gaining and building camaraderie on the common ground of how they sexed you—describing how you performed and what your genitalia looked like.

When you're the woman guys love bragging about having been with, you can never be comfortable about why men approach you. Is it because they want to know the real you, or because they want to see what everyone else has seen and be able to prove it to others, while adding a notch to their bedpost? Men are notorious for acting, upon first meeting you, as though they know nothing about you and are completely ignorant of your reputation, good or bad. Trust me, they know. Not only do they know, they want to see it for themselves. This is the collateral damage that casual sex begets. Having a reputation is a hard stain to remove. No matter how you try to leave it behind or rise above it, there's always someone who remembers and wants to bring it up. In these times where everything is on the Internet, someone will Google it if it's out there. Remember, girlfriends, you are responsible for your actions. They will follow you all your life. You can spare yourself from traveling down this road of humiliation by treating your body as precious cargo with respect and not giving away sex as if it's meaningless.

You shouldn't be afraid of abstaining from sex until you've found a man you feel certain will give you what you want and need, if those wants and needs come from a place of maturity. It's okay to wait. There's nothing wrong with a sexual fast. When you have sex, especially with multiple partners who have nothing more than a superficial connection to you, you take on all the energies of those people, both negative and positive. We as women are receptacles for that because of how we're built and how we're socialized to be the more outwardly emotional sex. By giving yourself a period of rest, you allow your body, soul, and mind a chance to cleanse, just as you would during a food fast. The you that will emerge will feel lighter and much more in control. Any wise man, or woman, will tell you: there's nothing sexier than a woman who can have sex, but won't.

I wouldn't tell you this if I wasn't sure it was highly effective, and I know it is because I've done it, having enjoyed celibacy for nine months at a time. It was the most cleansing, clarifying period of my twenties, at a stage when my toxic relationships with men were clouding my judgment and blocking my blessings. When I say blessings, I mean those beautiful, unexpected things that happen along the way. The moments and events that change your life for the better and open your eyes to all life has to offer.

Sometimes—and I think you can all feel me on this—certain types of men tend to get in the way. These types, with their charisma and machismo, their nonsense and their bullshit, tend to override what's really important and impede us from taking care of ourselves and doing what's right for us in the long run. During my nine-month dick desertion, my goals became clearer and my first five-year plan was devised. Between the ages of twenty-five and thirty, I was determined to utilize associates in media to help draw attention to myself in order to obtain my first publishing contract; I would become a best-selling author, jump-starting a new career and making enough money to buy my first home. Also included in my five-year plan was the intention to begin saving for my retirement and for my son's education. For that brief moment in time, I was saving all my love for me and treating myself with the same care and consideration I would have usually given an undeserving male or a casual sex partner. Instead of looking for a man to make me whole, I was working hard at becoming self-contained and content so that when the right man came along he would find a complete woman, not a woman looking to be completed.

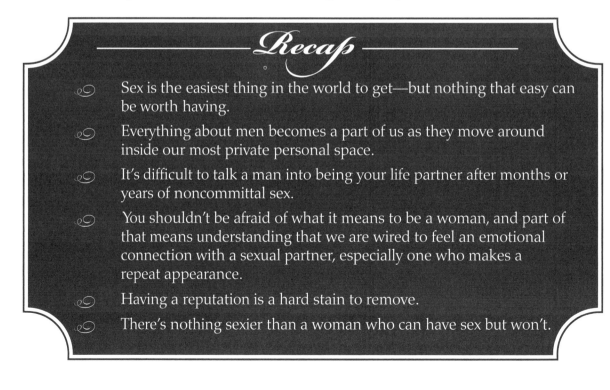

Recap

- Sex is the easiest thing in the world to get—but nothing that easy can be worth having.
- Everything about men becomes a part of us as they move around inside our most private personal space.
- It's difficult to talk a man into being your life partner after months or years of noncommittal sex.
- You shouldn't be afraid of what it means to be a woman, and part of that means understanding that we are wired to feel an emotional connection with a sexual partner, especially one who makes a repeat appearance.
- Having a reputation is a hard stain to remove.
- There's nothing sexier than a woman who can have sex but won't.

Chapter Five

Independence vs. Loneliness

Since entering into the realm of publishing, I have been introduced to not only a new business, but to lots of businesswomen. These are women who followed the independent woman's blueprint: get your education, don't get pregnant (if you can avoid it), graduate at the top of your class, find a respectable career and not just a job, and be independent, not relying on a man in order to make a successful living. Well, it's a nice little blueprint—in theory. I'm not so sure how much practical application it has for long-term happiness overall. As one woman in publishing so bluntly put it one day over the phone, "I should've been a hoe! I should've just not listened to my mama and been a damn hoe!"

Now maybe that statement was a little harsh—and you'll see me reference it again in a later chapter; that's just how much of an impact it made on me—but I understood the gist of what she meant, given the conversation we were having. There she was, an accomplished woman with her own property in the heart of Manhattan, her own financial stability, a college degree, and a fabulous career in publishing. She followed the independent woman's blueprint and got everything she set out for. Now in her forties, having achieved much of what that blueprint dictated, she could no longer ignore the obvious: she didn't have someone to share it all with. Sure, there was her dog, Mr. Sniffles, and he was nice and cuddly and awful cute, but as she listened to the ticktocking of her biological clock, she knew Mr. Sniffles would never be enough. She longed for more.

In between all the studying and sticking to the blueprint, she forgot to make the time to fall in love, find a mate, and start a family, all the things she was now longing for once she entered her forties. She's not the only woman I've heard this story from. I have come across plenty of businesswomen who have reached amazing heights in their education, career, and even in their personal lives as single women. Then one day, they look around and there's no one there but them. Even though they have the most spacious apartment in the city, there's no room for anyone else. They've built a life that only they can fit into.

The thing about independence is that too much of it can be a bad thing. Since the nineteen sixties and the advent of the women's movement, we've been taught and encouraged to assume what have historically been very masculine roles. There are many of us who grew up without fathers and were taught by our mothers to make it on our own, to be both man and woman. We've had to learn how to bring home the bacon, fry it up, and not forget to wash up the dishes when we're done. As a result, we have made no place at our table for a man. Some of us simply don't know how. But if you don't make room for him, how can he ever sit at your table? How can he share in the feast that is your life?

Vixen Tip

Compartmentalize your life. Leave your outside life out there. When you're home, be the woman your man and children need you to be. Turn off your mobile phone, give your laptop a rest, and sit at the dinner table and enjoy a meal with your man and family. Make the weekends, or your time off, theirs and take that time to manage your home, giving them all those creature comforts that make a house a home.

There is a fine line between independence and loneliness. It's one thing to know how to thrive on your own and enjoy your own company. It's another to have learned to exist on your own because you don't know how to include someone else. A man needs to feel needed. There has to be an opening, a place for him to fit. If we become so independent that we begin to act and talk as if we don't want or need a man at some point in our day and in our lives, no man will ever be there. Of course, there are some people out there who don't want a mate and are more than happy to grow old alone, fall out of the shower, and press one of those Life Alert buttons to summon for help or, even better, teaching Mr. Sniffles how to dial 911. If that's you, that's okay! For those of you who would like to spend your days with a mate and maybe a couple of kids and a dog, be careful how you present your independence. Never be ashamed of it, but never, ever use it as a shield.

Any one of us can be guilty of this. I think realizing the difference between independence and loneliness was one of the most difficult things for me to do once I felt I'd successfully completed my first five-year plan. Becoming a homeowner, as a single mother, was a proud moment for me and I wasn't afraid to let everyone know it. It was as if I suddenly had this Daffy Duck complex, this, *Mine, mine, mine!* and *You can't do anything for me that I can't do for myself!* attitude. My partner had to point out these flaws to me; it also took my own constant cognizance and practice to curb my way of thinking and speaking about my accomplishments and independence. Yes, I had come a long way from sleeping in my car in just five years, but instead of sharing my life, I was using it to keep him and others out of it. My "Mine, mine, mine" demeanor, with its off-putting tone, would have eventually reduced me to a world with just "me, myself, and I." A strong, supportive, and confident man with just as much to offer would not be able to tolerate all that *me, me, me*-ing. Not for long, anyway.

When we cloak ourselves in our independence, it is the equivalent of making an escape route. If a man believes that you don't need him and might possibly bounce, or bounce him, if he makes one false move, he's never going to feel secure. He needs to feel that he has a necessary place, especially if you are the more financially successful one in the relationship. It's no myth that a woman who makes more money than her mate can be perceived as a threat to his masculinity. You have to walk that line gingerly and with great consideration. Don't be afraid or ashamed to play the damsel in distress on occasion and let your man take care of you. There's nothing wrong with that. It's not the equivalent of playing dumb or surrendering your sense of self. What it does mean is that once in a while, it's okay to act as if you don't know how to solve a problem and need to seek his help. It will bolster his confidence in himself and his standing with you. It will make him feel useful. Let down your guard. Let him in. When we don't know how to allow others to assist us, it makes us less apt to grow in a relationship and jointly deal with the challenges that present themselves.

Vixen Say What? A woman who cannot stand down may find herself standing alone.

This isn't to say that independence has no value. There's *worldbound independence*, where you are able to hold your ground professionally just as much as a man. That's fine when you're on the phone handling business or brokering major deals. When your man walks through the door, however, there's a softer, more *homebound independence* that you can show. It means you know how to cook and clean, and you don't need someone like his mother (or your mother) showing you how to do so. You can do laundry without turning his whites pink. He can relax in knowing that his woman has mastered their domestic terrain. Just don't look up and find yourself lonely because you were trying to be too worldbound and dominant at home.

Men need to plant flags and claim a place of their own in the world. If you make him feel there's no claim he can stake with you in your world, he will move on to a woman who's more open and accommodating.

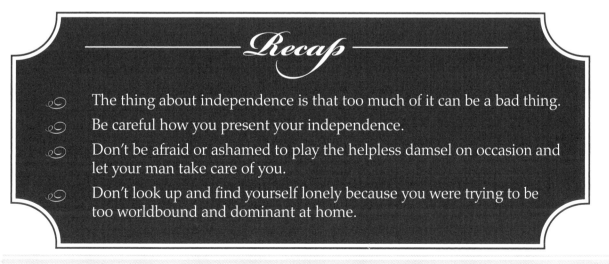

Recap

- ☙ The thing about independence is that too much of it can be a bad thing.
- ☙ Be careful how you present your independence.
- ☙ Don't be afraid or ashamed to play the helpless damsel on occasion and let your man take care of you.
- ☙ Don't look up and find yourself lonely because you were trying to be too worldbound and dominant at home.

Chapter Six

The Single Mother

Dating as a single mother has to be one of the trickiest forms of dating. There is so much to consider and so many pitfalls to negotiate.

First off, there's always the underlying guilt of leaving your child for a night out with some guy you may or may not like. The whole time you're on the date, you're wondering if your little one has awakened during the night and is wondering where his mommy is. You feel as if you're doing something wrong, as if you're choosing this man you're out with over your child. While that hopefully isn't the case, what it means is that you have to be strategic about introducing the element of dating into the secure world you've created for you and your child.

As a rule, dating should happen only after your child's bedtime and before he or she wakes up. That's when you should plan to have the sitter on hand. Your child should never even see the sitter in the initial stages of your dates. In my case, my son would be in bed by 8:00 p.m. I always scheduled my dates for 9:00 p.m. and would have my sitter arrive shortly before. In the event I thought I'd found the love of my life (insert chuckle here) and wanted to stay out overnight, I made sure to return before my son awoke. Even during my dating frenzy, I believed my sitter should never be the one to rouse my son out of bed, prepare his breakfast, get him ready for school, or anything else. I never wanted him to see the sitter come or go, especially when he reached school age. At that point, his sensitivity heightened as he became more cognizant of my actions and our schedule as a family. Everything I did, if not properly handled, had the potential to become detrimental to his feelings and behavior. I don't believe your children, during their young, formative years, should ever see you leaving for or coming back from dates. Your departures can be traumatic for young children as it is. If they see you leaving for a date, it may seem as though you're picking someone else over them. If they never see it happen, then they never even know you were out and won't be impacted by it.

Despite knowing this, there was still a time when I was so sure I had found the man I'd spend the rest of my life with and, without thinking, allowed him and our relationship to take precedence over my better judgment and my responsibilities as a mother and the figurehead in my young son's life. I lost myself in the moments of excitement brought about by his private jets and fancy red-carpet events. Like many of us, I felt I wanted to be more than just a mom. I wanted to enjoy life and find my own identity, one that was not attached to the PTA and play dates. On paper, the theory looked solid, but in actuality, by the time my son was five and began kindergarten, I'd disrupted the balance I'd created for him just a few years before. I became determined to break away from mommydom each and every single weekend, and the adverse change in my son's behavior became painfully evident. He began acting out in school and lost his ability to focus and uphold his good grades. When I realized how selfish I'd been, I became as devastated as he had been when, in his eyes, his mommy had found a replacement for him. As with anything else in life, we as mothers have to find balance in our dating habits.

So, Vixen, you ask, what if my child wakes up during the night, comes out for a glass of water or to go to the bathroom, and sees the sitter? Now what? Is he going to be traumatized because Mommy's not home?

Vixen Tip

Your sitter should be someone you know, someone with whom your child will feel at ease in your home. It should be a family member, a best girlfriend, or someone close to you whom you and your child trust. If it's someone you have to hire, you should find a way to make this person your friend. Treat the sitter the way you would a suitor. You take the time to get to know a suitor—do the same with the sitter. Visit the sitter's house. Get to know the sitter's family and friends. Ensure that this person is trustworthy. Once you've gained a certain level of confidence, then, and only then, introduce the sitter to your child as one of your friends so that your child will view the sitter as such. The sitter should not just come over for work but should be welcome during times outside of work. She (or he) should genuinely become your friend. That way if your child wakes in the night and sees the sitter, it doesn't necessarily mean Mommy went out. It just means Mommy's friend came over to hang out like she always does.

Many of you who work outside of the home may already have day care for your child, which you use during the workweek. You may find equal success using them for aftercare services, if available, since you and your child will already be familiar with them and have a certain comfort level.

Ideally, make a friend your sitter, but if that's not possible, make your sitter your friend. For those of us who don't have family or friends to depend on, there is an added stress of trusting a sitter with your most precious possession. Even though you've befriended your sitter and gotten to know her background, you'll still find yourself calling home throughout your date, checking to make sure everything at home is okay. Eventually, you will adjust, and as long as you have found balance between your dating and your family life, so will your little one. But it's usually awkward in the very beginning.

Once you've gotten past the sitter issue, an even greater one has the potential to present itself. What happens when you meet a man you actually know (and not just think) might be the one, but he hasn't met your child yet, since you've been cautious and deliberate about introducing men into your environment? This is the part where your heart jumps into your throat—the day the kid meets Mommy's "friend."

This can be terrifying for a single mother and terribly overwhelming for our children. You wonder what your child will think about all this. Our kids are so fragile, capable of being enormously impacted by what we bring into their world. You wonder, *Will he like the man?* What title and description have you given identifying who this man even is? Have you and your man definitively concluded that you are, in fact, in a serious relationship? Real relationships don't just happen. They have to be decided upon and agreed to mutually before you begin to get your children involved. You and this man should have common objectives and plans with every intention of moving toward them and which include your child. When you finally introduce your child to your man, it should be with the explanation that this is your mate, and he has come to be a part of both of your lives.

Your child should be included in the decision of bringing a man into your family. When children aren't included, they often act out, and you end up having two separate relationships—one with your lover and one with your child, which is the mistake I made and explained above. Having two separate lives may sound as if it can work, but it can't—not successfully. If you're in a relationship, it means your child is in that relationship, as well. The nature of your romance should be explained to all the necessary members of both your families so that there's no confusion. Your children should never feel uncertain about the standing of the person you are bringing into their lives, having to guess what this man's role will be. Even more important, he absolutely has to make his intentions evident through his actions: taking time to get to know your child, allowing your highly impressionable young one to see him being a helpmate to you and not a hindrance.

Your children have to see this man making you happy, helping you around the house, and helping to make a difference in their lives without forcing his presence upon them. Ever so gently and cautiously, your mate should interject those male wisdoms that only a man can.

Even though so many of us have been told, or convinced ourselves, that we can be both mother and father to a young girl or boy, this is one of the biggest lies being passed off today, to the detriment of children and families everywhere. There are things a man can give to both you and your children that will enrich your family beyond your expectations, if you've taken the time to be sure your man is the right man for all of you. Between teaching your young son about household and financial responsibilities and the proper way to care for and about women, and instructing your young daughter on how to pay those fresh little boys in school no mind and hold her chastity close, a man's words can be highly influential and life-altering.

It is imperative that we make sure to date only men who want to have children, are fans of and champions for them. To do otherwise will create tremendous drama, frustration, and conflict for you, your man, and your child. This was the underlying reason why, in the relationship I referenced earlier, I was unable to include my son in activities with my man. I wound up creating an alternate life and a lifestyle that allowed no place for my son. The moment I heard this man was no kid lover, I should have walked away and found a man worthy of us both. This was my mistake. I only hope you will do the opposite and spare both you and your child unnecessary pain.

And let's not forget your child's father. Whether he's a baby daddy or your ex-husband, he'll need to be notified as to who the new man in your and his child's life is going to be. Be careful, however. Make this introduction only when you're sure it's the real thing. Real, as in engagement-ring real. Even if your ex is the worst man in the world, you have to respect him enough to make him aware that another man is coming into your world, thus having the ability to affect his child. There are plenty of good men who are concerned about having their children around someone who could potentially cause them harm.

Vixen Tip

Meet your ex to discuss it, preferably in a public place, over lunch or coffee. Ultimately, you must introduce him to your man so that your ex can be assured your man is safe. Depending on the type of baby daddy you have, he may not give his full support, but he will appreciate your making the effort to include him. If he is a truly fair man, he's already an active part of your child's life and has a good relationship with you. If he's the violent, brooding type, however, you may have no choice other than to forego this option. Whatever the case, as long as you take everyone who matters into consideration, the dating process should flow much more smoothly.

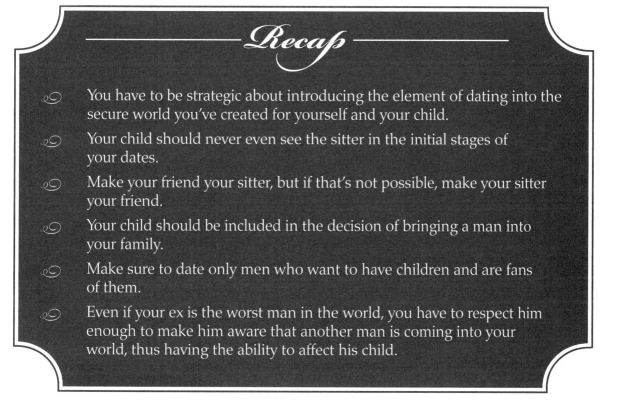

Recap

- You have to be strategic about introducing the element of dating into the secure world you've created for yourself and your child.

- Your child should never even see the sitter in the initial stages of your dates.

- Make your friend your sitter, but if that's not possible, make your sitter your friend.

- Your child should be included in the decision of bringing a man into your family.

- Make sure to date only men who want to have children and are fans of them.

- Even if your ex is the worst man in the world, you have to respect him enough to make him aware that another man is coming into your world, thus having the ability to affect his child.

Chapter Seven

Getting Older

Okay, don't panic but…you're not so young anymore. And if you are, you won't be for long. That's right, honey, you're getting older by the minute, and for those of us who have already been introduced to a hint of crow's-feet and impending varicose veins, this is not a new revelation. Growing older is a fact of life, but it doesn't have to be an agonizing and annoying one. For every woman out there who fears the aging process, there's another who's not anxious at all, one who's actually excited about it! Why would anyone be excited about getting on in years? Because there's so much to look forward to! There is a special glow about a woman who wears the passage of time with honor and grace. She realizes that with age comes a considerable amount of wisdom, experience, clarity, and overall advancement—if you do it right.

But what happens if you're getting up in age and, with each passing birthday, you're also getting more and more single? You've got a string of failed relationships in your wake, each disappointment making you feel as if your chances at happiness are growing further and further out of reach. After a while, you begin to buy into the rhetoric that all the good men are married or dead and the rest are gay, bisexual, in prison, or are lying, cheating dogs. Most of your friends seem to be coupled off, but there you are, all alone. Even worse, you're starting to feel as if you're destined to die that way. At least, that's how you feel on your worst days. Another birthday passes, pushing your dream of a family and a husband even further away. And now you hear the ticking of that dreaded biological clock. Panic sets in, waking you with the cold slap of reality first thing every morning. Nudging you in the back throughout the day every time you see a happy couple pass by or a woman cradling a gurgling baby. Cozying up to you with its blood-chilling dread at night as you lay in your sumptuous, sprawling bed—a bed more than big enough for two—faced with the stark reality that it just may remain this empty forever. And then it happens: you officially become the clichéd "Desperate Broad."

> **Vixen Say What?**
> Stop being a pussycat. They don't call you a cougar for nothing!

Ladies, please. No matter what, don't let it come to this. Desperate women make desperate moves, many of them resulting in some duplicitous man, one who can smell your desperation from miles away, suddenly appearing in your life and—*voila!*—saving the day. Trust me, a guy like this won't save you or your day. If anything, he's probably going to ride off with your life savings, your dignity, and everything else you make readily available to him because you were so terrified of growing old alone. He may destroy your self-esteem, already fragile from you convincing yourself that you were destined to be alone had he not come along. These kinds of men know how to seize upon this kind of vulnerability, beating you down emotionally and physically until you're completely subject to their cruelty and whims. And once you're completely broken, he may still abandon you. But wait! He might leave a little something behind for you, though. Perhaps it'll be the child you've always wanted. Still, you'll be hard-pressed to get a man like this to play an active role in your child's life and you may find yourself chasing him down for child support. Because that's what we get when we make desperate moves. Broke, conniving men, abusive losers, and absentee fathers. Your potential child deserves better. *You* deserve better!

Vixen Tip

First of all, calm down. Breathe in. Breathe out. Look at yourself in the mirror and know that there is a beautiful, amazing woman gazing back, one who any man would be lucky to have. Make the conscious decision RIGHT NOW to change your desperate attitude to one of positive conviction. Remember, you get what you believe in. If you don't believe there's a man for you, he'll have a hard time making you believe it when he finally shows up. Know from this point forward that there *is* someone out there to share your life with. Do you think God would have made all these people and not set one aside for you?

Second, here's a revelation: getting older is a victory! It's like having seniority in life, especially when you utilize the experience of the years to your greatest advantage. With an education and a career under your belt, with your life goals and principles intact, you don't have to panic or accept less than what you deserve. It's critical that you realize you're not the last of the Mohicans.

Just take the right steps to make sure you're ready when the man for you—the right man— arrives. That's what we've been talking about all along in the prior chapters and what we'll discuss throughout the rest of this book. It's all about preparation. You've got to be ready, ladies. But you don't have to be alone.

Embrace your maturity. Use it to your advantage. The wisdom that comes with age should be the very reason you don't fall for the same tricks you did when you were a more impressionable twenty-something. Revel in the liberation that comes with knowing better by declaring *I'm too old for this shit!* when some man tries to step to you with a half-assed hustle that was sure to work on you a decade before. What can a man say in response to that? "No, you're not"? Ha! Of course, he won't. He'll just keep it moving, targeting someone more gullible, and perhaps younger, because *you* know better.

Now, I'm sure those of you reading this who are older than I may be wondering what the hell I know about getting older. Well, hey, I may not be forty, but I damn sure ain't twenty anymore. Just like you, I'm getting older, too, growing and learning with each moment that passes. Like many of you, I find that, as the years go by, I hear that proverbial ticking men always like to tease and semi-demean women about. Awareness of that ticking is what makes us women, attuned to the design of our bodies, our natural inclination to mate, the ability to procreate, be the backbone of families, and, yes, conquer the world, if that's what we desire. Those feelings are nothing to be ashamed of and should not be diminished, but as we all know, it's not always good form to talk about such things in mixed company or on first and second dates. That doesn't change the fact that these feelings exist. Like many of you, I feel a little desperate at times; as if I want my whole life to happen *right now*, before it's too late! Sure, I'm still young, but in this moment as I write this, this is the oldest I've ever been, and the fact that I haven't accomplished everything I want to do is scary just the same. By the time this book is published, I'll be even older and, hopefully, even wiser. As my prior memoirs have explicitly detailed, even though I may be younger than some of you, I've experienced much more—both positive and negative, in a concentrated amount of time—than many women will (and should) over a lifetime. I can definitely contribute on the wisdom tip. Besides, when it came to preparing advice for this chapter, I made sure to consult women who managed to survive their twenties and withstand their thirties, because I know I don't know it all, and I'm not afraid to admit it. Ha!

Oh, and before I wrap this up, here's a tip for you twenty-somethings, a little something to remember every time one of those suspiciously smooth-talking guys slithers toward you with his transparent game: *you're* too old for this shit, too. You probably just don't know it yet.

Recap

- There is a special glow about a woman who wears the passage of time with honor and grace.
- Calm down.
- You get what you believe in.
- Getting older is a victory.
- The wisdom that comes with age should be the very reason you don't fall for the same tricks you did when you were a more impressionable twenty-something.

Chapter Eight

Dating Younger Men

Disclaimer: Younger men are delicious. Yes, I said it. *Delicious.* But depending on how young they are, they can also be very dangerous, as in federal-case dangerous. So please, ladies, check ID when dating someone significantly younger and be sure you're not breaking any laws.

Now, having said that…

Younger men are delicious.

How do I know this? Honey, been there, done that, got the T-shirt and the key chain, okay?! And I'm not just talking a couple of years here, oh, no. I'm talking eleven years! I was a cougar in my twenties. Now, this is the part when you say, "But Vixen, you've only just turned thirty, been in a committed relationship for a couple of years…hmmm…what the hell?" Yeah, well, what can I say? Actually, I can't say much more than that, except—be sure to check IDs, ladies. These young boys are growing up fast and are putting it down hard, and by the time you figure out he's too young for you, you could be locked up in the pokey. Speaking of poking—boy, could he ever! What a thrilling ride it was! He was amazing in bed and a joy to goof off and get off with. He took me away from my grown-up problems and was so eager to please and learn. There really is something special about being with a younger man.

They have a swagger and a confidence that hasn't been eroded yet by the weight of responsibility that comes with the passage of time. They step to you boldly, like Superman incarnate, and they are, indeed, Supermen of sorts, with their sinewy, muscular bodies and promises to satisfy you all…night…long. Most of these promises are easily fulfilled, since their youth places them at their sexual peak. It's a perfect physical match for a mature woman who's had her fill of men her own age or older who can't, um, keep up—not without the assistance of a certain medical drug that threatens four-hour erections requiring emergency medical assistance. We peak sexually as we grow older. A virile young stallion plus a horny older woman equals happiness all around, especially in the bedroom. But we can't live in the bedroom all the time now, can we?

Initially, you'll find him fun and exhilarating. It'll be like reliving your own young adulthood or experiencing it fully for the very first time. There'll be silly jokes, cute little text messages, lots of steamy e-mails, and wild nights out followed by even wilder nights of sex with an energetic fellow who has lots to prove. Satisfying and pleasing someone with several years' advantage will be very important to him. Lucky you!

Vixen Say What?
The younger the man, the stronger the attachment.

Be careful, though. A younger man has a greater potential to become attached to an older woman who has been showing him the ropes. He'll have the stamina, but you'll have the moves. You know, flipping him over and working muscles he didn't even know he had. Do that enough times and that young man will be on you like wet on rain! After that, you won't be able to shake him so easily. He'll want more, eager to learn as much as he can. That's when that fine line will emerge, the one where you carefully tread somewhere between being his lover and—*gasp!*—his mom.

Because of his youth, it won't have been so long ago that he was under his mother's care. And while I don't know the actual stats on this, I'm willing to bet that men who are attracted to older women already have a bit of a Mommy complex to begin with. That doesn't mean they want to *be* with their mothers, you know, biblically. It does mean they can appreciate the guidance, wisdom, and nurturing that an older woman can offer. Older women know more, just like their mothers. Older women can do it all, and your young man will bask in the glow of watching you take the lead, praising you all the way. He'll want to be with you all the time. You represent the good stuff. Your place is cushy, always stocked with food. It smells good. *You* smell good. He loves your body. He loves your mind. He just wants to eat you up. And he will! So just be sure that's what you're ready for if you let this man into your home.

Equally dangerous is your ability to become addicted to his energy and the thrill of having a man you can boss around a bit, a man you can belittle once in a while. He even likes it! You'll find yourself feeling like his mother one minute and his sadist the next. This can be a new, higher form of eroticism for you while simultaneously being very tedious. Keeping up with his energy requires a certain amount of energy of your own, in addition to all the other things you have going on in your life. Eat your *Wheaties*, girls. This one's going to wear you out, in more ways than one.

Vixen Tip

There are myriad reasons for dating younger men. Some of you may actually find a true soul connection in a man many years your junior. In that case, you definitely shouldn't let age get in the way. Once you establish the necessary levels of trust, feel free to open your heart and your life up to him without bias, just as you would with a man your age or older.

In contrast, some of you may just want to experience the legendary passion and abandon that comes with being with a younger man. You want to partake of his stamina that can truly go on All. Night. Long. You want a boy toy and nothing more, and you certainly don't want your physical desire for him to spill over into other areas of your life. If that is the case, then there are measures to be taken. Here are some rules to keep your young stud at a distance:

1. Give him only your mobile number.

2. Allow no calls after a certain hour; turn off your ringer or send him straight to voice mail.

3. Go apeshit on his ass if he shows up at your home unannounced. Call the police if you have to.

4. Chastise him as if he were your child; give him punishments, such as groundings and time-outs.

5. Never be seen with him in public.

6. Never hang out with him and his friends. You are a cougar; see him only in your den.

Eventually, all those funny inside jokes you once shared may begin to feel like silly, distracting nuisances as you become increasingly aware of how unequally yoked the two of you really are. Perhaps he doesn't watch the news the way you do. He never reads the paper. He wants the two of you to go out clubbing, but you've got to be at work in the morning. He doesn't work because he's still in school (college, hopefully, not high school!), or he's just getting started in his career and his income is woefully deficient compared to yours. He looks to you for help when his bills get behind, and you find yourself feeling more and more like his mother than his lover. Every time you serve him dinner or wash his clothes, the mother feeling becomes more evident. Soon you find yourself with a grown baby on your hands, and all the fabulous sex in the world can't make that feeling go away.

That's not to say a younger man can't be the one, the real one, for you. He just might be. It depends on your ages and what both of you are seeking in your lives. There's a marked difference in being a thirty-year-old woman dating a twenty-five-year-old, and being a twenty-five-year-old woman dating a nineteen-year-old. The same is true of a woman in her forties dating a man in his thirties. The more life experience and wisdom you have between you, the better the chances of your relationship surviving.

If you're not serious about your younger man, however, you have to be very careful. Odds are he's growing serious about you. Separating from a younger lover can be much more difficult than parting with one your own age or older, one who's had more experience with breakups. Your young man might not take the words "It's over" that well.

Go easy on him. Keep in mind you're helping to shape him for the next woman that comes along. Pay it forward, ladies. You'd want another woman to do it for you!

Recap

- Check ID when dating someone significantly younger and be sure you're not breaking any laws.
- A virile young stallion plus a horny older woman equals happiness all around.
- A younger man is more likely to become attached to an older woman who has been showing him the ropes.
- You'll find yourself feeling like his mother one minute and his sadist the next.
- The more life experience and wisdom you have between you, the better the chances of your relationship surviving.

Chapter Nine

How to Handle Rejection

So, he doesn't want you anymore. He's through, done, over it. He's changed his numbers, his schedule, and the route he takes on his way home from work. You've been dumped, honey. Tossed aside. Told, in no uncertain terms, to kick rocks. In fact, he's already moved on. Now what?

Whatever you do, don't fall apart. Now is the time to bolster yourself. If you lose your cool, it will only be the first of several escalating irrational reactions, each increasingly darker and more desperate than the last. We tend to take things extremely personally when it comes to our relationships with men. In reality, you could be the very reason your relationships keep falling apart. For all you know, you could be an unbearable bitch and an emotional vampire, sucking the life out of everyone you come across, so let's not count that theory out just yet. You might want to put yourself in your ex's shoes for a moment and consider the following: would *you* want to be involved with you?

> **Vixen Say What?**
> If every time you walk into a room you smell ass, you may want to check your own.

On a related note, you may have a habit of choosing jerks, men who are incapable of commitment, or men who know that because of the low standards you've set for yourself, they don't have to put forth much effort to earn your time and attention. There can be a number of reasons why your relationships do not last, but all that matters is…they don't.

So, before you take another breakup personally and feel the need to add your ex to your shit list, think about what you may have contributed to the demise of your relationship and the ones that preceded it. If you find it impossible to rationalize the outcome of a failed relationship, especially in its recent wake, then focus your attention back on yourself. Do your best to grieve in a healthy manner. Pick yourself up and, as hard as it may seem to do in that moment, direct your energies toward moving on. People recover from breakups every day. So can you. If done correctly, you can emerge even better than you were before, much wiser about life and love. Whatever you do, don't direct your attention toward your ex. If you do find yourself, however, having obsessive thoughts about him and what he's doing now that you're no longer a part of his life, the following tip outlines ways to avoid or at least minimize engaging in further self-destructive behavior.

Vixen Tip

The following is a list of things you should *not* do.

1. Do not call him more than once a day, if at all.

2. If you do call him and he ignores your call, do not leave a psycho message.

3. After placing several calls with no answer or callbacks, do not go to his house and sit outside in your car.

4. If you find yourself stalking him, do not get out of your car!

5. Okay, if you find yourself getting out of your car, do not jump his gate, bang on his door, scream his name, or find an open window to crawl through.

6. If you find yourself jumping his gate, banging on his door, screaming his name, and crawling through an open window, do not resist arrest!

Vixen Say What?

Examples of the psycho message: You lose control of your emotions and demeanor; you make threats against him or yourself; or you call every few minutes to do so.

You don't want to wind up having your voice message played over and over to a roomful of his buddies as they knock back beers and laugh at what a loon you are. Or, worse, you don't want him and his cronies to film themselves laughing at your message and have it be one of the most played videos on YouTube!

Think of every message you leave as a potential sound bite that can work against you.

Perhaps by now you've figured out I know a thing or two about flipping out and stalking my man after or on the verge of a breakup. While I would love to recount every single last one of those embarrassing moments with you, that's a whole other book. Perhaps you've heard of it; it's called *Confessions of a Video Vixen*. What I can share with you is that each time I reacted adversely to some sort of rejection, it only frightened the men who were witness to my loss of control and further solidified their reasoning to let me go. I was a nut! A certified macadamia! After a bit of self-examination—and one court order later—therapy really helped me work through my separation anxieties and self-esteem issues. I highly recommend talking to a professional if you find yourself really losing it when your relationships stagger or come to an end. It can save you from disaster. It can save you from yourself.

No matter how badly you want someone to be yours, that doesn't mean it will change the outcome and make it so. You can't hold a man's emotions hostage or force him to be with you against his will. I mean, you can, but that's false imprisonment—also known as *kidnapping*—and is considered a federal crime. Are you sure that's what you want? Do you love this man so much that you want to hold him hostage and force him to love you, then risk having to go away for a long, long time? Really, ladies, it's not that hectic. Let him go—physically, emotionally, and spiritually. Release him to the universe as you bid him Godspeed. Not everyone is for you, and that's okay. Your life can still flourish in spite of this fact. We've all picked the wrong guy at one time or another and had to let him go, or, conversely, had a guy push us away. Sometimes it's happened over and over again. No matter. We do it until we learn the lesson and begin to figure out what we don't want in our lives versus what we do. If the two of you don't fit, it's not the end of the world, and it's most certainly not the end of you. Use the disappointment as fuel to motivate you to personal greatness. Let that breakup make you better, not bitter!

Vixen Say What? Nothing beats an ex like success!

There are plenty of ways to improve yourself that have the side benefit of allowing an ex to see just what he missed out on, if that matters to you (and for many of us, it does). For those of you ready to show him a thing or three about the prize he foolishly let go, the next set of tips is just for you.

Vixen Tip

The following is a list of things you *should* do.

1. Change your hairstyle and/or color drastically.

2. Spring for a new, sexier wardrobe that fits your body and your budget.

3. Put on those sexy new clothes and hit all the hot spots, especially the ones you know your ex or his friends frequent.

4. Upgrade everything possible in your life—your job, house, car, and jewelry.

5. Never let him see you sweat. Always smile, even when you feel like crying.

6. Save your tears for your friends, for family, or for when you're alone.

Experiencing rejection doesn't have to be a bad thing. If you recognize moments like this as opportunities to up your game and, in the process, learn more about yourself, you can continue to evolve into the kind of woman who is more than ready when a deserving man comes along. And he won't have any problem recognizing it, because you'll have a glow that lights up everything around you. You'll know you're a prize, and no man will ever make you feel like anything less, even if you're not the one for him.

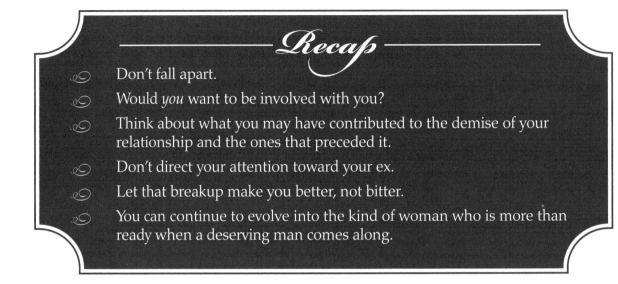

Recap

- Don't fall apart.
- Would *you* want to be involved with you?
- Think about what you may have contributed to the demise of your relationship and the ones that preceded it.
- Don't direct your attention toward your ex.
- Let that breakup make you better, not bitter.
- You can continue to evolve into the kind of woman who is more than ready when a deserving man comes along.

Chapter Ten

Preparation Meets Opportunity

Ladies, if you find yourself wandering through life intently focused on looking for a man, odds are you'll probably never find him—sad, but true. That's how the math of the universe works. The more desperate you are in your quest to obtain something, the more elusive it becomes. The reality is, you stand a better chance of finding what and who you want if you take your life one day at a time, enjoying each moment fully as if everything you desire is already here. It requires changing the way you think, focusing on the positive instead of the negative, but if you're a woman who's determined to realize her highest potential, you should already be leaning that way. Let's take this a step further to something even more radical: What would happen if you lived your life as if you already have a man? Talk about a tremendous burden being lifted! Imagine all the other wonderful things in life you could finally start focusing on, now that this major issue has been resolved.

Okay, okay, calm down. I can already hear the disbelief in your voice. *Vixen,* you snap, *what the hell do you mean? Are you suggesting that I come up with an invisible man, like the invisible playmates I used to have when I was a kid?* That's exactly what I'm suggesting, ladies! Laugh all you want; it works. If any of you have ever experienced the power of prayer or spoke your requests into the air with the absolute faith that they will come, then just went about your business waiting for what you asked for to show up, then you know that what I'm talking about works. That's exactly how it's been designed. The universe always delivers, as long as you believe, which is why we've all heard the phrase, "Be careful what you ask for, because you just might get it." But what if you've asked for things and didn't get them? Well, there's an answer for that, too—a very simple answer. It's because *you* were the weak link in the equation. Something inside of you either feared, doubted, or both. Fear and doubt are the natural opposites of faith. You have to know what you want is on its way, and then proceed as if all it has to do is show up. But hold on…that doesn't mean you can just lay back and wait. You have to prepare for its arrival so that you don't miss out on what you asked for when it comes. These are principles that have been in play since the dawn of man, laws that are present in every religion and philosophy throughout the world. No matter what walk of life you're from, all roads lead to the same answer: you get what you believe in.

If you don't believe your man is out there, then guess what? He isn't. If you believe he is and just hasn't made it to you yet, why not use your time wisely and start getting things ready for when he shows up?!

Vixen Tip

Start by imagining your life the way it would be if there were a man around. Visualize it. Having a picture in mind is one of the strongest ways of bringing things to fruition. How would your home look? What kind of furniture would you have? Would it be the same as what you have now? Would you have your dirty panties and socks scattered all over the floor? Would that tub of Breyer's Double Vanilla ice cream still be melting all over your end table? And what about your bed? Would the same sheets from three weeks ago *still* be on your mattress? Would a man be thrilled to be in your home right now, at this very minute?

And what about *you*? When was the last time you had your hands and feet looked after? Let's not even talk about your body. No, I take that back…let's. Be honest. What kind of shape are you in? Are you waxed or shaved, feeling as fresh as one of those embarrassing douche commercials? Does your skin give off an inviting scent? Would a man salivate at the very thought of being near you? No? Double no? Then, girls, you have some serious work to do.

You must prepare yourself for the moment when your man arrives, even though you don't yet know his name or what he looks like. Maybe you do know him, but he's someone to whom you haven't given much consideration or who currently plays only a peripheral role in your life. No worries. What matters is that you already know that he will be right for you when he does show up, because you've put your faith on it.

Now, consider this scenario: what if the man of your dreams happens to be the guy who just moved in next door and, being a friendly neighbor, has decided to pop over and introduce himself? Upon hearing the doorbell, you shuffle to the door in your ratty pink bathrobe, holey bath slippers, and a hairnet. You trip over your fat, lazy, ever-shedding cat, damn near breaking your neck on the sweatpants you quickly kicked off when you got back from Cold Stone Creamery and heard the theme song from *Sex and the City* playing. You open the door and there he is: a Boris Kodjoe–meets–George Clooney–esque stunner. And there you are: Dirt McGirt. *Ugh!* Preparation: none. Opportunity: blown. See what I mean?

Now, I'm not just pulling this stuff out of my ass. I've actually applied this to my life and have seen it work every single time in every single scenario, eventually. Ever heard the phrase, "Fake it 'til you make it?" Okay, well, it's sort of like that. As I prepared to exit my twenties, after finding satisfaction in my career and a real sense of accomplishment as a mother and an overall human being, I wanted to share all this good news with a tall, dark, handsome, and sexually compatible man looking for a long-term commitment. I wanted it all, honey, so I decided to pretend as if I already had it.

This may sound a little nutty, but I swear by it. When I met new men, I told them I was married. Shit, I even called the men I'd been seeing and told *them* I got married! I made my home comfy for me but male-friendly as well, and I kept up all those girly beauty rituals that men find alluring. I went to bed early and woke early, preparing breakfast, lunch, and dinner every day. I stayed on top of all my household chores and basically did everything I talk about in this chapter, things I thought a man would appreciate in his woman. I expected the love of my life to show up at any minute. I was calling out to him in my prayers and in every move I made, especially when it came to making sure my personal and business affairs were in order. I wanted my new man to have a complete person as his partner, an asset to his life, and a woman who could be all things to him. I wasn't sure who he would be, but it just so happened he'd been right under my nose. But neither he nor I noticed, not until I began living my life with the intent on being prepared when the opportunity presented itself. Once things were in order in my world, clarity happened, and *whammo!*

Prepare thoroughly, ladies. Your preparation goes further than just your looks and the order of your home. It includes educational, financial, and emotional preparation, all of which are discussed in this book. No truly worthy man wants to be with a woman who can't carry a conversation on various topics with both specific and general knowledge. This same man wouldn't want to be viewed as a cash cow, there to meet your every financial whim. He would want you to have your own money, at least enough to support your current lifestyle. That doesn't mean he's a miser. It means he sees the way a woman handles her finances as a pointed insight into how she handles herself overall. He also doesn't want a basket case, an emotional wreck of a woman carrying around so much baggage from past relationships and family issues that there's no room for healthy emotional interaction with him, and the little space that is available is cluttered with drama.

Clean up your life, ladies. I mean that figuratively and literally. Take the time today to make the world that is You a place that not just your future man would be proud to inhabit, but one you would be proud to swing open the door and let anyone into. When you take the necessary steps and prepare for everything you've asked for, it not only uplifts everything around you, it means that when opportunity comes knocking, you won't be caught covered in cat hair, wearing ratty panties, and with a smear of ice cream on your cheek. You'll be on point, ready and eager to step into the next level of the bright, shiny life that you already knew was yours to begin with.

Recap

- The more desperate you are in your quest to obtain something, the more elusive it becomes.

- The universe always delivers, as long as you believe.

- If you don't believe your man is out there, then guess what? He isn't.

- Start by imagining your life the way it would be if there were a man around.

- Your preparation goes further than just your looks and the order of your home.

Chapter Eleven

Dating for Love or Money

The society we live in is so much more than a capitalistic society. It is a virtual reality where, for a new urban generation, money truly has become the root of all things. For women, in many instances, it's the basis for romantic and sexual relationships. Nowadays, if a man isn't *ballin'*—making and spending money in a grand display—he's considered by many women to be not worth their time and respect. This is very prevalent among women of my generation and even of my mother's. All of them are looking for the same thing: they want a man to rescue them from themselves.

Dating or marrying for money is not a new concept. It's been a way of life for the elite and nobility around the world for centuries. Marriages were frequently prearranged, sometimes at birth. Families of so-called good stock and great wealth wanted to assure that their children married into a family of equal or greater stock, thus stabilizing or improving the family's overall social and political stature. So, "marrying up" isn't an issue. It means you're smart and practical enough to have a plan for the place you want your future family to have in the world. We should all want to financially improve our lots in life, not diminish them. The real issue, however, is that it has to be a fair trade.

Even in those prearranged marriages of old, the bride's family always made sure they had something to offer the groom in exchange for him taking on their daughter. She couldn't just show up. She had to come with something. This something was known as a *dowry*—an offering which included things like money, livestock, and/or land—and it was presented along with the bride. What, exactly, is *your* "dowry"? What do you have to offer? I'm not just talking about money. I mean, overall. For instance, you can't be in your eighth year of nail school, living in your granny's basement with nothing substantial to speak of, expecting a man to come and rescue you!

We all want to shoot for the stars, but are you really bright enough to live among them? Think about that, ladies. It's not meant as an insult. It's a bona fide question you should be asking yourself. I'm not talking about whether you're worthy to live among the stars. We all are. I asked if you were bright enough. Do you have what it takes to strive for excellence and maintain it, not

Vixen Say What?
When a man knows you don't need him to live, he won't want to live without you.

just have it handed to you by way of a man? It's a shame that we expect more from our men than we do from ourselves. Many men find it difficult to respect a woman who thinks this way. No one wants to be saddled with the responsibility of saving you and, as we discuss in another chapter, even if a man gets swept up in the romantic notion of doing so, that feeling will soon wear off once he realizes that he's got dead weight on his hands. If you enter into a relationship based on a man's ability to support you financially, the likelihood increases that either he will begin to resent what he'll view as your gold-digging ways, or he will use your laziness and lack of ambition against you by abusing you financially.

What? You've never heard of financial abuse? You probably have, even though you might not have given it a name. It is a very real form of abuse in which a man uses his position as the breadwinner to control you and your lifestyle. He'll remind you at every turn that everything around you is his and there by the grace of his generosity. You'll constantly be told that it's his money that keeps it all together. He'll start dictating what you do and when you do it, and if you are resistant, there will be a penalty. It may be something small, like not giving you money for something you really want while he overindulges in all his desires, rubbing it in your face that he is the gatekeeper.

Trust me, I've lived through that, and it was compounded with physical and verbal abuse. But just because you're not being thrown around a room or having your teeth knocked out and being calling a stinkin' bitch doesn't mean you're not an abused woman. The man who took care of me was in control of every move I made, everything I thought and said. He knew he had power over me and I knew it, too. I could do or be nothing without him because he held the purse strings—or so I thought. After four years of living under his rule and with his financial manipulations, I left him and I took nothing but my son.

Getting out from under a man who uses his monetary standings to control you is difficult, and serious sacrifices may have to be made. Some men have said, "It's cheaper to keep her," but more often than not it costs us more to stay. Yes, it's okay and quite natural to be attracted to a man who has the ability to provide, but just because he has the ability doesn't mean you should depend solely on that ability to survive. Never date or marry for money. It will never buy you love and honor.

While being a kept woman may sound like fun, I can tell you from personal experience that it very rarely is. We live in a country where the divorce rate soars well over 70 percent. If that holds true—and the reason it isn't even higher is because it can be a pretty harrowing legal process that some people would rather not undertake—then it must follow that the breakup rate must be at least somewhere around 98 percent. There are no legal repercussions to breaking up with someone. Sure, there are emotional, monetary, spiritual, and maybe even physical ones, but no courts need be involved. So what's my point? you ask. My point is this: If you're dating a man for his money, odds are he's already figured that out. Odds also are high that once he's gotten what he wants out of you and becomes bored, he'll replace you. Then where will you be? If he was the sole breadwinner, it means you'll most likely be right back where you started, in that raggedy old apartment you hate so much, or, worse, in Granny's basement, back on the prowl for the next well-to-do man to swindle.

Does the thought of this excite you? It shouldn't. This is no life for you. This is no life for anyone.

Vixen Tip

Be sure you're with him for love and not money.

1. Follow your heart, not trends.

2. Offer to pay for meals and activities from time to time. A real man will not accept but will note your willingness to share the burden.

3. Don't take advice from friends on who to be with, especially those not in relationships or in miserable ones. *You* decide who's right for you.

4. Be careful not to pass on a man with great potential, who will love you for being with him in leaner times, for a man with money who will question your motives.

5. Do not lie to yourself or try to fool him. If you have chosen a man because of what he can do for you, you don't deserve his love and he most certainly deserves better. He will eventually see through you.

Ladies, the best way for you to not end up in this situation is for you to achieve success on your own. Money should never be the driving motivation for entering a relationship. You may end up living a fabulous lifestyle as a result of the promise of financial security, but that is never enough on its own. There are several other factors to take into consideration when selecting a man, many of which are addressed throughout these chapters. If a man happens to be well off in addition to those factors, then good for you! What matters most, however, is that he's honest and genuine, works hard at whatever his profession is, loves and respects you and his family, loves God, and can help you and your family maintain a comfortable life. You should be a helpmate in every way, including financially. This increases the chances of success for your relationship. *Be* the dowry. A woman who offers plenty will always get plenty in return.

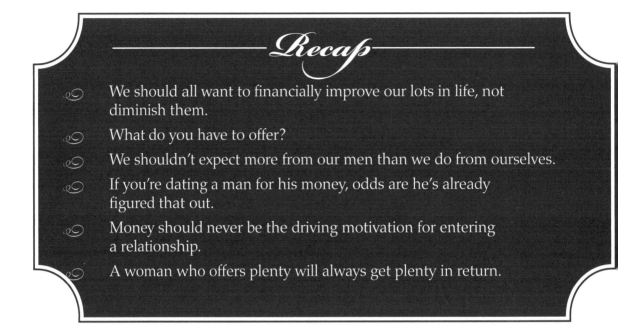

Recap

- We should all want to financially improve our lots in life, not diminish them.

- What do you have to offer?

- We shouldn't expect more from our men than we do from ourselves.

- If you're dating a man for his money, odds are he's already figured that out.

- Money should never be the driving motivation for entering a relationship.

- A woman who offers plenty will always get plenty in return.

Section 2

How to Attract Him

I am a firm believer that women and men misunderstand one another

nearly 100 percent of the time. Men are very simple creatures, needing

very little to attract them and make them happy. Women tend to complicate

things with overthinking and emotional excess. Get yourselves together, girls,

and the men will take notice!

Chapter Twelve

Goals

Who are you? Where are you going in life? Where do you *want* to go? As a woman who exists in a society historically built upon women looking for men to save them, make them whole, and, essentially, define who they are—even in these postfeminism times—let me say that not only is this notion impractical and absurd, it's plain old dead wrong. You'll never get anywhere thinking like this! If you want to gain and maintain control in your relationships, romantically or otherwise, you have to gain and maintain control of yourself. This means having a sense of direction. In order to achieve anything, ladies, you have got to have goals!

Who would we be if we didn't have goals to motivate us and propel us forward? A woman without focus is just an aimless soul walking the earth, unaware of her purpose and the steps necessary to be successful in her life and in the lives of those who care for and depend upon her. Defining who you are and what you want in life should not be done for the sole objective of getting a man, but they are essential elements in doing so. Men can spot an unsure, unformed woman. Those kinds of females make for excellent prey. Duplicitous men love someone whose mind is malleable. A woman like that can be tricked into everything from making herself available for booty calls to bankrolling a man without expecting anything in return. If you fall into this category, you will find yourself not just manipulated by men but buffeted and bruised by the fancies of chance, because you don't know how to gain your footing. Why?—because you haven't even determined what your footing is.

A woman with a clear sight of her goals not only knows what she wants, she makes a plan to ensure that she gets it. Once you identify a direction for yourself and lay out a plan for achieving it, understand and accept that not everyone will be supportive, especially if what you set out to do defies their idea of convention or is something much

Vixen Tip

It is important to organize your thoughts and start small if you have to, leading into your bigger, more long-term goals. Part of planning for those long-term goals is accomplishing the hundreds of short-term goals that will get you there. It's good practice to start with organizing even the tiniest of tasks on a daily basis by writing them down in a daily planner.

bolder and higher than they would attempt. Do not let this prevent you from going forward. Having a strong sense of conviction and refusing to be taken off course are necessary to stay focused and geared toward a better quality of living.

Vixen Tip

I find it helpful to make a daily list of everything that needs to be done in both my personal and business lives. I keep track of everything in a yearly planner. Each day, I mark off the accomplished tasks and move on to the next. However, since I often bite off more than I can chew, I sometimes carry unaccomplished tasks over to the next day. This goes on for weeks until most everything is done, yet by the end of the year, there always seems to be a few things still left untouched. It's usually the little, more tedious chores, like changing the windshield wipers or cleaning out the closet. In December, I put together a list of all those little things that weren't checked off in my planner throughout the year and make those my end-of-the-year goals. This ensures that I go into my new year unburdened by the year before.

By now, you're probably saying, *What the hell does this have to do with snagging a man, Vixen?! I bought this book for the good stuff, the steamy stuff. Get to the blowjobs and pole dances, already!* We will, we will. But before we do all that, we must lay the proper foundation beforehand. Trust me, this will allow you to get whatever you want from a man. More importantly, it will ensure that everything is in place for you to get what you want out of life in general. A good friend once told me, "You can't build castles in the sky." I never used to know what this meant, but now it makes so much sense. Without a sturdy foundation, everything you reach for and build will fail.

So read on, ladies, and do so in the spirit of feminine camaraderie. Know that I only want to impart to you the benefit of my wisdom, wisdom I wish someone had shared with me when I was younger. This is especially significant if you are twenty-five or older but haven't yet figured out where you're going with your life. While it's true that it's never too late, the sooner you get yourself together, the sooner you can begin laying out a plan to, ultimately, realize your dreams.

I'll use myself for an example here. At the age of twenty-five, I discovered there were bigger, much more pertinent goals in my life that needed to be met, many of which were way overdue. That was the year I knew that there'd be no more excuses for me. I had to make a move for the positive. It was a case of either sinking or daring to swim—with strong, bold strokes. Twenty-five is a very significant age for a woman. It is a critical mile marker of sorts. By this point, most of us have been out of high school for seven years already and may have also graduated from college. You may be married and/or have already had children. You're a quarter century old!

If you've reached this age and you still haven't figured out what it is you would like to accomplish in the long term or begun to map out how to do so, you're already operating at a gross disadvantage. If your personality isn't clearly shaped and your self-esteem is shaky, you're even more in the hole. Don't be misled by those around you saying things like, "It's okay, you're still young." People love to throw that phrase around, but those same people will hold you accountable a short time later if your life is still in disarray. Then their judgment will be harsh and unforgiving, filled with comments like "You should have your act together by now." Time is a commodity. Treat it as such. It is not something to be squandered once you've become an adult.

Picture a twenty-five-year-old man living in his mother's basement, jobless and with no goals or ambition. Now, picture yourself saying to this person, "It's okay, you're only twenty-five." How ridiculous would that be? After twenty-five, there are no more excuses and very little leeway. That's why this is a good time to come up with a five-year plan, if you haven't already, and put the wheels in motion to accomplish your bigger, more life-changing objectives.

Vixen Say What?
Crucial topics for your five-year plan should include, but should not be limited to, education, career, family, and physical and even emotional goals.

I believe you should have a clear idea of your life goals as early as high school, but whenever it is that you begin to formulate them, each day should be spent moving forward. These can't just be casual steps forward. You need to fix it in your mind, always strategizing and preparing. You have to become obsessed with being whom and what you wish to be, letting nothing deter you.

I clearly remember when I decided I would make my lifelong dream of being a writer come true. I was kicking around the idea of writing my first book, *Confessions of a Video Vixen*, and mentioned this to my then-attorney. His response to my life-changing goal was, "No one will ever care about this." Right then, I knew that someone would. Seeing his words as a gauntlet—a challenge—rather than a deterrent, I began to write feverishly. Soon after, *Confessions* was published and very quickly hit the *New York Times* bestseller's list, followed by *The Vixen Diaries* just two short years later. My point? That attorney's words meant nothing in the scheme of my life. They weren't important because I chose to not let them be important. Imagine where I'd be now if I had taken his comment as gospel. Look at what happened when I made the choice to follow my own plan for myself and not someone else's dismissive, limited vision of me. That attorney is probably still greasing up his lips, trying to pull his foot out of his mouth.

Let the adversity and resistance you encounter from others have an energizing effect instead of a depleting one. If necessary, use their negativity as the incentive to prove them wrong, but don't let that be your guiding force. Personal fulfillment should be the beacon that motivates you. Approval from others is usually the last thing you will get when your goals are still in the dream

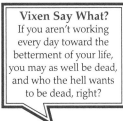

Vixen Say What?
If you aren't working every day toward the betterment of your life, you may as well be dead, and who the hell wants to be dead, right?

phase. Don't look for or wait around for approval. If I had, God knows, I would have never become the best-selling author I'd always dreamt of being, and you wouldn't be reading this book.

It's encouraging to have dreams of college, careers, and personal and financial success, even though those things may seem impossible to touch from where you are in your life right now. Everything is possible and there is a path around every obstacle. Before I had a computer and access to the Internet, I would spend hours at either the public library or at my local bookstore. I wanted to know how to write and sell everything from treatments to screenplays to television shows and books. I bought or checked out books on these subjects and started writing—on paper, with a pencil, since I couldn't afford a computer. That was how my career was born. Those were the first critical steps to the realization of my dreams. Even if your financial resources are limited, there's a way to access the information and inspiration you need to be whom and what you desire.

Vixen Tip

Spend a lot of time reading about the things and people that interest you. Emulate those who have been successful in the craft and field you wish to be a part of. Be inspired!

Utilize your local library and bookstores, especially the ones with cafés and couches in them! There is no reason to go hungry or be uncomfortable while getting your act together!

I had goals, as we all do, of owning things. This desire was a strong motivator, making me determined to accomplish my long-term objectives. Like many people, I wanted a big house, a nice car, vacations, fancy clothes, and many other luxuries that I saw on television and in films.

Vixen Tip

I would go through magazines, cut out pictures of what I wanted, and tape them to my wall, poster board, refrigerator, or bathroom mirror. We usually think of teenagers as the ones always taping things all over the house, but these weren't photos of pop stars and pop-culture icons. These photos represented my future accomplishments and my incentive to move toward my long-term goals. There were photos of cars, homes, vacation destinations, and people I always admired. I have accomplished all of those goals and have now moved on to others. I still post pictures. It works, and I strongly recommend that you try it.

These tidbits are just some of my suggestions for becoming a more focused, goal-oriented woman who will achieve everything she puts her mind, skill, and energy toward. So many of us feel stuck because of our circumstances. Perhaps no one's ever told you that you can be more than what you are now or offered advice on how to move toward your dreams. Maybe you already know what you have to do to reach your goals, but your spirit has been broken by a bad relationship or a distracting home life, and you just need a little pick-me-up. I've been there, and it wasn't that long ago. Believe me, ladies, when I say that these simple steps helped me, and they can work for you. By having your goals and a strategy to accomplish them intact, you are one step closer to having the types of relationships you desire.

Recap

- In order to achieve anything, ladies, you have got to have goals!
- Men can spot an unsure, unformed woman.
- Not everyone will be supportive, especially if what you set out to do defies their idea of convention.
- Without a sturdy foundation, everything you reach for and build will fail.
- The sooner you get yourself together, the sooner you can begin laying out a plan to ultimately realize your dreams.
- Time is a commodity.
- After twenty-five, there are no more excuses and very little leeway.
- Let the adversity and resistance you encounter from others have an energizing effect instead of a depleting one.
- Everything is possible and there is a path around every obstacle.
- By having your goals and a strategy to accomplish them intact, you are one step closer to having the types of relationships you desire.

Chapter Thirteen

Principles

We all have principles of one kind or another. Our principles and values play a major part in defining who we are. And as sure as there are differences in our fingerprints, so are there differences in what we will and will not stand for in our lives.

While one definition of the word *principle* has to do with morally correct behavior, I try not to let the morals of others get in the way of my decision making. Most of the mores we are told to live by are based upon the double standards of a patriarchal society, based upon rules set by men to keep women in their place. If you take that fact out of the equation, you'll realize that what an individual considers right and wrong is typically directed by an internal compass, a compass that is, for better or worse, often shaped by that individual's upbringing. One person's outrage might therefore be another person's no big deal—it's all subjective. And although we live in a world that is quick to categorize and demean others based on their behavior, none of us have the right to judge another's moral correctness and principles.

As for your principles, do you even know what they are? And as it relates to dating, are you aware of what you will and won't accept? Have you even thought about it before?

Most women, by the time they've reached their early twenties, have experienced some form of teenage heartbreak and, perhaps, the reckless intensity that comes with first love. Your emotions, untested up to that point, were allowed to run rampant. No boundaries were set because there had been nothing by which to measure. You loved hard and heavy, soaring high, and when things eventually ended, you hit the ground at crushing speed. You probably thought you would never get over the pain of that first breakup, but, miraculously, you do, and you learn to do this dance over and over again, each time learning more about yourself than you knew before.

Once you began to experience joy and excitement, pain and disappointment, and all the feelings in between, you start to set parameters for yourself for what you like and don't like based on these early learning experiences. If you don't set boundaries for yourself, you soon find yourself repeating the same thing again and again until, ultimately, it becomes a pattern. The only way to avert this kind of serial situation is to be clear about what you want and what fits within the guidelines of your life; otherwise, you'll find yourself constantly recovering from emotional devastation. To paraphrase a popular adage, a woman who stands for nothing will fall for anything.

Who wants to be a pushover, anyway? Ladies, it's important that you not lose sight of the rules and expectations of your life. Always fight for what you believe in and never settle for less. Don't allow anyone to make you feel ashamed for only wanting to date a man who is successful in his chosen line of business and financially independent, or a man who commands respect among his peers or even unconsciously provokes fear and envy in them. If you fall for a short, thick, bald man and all your friends have tall, athletic boyfriends with magnificent heads of hair, so what? If that's what you like, then, damn it, that's what you like. Don't let the judgment and pressure of others deter you or make you bend to their will.

I find it absolutely silly and hypocritical that some men do everything in their power to become financially successful and acquire all the trappings that indicate their wealth (a big house or an apartment, luxury vehicles, the finest clothing), all in an effort to get the most attractive woman they can—a woman whose sexiness and overall desirability can be a testament to the virility of the man who got her. These same men then turn around and accuse the women they attracted of being gold diggers. Where's the sense in all this? If the man didn't want to attract a woman who found a successful man sexy, ambitious, and would be a great provider for her and a future family, then why did he work so hard? Was it to turn women off? Of course not.

We all know that an accomplished, driven man will not be ignored. He'll buy the biggest luxury vehicle he can and trick it out to within an inch of its metal, all in an effort to shout to the sexiest women around, *Pick me! I make money! I can afford things! I can afford* you! and to declare to his fellow men, *I am a man apart! Above all others! Look at my big toy! It's bigger than yours!* It is a formula evident in the mating rituals of almost every living creature. Males in the animal kingdom typically choose females for their ability to reproduce and nurture their young to adulthood. Females typically choose males for their power and exuberant masculinity above other males. This is why male peacocks will fan their lustrous tail feathers, strutting their stuff, demonstrating that they possess the best plumage and should therefore get the prize peahens.

A perfect example of this played out in my living room one night on the Discovery Channel.

There was a family of four lionesses, their cubs, and a male sire. One day, a lonely lion in need of his own family came across this one and challenged the sire to a duel. The lonely lion won, killing the sire, then killed off the cubs as the lionesses looked on. The lionesses didn't fight for their children but allowed them to be murdered, and then submitted to the lonely lion, who was lonely no more. Not long thereafter, the lionesses bore him his own sets of cubs. Now *that* is male prowess!

So what's your point, Vixen? you might ask. My point is this: it is instinctive, even in the wild, for a woman to be drawn to power and success, so there's nothing wrong with you being drawn to the most successful, most powerful men who can provide for you. That doesn't make you a gold digger. That makes you smart. That being said, however, if it is part of your dating principle to be with a man who can comfortably provide for you and his family, make sure you are worthy of it. This should be a fair trade. No man wants to take on a woman who just wants to enjoy the spoils of his hard work and contribute nothing of her own to complement and enhance their union.

So many times throughout my life, I sacrificed my own principles in order to feed an immediate need for companionship or acceptance. In retrospect, I have learned that instant gratification is not worth sacrificing long-term peace of mind. Many of us accept less than we deserve, often settling for a lifestyle we would have never wished for ourselves. Whether we take a job that makes us unhappy or leaves us unfulfilled, or a mate who does the same, or live in a place that makes us uncomfortable, or keep friends that only drag us down, all of it is a form of settling and, therefore, ignoring our own values. Living an unfulfilling life is a form of unconscious punishment, usually brought on by feelings of unworthiness. Daring to live according to your principles, refusing to settle for less in your life and not just defining yourself by the moment and unfortunate circumstance can make all the difference.

Vixen Say What?
The woman who stands for nothing will fall for anything and lie down for anyone.

Vixen Tip

Just as I have done with the goals I have set for myself, I also keep a list of the principles I most believe in, which I also recommend you take the time to do. I do not believe that your principles should be exactly the same as your mate's, but they should, at least, be similar or easily blended. The worst thing is to be in a relationship and be unaware of what your man stands for or who he wants to be, then one day realizing you are at polar opposites on some of life's most critical issues. I believe that basic beliefs and principles should be discussed, along with personal and professional goals, soon after meeting a man with the potential to be a future mate. It's an important step in the selection and elimination process.

Principles are not something you are born with, but are taught and acquired as you experience life. Each of us must have principles and rules to live by, otherwise we will find ourselves mired in chaos. People will be able to take advantage of you because they'll know that you have no sense of self.

When you have no sense of who you are, you can be easily persuaded to do the bidding of others. So many women, myself included, were born into families that were unclear on how to give their little girls decent principles to guide them through life. The more fortunate were born to parents who instilled into them a strong sense of self and personal potential by teaching them what to expect from themselves, as well as from the world around them. Everything I have ever learned was as a result of life experiences, heartaches, and letdowns. Once upon a time I viewed this as a curse, but now I realize that it has brought me the greatest gift—wisdom—one that I am eager to share with others.

> ## Vixen Tip
> Your list of principles should include, but should not be limited to, the ways in which you wish to run your dating, home, and business life, as well as your physical, emotional, and spiritual one.

I have sat down at my computer three times now to pen books I have known would be ill-received by some. And even though I may not have had the same principles instilled into me as some of the so-called gatekeepers of morality, I have always had my own set of principles and have stuck by them. Thankfully, over time they've changed to reflect growth and maturity in my life. Even when no one else believes in what I stand for and who I am, I cannot waiver—not if I believe a word I have written. In the face of ridicule and a good old-fashioned biblical stoning, I stick to my principles, knowing some of them differ vastly from those of others, and at day's end I am always vindicated by what I believe. Don't be afraid to stand firm on your truths and values. You are the author of your destiny and what is true for you may never work for someone else, but it's *your* compass. Use it to navigate. Never abandon your code of ethics. You will always be rewarded for sticking to your guns.

Nowadays, when given lemons, instead of bemoaning the situation, I opt to make lemonade, a dazzling lemon chicken, and one hell of a lemon meringue pie. And while there are many rules we can have for our lives and relationships, there are a few that should be universal. Never allow anyone to degrade you. That includes both physically and verbally. Hitting, choking, shaking, spitting—none of it is acceptable for a man to do to you. Don't even allow anyone to look at you in a way meant to demean you. Bottom line, any form of abuse is absolutely unacceptable. You set the terms for what you allow others to do to you. They take their cues from you. If you cower when others yell, then they know you can be overpowered. Never be afraid to walk away. When you have your life in order, it becomes much easier to do so.

I cannot stress how important this is. Sure, lap dances and dildos are more fun to talk about, and as I said before, we'll get to them soon enough…but *you* are more important than anything.

Once you've got your life in order, you can have all the lap dances and dildos you want!

Recap

- None of us have the right to judge another's moral correctness and principles.
- A woman who stands for nothing will fall for anything.
- Don't let the judgment and pressure of others deter you or make you bend to their will.
- If it is part of your dating principle to be with a man who can comfortably provide for you and his family, make sure you are worthy of it.
- Any form of abuse is absolutely unacceptable.

Chapter Fourteen

Power

Sex is power. Money is power. Education is power. Beauty is power. Property is power. Position is power. There have been many things offered as definite sources and proof of power, too many to count. All of these suggestions can be correct, based on what your objectives are. Personally, I find that power doesn't exist in just one thing, but in a combination of many. What good is sex if it's with an unmotivated nonintellectual who doesn't have the wherewithal to at least strive to own something in his or her corner of the world? How would you be able to reach full emotional or physical orgasm with someone like that?

Now…what if this person is you?

Vixen!

That's right, I said it.

Forget about what you want the man you attract to have. What exactly do *you* bring to the table? Are you banking solely on your good looks to earn a powerful position in life and relationships? Do you really believe that if all you have to offer is a gorgeous face, a killer figure, and a hefty sexual appetite, you can keep a man's attention? Ha! That must mean you've never heard the running joke, "For every beautiful woman, there's a man who's sick of fucking her." That means *you*, pretty girl—so much for beauty's power. I'm sure you've figured that out by now, if you've ever found yourself eating the dust of a man who couldn't get away from you fast enough because he was fed up with your limitations. "How could he leave a woman as fine as me?" you ask yourself. Because, girlfriend, looks are not, and never will be, enough. Not to mention the fact that they have a very limited shelf life. If beauty is your sole currency, what happens when that beauty fades?

Maybe you think that being smart, having a degree, landing that high-paying corporate job, and buying that beautiful new town house overlooking the park will attract him. Now that's power, for sure. What? He still left you? But you're smart, damn it! You graduated summa cum laude from an Ivy League school! And your town house…it's so lovely, with lots of expensive artwork and furniture. How could he leave?

Vixen Say What?
Good looks will always get you in the door, but what's going to keep you in the room?

So many women offer too much of one thing and none of the other, believing that they can't do it all. Nothing could be further from the truth. We as women are incredibly constructed creatures, designed with the capacity to accomplish a broad range of things…simultaneously. That doesn't mean you have to be Superwoman. What it does mean is that it's in our best interest to work and live to our fullest potential. *This* is how you gain power. A woman who knows her craft, works hard at it, and is successful in it, and can contribute to the financial responsibilities of a dual-income household or hold herself down just as well as or better than a man is powerful. A woman who can do that and still come home to care for her children, fix a delicious meal, and keep a clean and organized home is powerful. That same woman also takes impeccable care of herself, keeping her skin, hair, nails, and figure well-maintained, and she still manages to find the time and energy to please her man in ways usually only found in their fantasies. This woman exudes power. You don't see men walking away from this kind of woman every day.

Sound like too much? It's not, especially if you are truly living up to your potential. And I'm not suggesting you do this just to get a man. Do this for you. This builds up your ego and keeps you living and moving in your purpose. That's the secret of power. It's already within you. All you have to do is tap in to it.

Vixen Tip

Pick a day, just one day, when you will do everything you've always wanted but for which you never thought you had the time, energy, or gumption. Get up, make your bed, head out for a bit of exercise, then come home and get into a steamy shower. While showering, pay close attention to yourself. Be sure to shave all that hair you've been neglecting over the past week or so. Prepare a healthy breakfast, put on an outfit that makes you feel beautiful, and head out to work. Hopefully, you enjoy your job and are able to perform with vigor and enthusiasm. Come home, prepare or buy dinner, straighten up your place, and slip into the shower, then into something sexy. Invite the man you are dating over or jump on the one you have at home. Ride him until you can ride no more, then either allow him to go home, or curl up next to him and end your day with a smile. Will you be exhausted? Yes! (Even more so if you have children.) But you would have done it all. Even though this may not be an everyday routine, try it once or twice a week. You'll feel so accomplished, so complete, and so very powerful. And guess what? You are!

Power is something that eludes many women. We're not always sure of how to harness it, often falling back on the only tools we believe to work, mainly beauty and sex. At some point during the course of history, power seems to have been set aside as something strictly for men. Yes, there are instances of women ruling monarchies and the like, but there's no question that this is a proverbial "man's world," and they seemingly have most of the power. The word power itself is masculine in tone and implies a certain indestructibility of those whom it is used to describe. Power is not easily earned but is absolutely necessary in order to be successful.

Part of gaining power is being in control of every aspect of your life. I believe it is important to have the exact components in your life that the average successful and powerful man has in his, all the while retaining your feminine qualities and sensibilities. In general, men do not rely on their emotions to guide them through their personal or business lives. They seek facts and are solution-oriented, examining what's in front of them and rationalizing the cause and effect of everything. If something goes wrong, they don't stop to get emotional about it the way women do. They immediately go into fix-it mode and try to change the outcome. If a man hates his car, he will take steps to buy a new one. If he does not have enough money to buy the car of his choice, an industrious, driven man will find a way to make more money in order to do so. He will not look for someone else to buy it for him. He will not blame the establishment for his woes. He will *become* the establishment and destroy his obstacles. These are obviously generalizations and are not true of every man, but they are certainly true of successful men.

Vixen Say What?
Nothing moves without power. Nothing changes without motion.

If you wish to gain more power, you will need to become more rational in your approach to life. Decide to become more practical and proactive and less emotional and reactive when critical thinking is required. Examine your dreams and aspirations. Realize that *no* dream is out of reach. You can be who and whatever you wish in life and, in turn, be the best. Once you have made this realization, you should educate yourself in your desired field and interests. Do so to the fullest extent. Do not rely on others to give you shortcuts. Fix your eyes upon your goals and be willing to do the work to achieve them. Constantly think of and picture yourself as you would like to be, always imagining and moving toward the next step in the creation of your future. Like so many powerful and successful men, you should be unrelenting and undeterred in your aspirations. Get excited about your life! By focusing on fulfilling your potential, you are giving yourself the greatest gift you could ever have. It doesn't matter if your goal is to be a successful wife, homemaker, mother, and/or CEO. This principle of commitment and focus applies to everything you are and wish to be.

Once I began putting together the pieces of my life, somewhere around the beginning of 2002, I realized what I had been doing wrong throughout the years and that the use of just one word would have been able to save me an enormous amount of heartache and regret. One of the most important pieces of advice I have ever given to women, both young and old, is to become the ultimate authority on the word *no*. A powerful woman can never be persuaded to do anything she does not want to do. Her opinion may not count to the entire world, but when she speaks, everyone in *her* world listens. This doesn't mean that it's either her way or the highway, since in a relationship both compromise and understanding are required. What it does mean, however, is that her opinion counts and holds weight within her relationships and household. As a result of commanding this kind of respect, you may find words like *bitch* and *diva* being applied to you. Don't let it break your stride or alter your mind-set. Words such as these are impotent tools of the insecure, both men and women, who otherwise don't know how to deal with a woman who is confident in her identity. Personally, I don't see anything wrong with either of those words. I've been called worse, and it hasn't stolen my thunder in any way. As long as I am in control of my own time and space, little else matters. You should never be afraid to assert yourself and be self-empowered. At the end of the day, only you can be held accountable for your life. There's a way to do this even when you have more than yourself to consider, such as a mate and/or children. By being comfortable in your own skin and assured of your value, accomplishments, and self-worth, you, in turn, empower and strengthen those around you.

Ladies, we are capable of having and being everything we desire. Know this to be true. In the process, it is necessary to understand how to shift among the many roles that we undertake in our multidimensional lives. Sometimes it's difficult to be one way at work and with our friends and colleagues, and not take that same dominant persona into our homes. We often operate singularly in the world, and when we arrive home to our mates, we continue in that singular mind-set. Part of a woman's power exists in knowing when there must be a changing of the guards, to know that it's okay to relinquish power to her male counterpart.

A powerful woman has her own everything, including her own educated opinion. You should take it upon yourself to be informed, and be able to hold an intelligent conversation about current events and stand your ground in a debate. You should have your own sense of style and not follow the lead of others. It is also imperative, in this day and age, to have your own money and your own way of making more as you progress in life. To be powerful, you must not *need* a man to support you, although you can *allow* him to. It is also a good idea to have a life outside of your home and relationship, taking the time to enjoy life with your own friends and family.

Even if you are possessed of all these things—your own opinion, money, and a place in the world—a woman of power knows when to speak and when to listen. She chooses her words carefully when she decides to interject and knows how to process the information she is being given. She utilizes it toward the betterment of her life and that of her family and friends.

I've made many of the classic mistakes women make, such as needing a man to support me and not having my own life outside of my romantic relationships. By not having a job, furthering my education, or having a plan for myself, I gave the men in my life tremendous power over me. I didn't believe in my dreams, never spent time with friends, and was often estranged from my family. I eventually figured it out through extreme trial and error, but imagine if I had known then how truly powerful I really am! You have this same power within you. It's waiting to do your bidding.

From Helen of Troy to Cleopatra to Mrs. Wallis Simpson, who was able to get a king to abdicate his throne just to be with her, women have been able to captivate men with the power of their femininity. Empires have crumbled, wars have been launched, and some of the most powerful men on earth have been destroyed in the battle for the love of a woman. Only when we realize that we are, indeed, the more powerful of the sexes will our true nature be fully unleashed. Yes, there is great power in your sexuality, but it can also be dangerous and addicting. Once you realize that you possess this power and that it works—whether you want it to or not, in both your personal and professional lives—you're going to have to harness it. It's unfortunate that men and women alike seem to believe in an "idiot theory," that a woman cannot be aware of herself sexually and still be intelligent. I have intense sexual feelings that I am not only aware of but also excited to discuss. Many women feel the same, but they have been taught to be ashamed of their bodies and their sexuality, especially if they are highly educated professional women. A powerful woman is aware and unafraid of all sides of her femininity and has learned how to embrace her masculine side, integrating it all to her benefit.

Know your power, ladies. Master it and make it your own. Use it to create a better you. The world, particularly men, will respond accordingly.

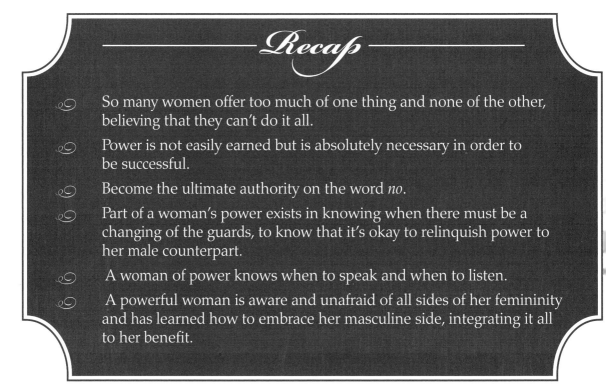

Recap

- So many women offer too much of one thing and none of the other, believing that they can't do it all.

- Power is not easily earned but is absolutely necessary in order to be successful.

- Become the ultimate authority on the word *no*.

- Part of a woman's power exists in knowing when there must be a changing of the guards, to know that it's okay to relinquish power to her male counterpart.

- A woman of power knows when to speak and when to listen.

- A powerful woman is aware and unafraid of all sides of her femininity and has learned how to embrace her masculine side, integrating it all to her benefit.

Chapter Fifteen

Position

Position. What exactly is that, anyway? Is it our career? Our financial status? Does it refer to our place in the world? It sounds like it may even have something to do with power. In truth, it can be all those things, but what I'm specifically referring to now is in relation to how you achieve it, particularly the manner in which you as a woman carry yourself and dictate the way in which you will be treated. Your comportment—and by that, I mean your demeanor, your presence, and the personal ethics that go with it—plays a major role in your position and how and whether you will excel in life and love. It can affect your career and how far you rise. That, in turn, can impact your financial success. And a woman's rank within her own home will eventually determine the type of relationship she'll have with her mate and how he will relate to her. A woman who upholds a powerful and meaningful position in life and relationships will inevitably find herself in control of both. She will be queen of her domain. Yet, you can't expect to be treated as a queen when you run your life with ragged abandon and act like nothing more than a common wench, a chambermaid, or a simple servant.

A strong position lends to an enormous amount of respect, which is most evident in the way we relate to men. In general, we as women find it difficult to respect a man with little or no position in life, a man who allows himself to be ruled by his mother even though he is an adult, or one who allows others to run his life personally and professionally. Whether he permits his boss to treat him condescendingly or gives in to his best buddy's every boyish whim, women don't appreciate a man who cannot run his own show and is not in control of his household. Men like this don't radiate the kind of confidence we need from a protector and a provider. He would never, ever do.

If that is the case, and if we apply such strict judgment to men, why should women today be held to a different standard? What man would want the female version of this? When it comes to women, men are just as attracted to strength and position as we are to those traits in them.

Though they have so many other things to distract them, like our bodies and looks, once the initial attraction wears off and they've gotten past our physical presentation, men begin examining us for other, more substantial attributes, like intelligence, self-esteem, independence, and ambition. Of course, I am speaking generally here, referring to a best-case scenario. There are plenty of men who don't care what you look like or where you're going—or where *they're* going, for that matter. Those are not the types of men you should be seeking, not if your goal is to be a woman to be reckoned with. You deserve a man who wants to see you rise to your highest potential, one who encourages you to thrive and does everything he can to support you, as you in turn support him. Keep in mind, ladies, that this requires a highly evolved man, one who is confident and secure enough in his own drive, ambition, and sense of self that your achievements and position aren't a threat to his masculinity and control. If you find a man like this, treasure him, for he is indeed a jewel and an excellent candidate for a relationship.

Many of us know from experience, however, that there are plenty of insecure, immature, stupid little boys running around posing as men, who would happily prefer you to believe you're much less than you're worth. These kinds of men can't handle a woman of position, and should you become involved with them, they will attempt to erode your esteem in every way possible in order to feel good about themselves. Vixen says stay away from them, for obvious reasons. These men want the opposite of everything I've suggested for you in the prior chapters, and everything I will suggest throughout this book. The right man will want a woman who has more substantial qualities, one who can hold her own in their relationship. As I've already noted

Vixen Say What? People treat you how they see you.

regarding your principles, we teach our men how to treat us. Somewhere along the way, after women's lib and the burning of bras, after fighting for the right to vote and for equal jobs and wages, someone convinced us that women are still following the lead of men. While there's nothing wrong with looking at how successful men have historically approached gaining position, remember that *you* are the master of your fate. You don't need a man to define your place in the world for you.

Men are following *our* lead and have been doing so for centuries. Women are and have been the foundation of civilization since the dawn of mankind. We are the nurturers, the child bearers, the dynasty creators, and, in certain matriarchal societies, the rulers. Today's woman can have a successful career and run a successful household, if that is what she chooses to do. While it is not unheard of, how often do you find that happening with men? Many of them look to be taken care of at the end of the workday. Our workday never truly ends, yet many women are able to manage this and never lose their stride. That's because we're made of tough stuff, ladies. You must realize that about yourselves. Don't ever let anyone make you think you're the lesser sex because you possess what is sometimes perceived as a delicate sensibility.

This is why it is so important to have and maintain a strong position in every aspect of your life. Men look to us for instructions on how to treat us. If you haven't cultivated anything of your own, you will be viewed as weak and unstable, and handled as such. In a relationship, both parties must know and respect the other's position, especially as it relates to the roles they will play. You must allow the man to *be* the man. By nature, and in theory, the males of most species set the atmosphere in which the relationship and family will be run. While this suggests that you should not be defiant when taking your cues from him, it does not mean that you should not participate in establishing that atmosphere. Once your man has set the initial tone of things and that tone does not conflict with your personal ethics and values, you can then set your own tone within those parameters, ultimately integrating it with his. This is how you mutually establish the relationship, instead of having it be defined for you, solely by him.

Vixen Tip

Let's say your mate decides to stay out past what you both have agreed is a respectful hour, without an explanation. You're sitting at home, waiting. While you're waiting, guess what happened? You've now gained the leverage needed to up the ante on things in your relationship. A power shift has taken place where you now hold the advantage because he has violated rules that were (and should have been) established by the two of you from the very beginning. Still, you must handle this situation lovingly, taking care to respect his position as the man of the house. Don't scream or carry on when he finally walks through the door. He already knows he's in for it. He's expecting it. Defy his expectation. Welcome him with a warm embrace. Take off his shoes. Help undress him and get him tucked into bed, even asking if he needs anything before he falls asleep. Whatever you do, just smile and play your position—that of a woman who has been steadfast and true to her role in the relationship. If you do anything other than this, you'll only relinquish your upper hand and sabotage the hard work you have done thus far in gaining a respectful position in the household.

Once you have exercised this kind of restraint, your position will change, strengthening in your favor. Being able to alter your position requires you being a woman of power, a woman who knows her worth. You can't be a taker, contributing nothing to your home and relationship yet demanding everything. You can't be needy and dependent and then try to pull rank. You don't have any.

When your man awakes the next morning after an unexplained late night out, breakfast should be cooked, the house should be spotless, and laundry should be done. Everything and everyone should be in order. You may be saying to yourself, *Vixen, are you crazy?* but trust me. There is a method to all this. You see, he'll actually be waiting for the fallout. He'll be expecting it. He already knows he broke the rules, and it will be hanging there between you, heavy but unspoken. Your calm, even demeanor will worry him tremendously, especially if this is the first time he's ever tested your boundaries. Smile and go about your usual business, happy and unconcerned. When he asks what's going on with you, say, "Nothing, honey. What's going on with you?" That subtext in those words alone with tell him everything. You've just given him a chance to explain himself, and now the burden is on him to eventually do so or potentially lose his footing with you. If he doesn't offer an explanation right then, continue about your normal day. Go to work. Go to the store or the mall. It doesn't matter where you go. What *does* matter is when you come back—and you won't, at least not when you say you are. Offer no explanation upon your return. You don't have to do anything drastic during that time you're away. Maybe you were only at your mother's house, or fast asleep at a friend's, having set an alarm to wake you when you planned on returning. He doesn't need to know that. Just make sure you're as late as he was the night before. Even if it's just for an hour or two, make yourself unavailable to him. Send his calls to voice mail if he rings your cell. Don't return his text messages.

When you walk in the door, he will most likely be waiting for you. In the event that he is, accept no quarrels. If he persists, ask him, "Did I say anything when you came home last night at four in the morning? Did I disrespect you or your position in any way? Or did I tuck you into bed and serve you breakfast this morning?" Your point will be well taken, and if you are a woman of power who has made her position in the relationship clear, he will know what to do next. Trust me, it won't involve disrespecting you again.

Some of you may frown upon this, seeing it as a game. While it may appear that way, this is an effective method for clarifying terms of respect in the relationship in situations where those terms are being tested. This method allows for both parties to reach a mutual agreement, with minimal conflict, of how they will treat each other. If conflict does arise, or if your man continues to stay out late in retaliation, using your actions as an excuse for continued disrespect, then your foundation wasn't set correctly in the first place. Perhaps you need to rethink this relationship. Maybe this is not the man for you.

This is an example of a worst-case scenario, yet the general principles are simple. Everyone is an individual and should be treated as such. Not even in marriage does the other person become your property. I was fortunate enough to learn this lesson very early in life, although it didn't register until I was about twenty-five. Even then, I wasn't able to utilize the wisdom I'd gained until I was nearly thirty. In retrospect, I was always trying to change my boyfriends, hoping to make them into what I wanted them to be. I would try to force them into loving and committing to me, into staying home, and staying over. That neediness and compulsion to own and control only resulted in the exact opposite of what I intended. Instead of drawing them closer to me, I repeatedly drove them further away. Eventually, I figured it out. It is not force that makes a man bend; it is positioning and acceptance, patience and restraint. Allow your man the latitude to do as he pleases, as long as he understands that the wind blows in all directions and he might easily find himself pissing in that wind if he doesn't govern himself accordingly. In that case, let's just hope that his mouth is closed.

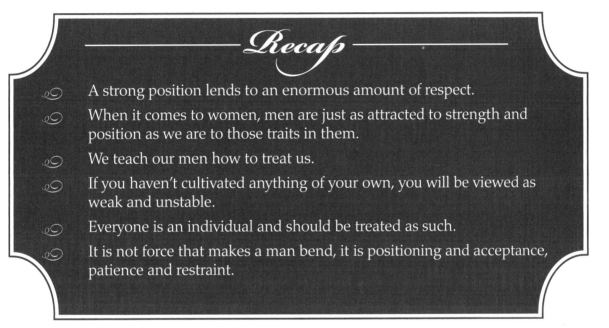

Recap

- A strong position lends to an enormous amount of respect.
- When it comes to women, men are just as attracted to strength and position as we are to those traits in them.
- We teach our men how to treat us.
- If you haven't cultivated anything of your own, you will be viewed as weak and unstable.
- Everyone is an individual and should be treated as such.
- It is not force that makes a man bend, it is positioning and acceptance, patience and restraint.

Chapter Sixteen

Worth

Worth is the mother of everything. When a woman knows her worth, all the other aspects—goals, principles, power, and position—are free to be manifested, pursued, and fulfilled. How a woman values herself becomes evident to anyone who talks to her for as little as five minutes. In that small amount of time, so much can be determined. A woman who believes in who she is reveals so in the music of her voice, her steady gaze, the swing of her hips, and the confidence with which she gains and shares information. A woman who does not carries with her an aura of disappointment and fear that can be seen in the slumping of her shoulders, the doubt in her eyes, and the hesitancy of her delivery.

We're all women of worth, but we don't all know it. When you do, however, your power and position are obvious. You command respect when you walk into the room. People around you treasure the impact you make on their lives. You become an energy source, one who nurtures and uplifts, imparting advice, comfort, and confidence to those you meet. People are instinctively attracted to you without even knowing why. That's because understanding your worth and existing comfortably inside of it is an irresistible thing to encounter. How you feel inside is often reflected in the way you navigate your life. Being cognizant of this is important because there are those outside of yourself who will attempt to define your worth for you, basing it upon your behavior. Always be aware of how you represent yourself in the world. A woman of worth gauges how to best utilize her strengths, understanding that power and position should be used as attributes and not weapons.

In her romantic relationship, she will do all the things a woman enjoys doing for her man and her family. She will strive for perfection as a wife, a mother, and a friend—perfection, of course, being defined as being a positive force to those who matter. When challenged, a woman of worth stands her ground, accepting nothing less than the standards she has set for herself, yet she understands compromise and the art of negotiation. Just as important, she knows when to stand down. Knowing your worth means understanding that phrases like *stand down* and words like *surrender* don't have to mean a loss of self or an abandonment of objectives. You can still get what you want by being willing to give in on the points that aren't most crucial. I know it can seem hard to do, ladies, but the payoff in knowing when to back off a position can prove very valuable for you in the long term. You can still be the queen, even though you concede points. It is your birthright. It is the birthright of all women. Every woman is equipped to be the queen of all things, if that is what she so desires. You just have to be confident and strategic.

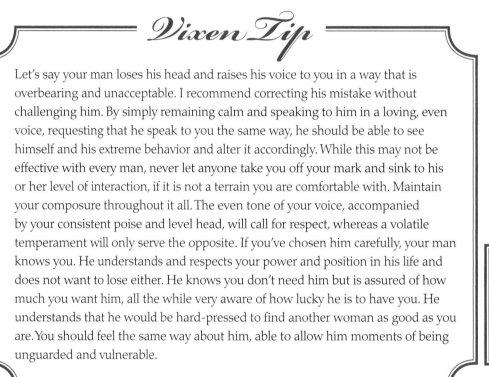

Vixen Tip

Let's say your man loses his head and raises his voice to you in a way that is overbearing and unacceptable. I recommend correcting his mistake without challenging him. By simply remaining calm and speaking to him in a loving, even voice, requesting that he speak to you the same way, he should be able to see himself and his extreme behavior and alter it accordingly. While this may not be effective with every man, never let anyone take you off your mark and sink to his or her level of interaction, if it is not a terrain you are comfortable with. Maintain your composure throughout it all. The even tone of your voice, accompanied by your consistent poise and level head, will call for respect, whereas a volatile temperament will only serve the opposite. If you've chosen him carefully, your man knows you. He understands and respects your power and position in his life and does not want to lose either. He knows you don't need him but is assured of how much you want him, all the while very aware of how lucky he is to have you. He understands that he would be hard-pressed to find another woman as good as you are. You should feel the same way about him, able to allow him moments of being unguarded and vulnerable.

Vixen Say What?
A man is only a man amongst other men, but to his woman, he can be all things

Worth is not something you earn. It is not something you are given. You are worthy from the moment you are conceived. It is your responsibility to uphold and maintain your value to yourself. Know that your worth isn't diminished by your mistakes, unless, of course, you refuse to learn and grow from them. When someone looks at you, they should see a woman who refuses to be broken, even by the worst of circumstances. They should see a woman who is well aware of her contribution to the lives of those around her, both personally and professionally. If you are secure in this, there will be nothing anyone can take from you. You will be independent, yes. But you will also be aware that although you are a singular person, you need to be especially careful to allow the man in your life to lead, if that is the kind of relationship the two of you have established. A woman who knows how to both follow and lead is more desirable than a woman who can do only one or the other.

I believe it is important for women, single and coupled, to be included on the titles and deeds of all or some property. If possible, you should contribute monetarily to the household. I am aware, however, of the very important, very necessary, often overlooked role of the housewife, who may not feel it is in her best interest to work outside of the home, away from her children. In this case, especially, you are worthy of sharing the same financial gains and luxuries as your mate. Someone once told me, and I have never forgotten or gone long without repeating it: power is in ownership. Ownership happens on many different levels. Find the one that's relative and right for you.

> **Vixen Tip**
>
> Consider your home a corporation and you and your mate co-CEOs. A a partner in this company, you are entitled to just as much as your counterpart, given you brought just as much in from the ground floor, monetarily or otherwise.

These principles are simple, but they require practice and awareness to develop. A woman who knows her worth is not afraid to speak up. A man will only do to you, and for you, what you have done to and for yourself. No one wants the responsibility of saving you. While there have been many relationships born of this romantic notion—the Prince Charming (sometimes *Pretty Woman*) theory, where the woman is rescued by a virile, heroic man—men soon tire of a woman who needs to be saved. That can be an enormous and exhausting investment on their parts, emotionally and financially. No one wants to be your all. That makes you a burden, a liability. You should want to be an asset to someone's life as well as an asset to your own. When a woman doesn't feel as if she is contributing to her own life and the lives of those around her, she may find herself depressed and envious of those who are doing well. She may become bogged down in a cycle of life that is far less than what she imagined for herself. Don't let that woman be you. You want to know and express your worth. And it feels good to know that others are noticing.

In a generation where we have so many young women waiting for a man to save them and make them worthy, it is critical that we change our definition of worth. I found it particularly tough when I was younger, being part of a monetarily driven society where tangible things, expensive things, hold importance and relevance. There was a time in my life when I believed that if I could only find a man who possessed things I didn't and I was well taken care of, then I would be happy, then I would be worthy. I could not have been more mistaken. The things a man has accomplished should never define what you possess or who you are. It is more attractive to a man when a woman is capable of taking care of herself, whether she needs to or not. What is even more attractive is the notion that if by some misfortune, the man of the house became unable to take care of his family, his woman could pick up the pieces and keep them in the same comfortable state his income has afforded.

A man once said to me, "If you can't be my helpmate, then what good are you?" (You will see me reference this statement again later; it really made an impact on me!) That man ended up being one of the many men unworthy of me whom I have encountered in my life. What he said that day, however, has helped me define my role in my current marriage. That goes to show you, ladies—even a man who's not good for us has the ability to prepare us for one who is, if we just pay attention!

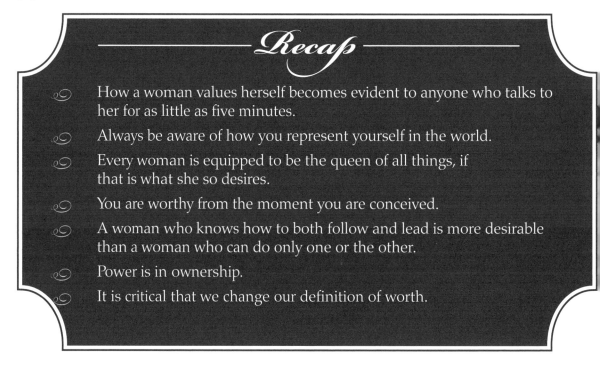

Recap

- How a woman values herself becomes evident to anyone who talks to her for as little as five minutes.
- Always be aware of how you represent yourself in the world.
- Every woman is equipped to be the queen of all things, if that is what she so desires.
- You are worthy from the moment you are conceived.
- A woman who knows how to both follow and lead is more desirable than a woman who can do only one or the other.
- Power is in ownership.
- It is critical that we change our definition of worth.

Chapter Seventeen

Physical Currency

Many of us have hang-ups about our physical appearance but aren't driven to do anything about it. Women often reach a point in their lives where they feel there is no need to try anymore, especially after marriage and children. If anything, marriage, children, and the myriad excuses we make to justify letting ourselves go ("He loves me no matter how I look!") should be the very reasons we become determined not to. The physical attributes a woman brings to her relationship at the beginning should only get better with time. A man doesn't want to bring home a princess only to find out later that she has turned into a toad.

> ## *Vixen Tip*
>
> Use your children as workout equipment! For infants, it'll be a fun game of Superman or airplane, but for you it's a workout. And with the older children and household chores, make everything you do for them part of your workout, as well. For instance, add squats to your laundry routine or leg lifts to your sweeping.

Being physically fit and attractive are just as important as being emotionally sound. Your body should be in its best shape possible. And no, ladies, I'm not suggesting you starve yourself or anything like that. Not everyone can be a size four, nor are they meant to be. Whatever your weight and body type, you should constantly be working to make it better. Your man's physical attraction to you, especially after being with you for a number of years, is very important to the health of your relationship. It should also matter to you for reasons relating to your own health. We all know that the way you look and feel can have a tremendous effect on your self-esteem. The longer your relationship lasts, the better it is to maintain an appearance as close to how you looked when you and your man first got together. Or better. So many women use children or work as an excuse to let themselves go. Because both work and children require a great deal of energy, these are excellent reasons to stay fit so that you can perform at maximum levels. We all secretly want other

> ## *Vixen Tip*
>
> Hate swallowing pills? Try liquid vitamins in your morning juice!

women to look at us and be inspired by our way of dress, style, and overall physical condition. We enjoy when another woman stops us on the street to say, "I love your hair," or, "Where'd you get those shoes?" Most of all, we love when women—and men, for that matter— compliment us on

Vixen Tip

A surefire way to feel good about yourself isn't to wait for someone to compliment you, but to compliment someone else.

our bodies. It is both attractive and unmistakable when you are healthy inside and out. Engaging in physical activities and knowing the importance of proper diet, vitamin intake, and drinking sufficient amounts of water are things we can all do to help ourselves feel and look more confident. Your man will appreciate a woman who takes pride in herself, and he will always be proud to have you on his arm.

With all that we have to do on a daily basis, it may seem impossible to always look your best, but it's not—difficult, yes, but far from impossible. It seems as if so many women have created a cop-out for themselves in order to not feel guilty about this very stealthy form of erosion of one's self-esteem and worth. It's not the kids' faults or that your schedule's too busy. It's definitely not because of all the work you have to do around the house. There are no excuses! No matter what, ladies, you should never leave your house looking less than gorgeous. Even in sweats and a T-shirt, you can be beautiful! The definition of beauty has changed constantly over the years. It has gone from skinny to slim to fat and back to skinny. Beauty has been white, black, exotic, and domestic, but in magazines it's always airbrushed and fully made up.

Vixen Tip

I have a regimen that works wonders for my face, and maybe it'll work for yours. Personally, I am a big fan of M·A·C makeup, yet I use very little of it. My makeup case has exactly the same few products in it, all year-round. I start with a *clean* face, washed with Neutrogena glycerin soap and a Buff Puff to exfoliate every day. Then, I *medicate* my face with Proactiv toner and repair lotion. At the age of twenty-five, my hormones began changing and brought on a case of adult acne. I was mortified! Within two weeks of using the Proactiv line of products, my face was healed. I have been using Proactiv ever since. As for the *makeup*, I start with M·A·C's Select Tint SPF 15, then powder my face lightly with M·A·C's Studio Fix. I then brush a bit of blush onto my cheeks and end with a very sparing application of mascara. Finally, I use a bit of lip balm on my lips instead of lip gloss, in order to appear more natural. I prefer the Hemp balm from the Body Shop, since it is made with coconut oil versus petroleum. This regimen is a great way to wear makeup without looking like you have any on. But hey, don't be afraid to go without makeup. It shows extreme confidence and men really appreciate a clean, natural face!

Because of this, there are women who think the definition of beautiful comes with a fully made-up face, both day and night, not knowing that natural beauty is always most appreciated. Sure, we all have flaws we would like to cover from time to time, but even that can be done naturally. The best part of it all, though, is that it's our flaws that make us even more beautiful.

Along with your face, your hair should always be neat, whether in a casual bun or let loose. If your weekend gear is common and very casual, make sure you wear it well. Your clothes should always be clean, pressed, form-fitting, or complimentary. No matter what size and shape you are, be confident knowing that you take good care of yourself. When you do so, and do it with a sense of flair, you can make even your weekend sweats by Hanes look like high fashion. People will notice the time and care you've taken to assure your appearance is acceptable, even enviable. And it's always nice to be admired, especially during those times when we are dressed down.

Vixen Tip

Okay, ladies, here's some super-important advice—be sure to pay very close attention to your most *personal care*. When your man slips into bed with you, he should feel smooth legs and feet. Take the time to shave or wax as often as necessary and arrange for pedicures regularly. If your time and budget are limited, handle the responsibility yourself! Smother your entire body with rich lotions and oils on a daily basis to assure your skin is supple year-round, especially during cold weather. I prefer Palmer's Cocoa Butter or the Hemp Body Butter by the Body Shop. You should always smell good. This is easy to do with a little trick I learned during my short stint as a salesperson at Victoria's Secret. It's called fragrance layering, and starts with adding perfumed lotion to your skin. I like to rub it into my thighs, chest, and neck. Then spray a light layer of perfumed spray over that, and even a bit onto your panties. Yes, your panties! Just make sure it has dried before putting them on! My personal favorite, especially during the summer, is to use a light coat of baby powder "down there," to assure that you stay free from wetness and odor. Trust me when I tell you the man in your life will notice and appreciate the time you take to care for yourself, inside and out.

There are many creative ways to take good care of yourself. Although I'm not a doctor or beauty specialist, I know what has worked for me, and I am happy to share as much of that with you as I can. It is critical that you do not underestimate the importance of your appearance. You must also recognize that how you look at home is just as important as your appearance in the workplace.

Just because you are plastered all over the pages of a magazine doesn't mean you don't have to look your best when you're relaxing in your home. We as women often underestimate how much a man knows and pays attention to. Ask any halfway astute man and he will tell you how important the upkeep of a woman's hands and feet are, as well as her scent and attention to personal detail. Take the time to pamper yourself. He will appreciate it. More importantly, you'll appreciate yourself.

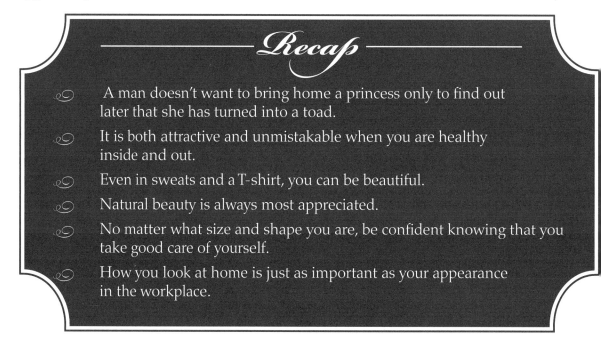

Recap

- A man doesn't want to bring home a princess only to find out later that she has turned into a toad.

- It is both attractive and unmistakable when you are healthy inside and out.

- Even in sweats and a T-shirt, you can be beautiful.

- Natural beauty is always most appreciated.

- No matter what size and shape you are, be confident knowing that you take good care of yourself.

- How you look at home is just as important as your appearance in the workplace.

Chapter Eighteen

Emotional Currency

We've all wrestled with our emotions at one time or another. We are emotional creatures by nature, designed to feel on a soul level and, therefore, be more compassionate and empathetic to our fellow man. It's important, however, to be in control of your emotions and not let your emotions dictate you. Ladies, this is something you seriously need to understand, if you haven't learned it by the time you're reading this book. For centuries, women have taken refuge in the excuse that we are "the weaker sex," thus more inclined to be led by our feelings. Many of us view that as license to lose our senses and rely solely on our emotional state, which is never healthy. In order to think more clearly in times of trouble or just during the course of an ordinary day, you should tap into and rely more upon your rational side.

It is extremely important that you remain emotionally fit. This is necessary for every aspect of your life, including the personal and the professional. This means learning to not harbor feelings for anyone who may have hurt you. You should not find yourself crying over years lost or become mired in blaming others for your own shortcomings and misjudgments. You are the master and commander of your own emotional destiny. You should realize that if someone has hurt you, it is because you somehow played a role in allowing them to.

I'm not talking about crimes against your person that involve you being a victim of circumstance, like rape, robbery, or physical battery. This is strictly in regard to relationships gone bad, friendships that have unraveled, strained familial bonds, disappointment at work, and similar issues. Many times, we fail to address why these things head south, leaving us distressed, sometimes devastated, instead of viewing others as having victimized us in some way. It takes real honesty to be willing to go inside ourselves and examine why we didn't get the emotional return we expected, and be truthful about the role we may have played in creating the problem.

I know it can be hard. I'm not oblivious to the process of pain and reconstruction that takes place after a disappointing emotional blow. It can result in an extended period of sadness, desperation, self-pity, anger—too many emotions for any one person to logically handle. But once the appropriate healing has taken place, once all of these feelings have come and gone, it is imperative that you let go and move on with the goal of being better than before. *But it's not that easy, Vixen,* you say. I know it's not. Trust me, I do. It takes practice, practice, then more and more practice. You have to train your mind to let go of those runaway emotions and focus on the positive and the practical. There are always other things you could be doing instead of bemoaning the outcome of a particular situation. You could be planning your next steps in life. You could be reading a book. You could be working out or spending time with friends. There's a reason for the saying, "An idle mind is the devil's playground." Life is so much bigger than whatever unchangeable thing it is you're allowing yourself to focus on. The more you dwell upon negativity, the more of a tailspin you'll find yourself in.

I have always said, "The one thing none of my exes could ever say about me is that I did worse after they left." That was always my motivation after a bad relationship and breakup, of which there were many. I would always go out of my way to do and look better. What I did varied. Maybe it was a change of hair color, a new car, a new attitude, a new style, or a thriving career, but there was always something I could do to make all those losers say, "Damn!" I'm willing to bet that many of you are not much different from me. It's normal to feel confused about which direction to move in once a relationship falls apart, but it's also normal and expected that you will pick yourself up and start a new life, even if it's just one baby step at a time.

I always had a fear of being one of those women—like my mother and others I've known—who never let go of the pain that someone, usually a man, had caused them. Those women held on to it, letting it stew inside of them until it formed a bitterness that they used like a weapon, wielding it against everyone and ultimately running them away. I dreaded one day being forty-five and alone, with my son all grown up, off somewhere happily living his life, and me left behind with no partner to journey with through my own life because I had chased them all away with a similar anger and bitterness. And to be honest, that's just what I was doing and had started doing very early in my dating life. I would pick fights with boyfriends, constantly comparing them to exes. Some of those comparisons left current beaus feeling inadequate and underappreciated. The fights I picked weren't always based on relationship baggage, though. Sometimes, pent-up hostility toward my family would pop into an argument. Most of the time what I found myself doing when drawing from past pain during a current relationship was projecting all of my insecurities onto the people in my life, blaming them for the way I felt or for the way someone else had treated me. To be superhonest, even now, from time to time, I fall right back into that old habit. That's when I have to read my own damn book to fall out of it! It can be difficult to unlearn learned behavior, especially if it was a negative muscle—and I'm using *muscle* as a metaphor in this instance—that you exercised time and again. Muscles have memory, so it's easy to snap back into old behavior if you're not vigilant. You have to want to change and be willing to do the work required to make sure you stay positive and forward moving.

Just as this sort of emotional baggage can affect your romantic relationships with men, it can also affect your relationships with other women. It's hard to maintain good, positive friendships if you are not living a positive and productive emotional life. They say that misery loves company, and I have found that phrase to be resoundingly true. You can never be happy with unhappy people around, and you will always attract those kinds of people if you don't take care of yourself emotionally. There will always be no-good men and drama-prone friends ready to swoop in and add more no-good drama to your life. Avoid this at all cost by maintaining your emotional health. Pick yourself up. Be encouraged. Take note of others who have lived through much worse than you and have still managed to thrive. Know that there is always a bigger, brighter outcome waiting for you. All you have to do is to take strides toward it.

When my son's father left my newborn son and me, the pain was so great, so devastating, I swore it would kill me. I went through all the clichéd responses to this type of tragedy—I couldn't sleep, I couldn't eat, and, even worse, I found it difficult to care for my son. Everything I had was wrapped up in my son's father. He defined all that I believed I was. Even though he was incredibly abusive and ran our home like a dictatorship, I depended on him to tell me who I was, even if that meant that I would always be abused. It took me a couple of years to really get over the pain of the abuse and the ruin of my life as I knew it. It was difficult to rebuild and to know who I was without him and without the abuse. It would take me an additional three and a half years to begin to understand and

Vixen Tip

Ways to move on from past heartache.

1. Find inspirational *music* that makes you feel stronger and understood, be it spiritual or secular.

2. Indulge in all the things that make you feel like more of a woman. Sugar scrubs, mud masks, and nail polish—all those *girly things* that make us feel even more beautiful.

3. Revamp your *wardrobe*.

4. Indulge in vigorous *exercise*. It will give you loads of energy and help you work out all the aggression you are harboring toward your ex and even his mother!

5. Further your *education*.

6. Completely *reinvent yourself* and make a point of reconnecting with friends who are very supportive and egg you on with good old-fashioned girl power. By the time your ex is completely out of your life, you'll be ready and able to start over, leaving that loser and all those bad feelings behind.

accept who I am without anyone at all, as a singular individual. Because of what I went through and the amount of time it took for me to get to the heart of the real me, I would never be the one to tell you that it is simple to be healthy emotionally after your spirit has been broken. It isn't. But it certainly is possible.

As for those losers who couldn't appreciate you, know that the best revenge is looking good and living well. You should also be aware, however, that this could very easily trigger a pattern as you begin to date again. If you repeatedly find that everyone ultimately leaves you and none of them ever returns, you might be the constant negative variable. Have you purged those bitter feelings from an earlier ill-fated relationship? Are you transferring those unhealthy emotions to the new man in your life? Even after you've regained your power, position, and sense of self-worth, you may still have issues regarding love and trust. If that is the case, no well-deserving man can be expected to stay, and won't, making it harder for you to differentiate between the bad boys and the good guys. You'll just mistakenly view them all as a series of bad men who left poor little you, the supposed victim.

Vixen Tip

In all your bad relationships, the common denominator has been you.

When you do find yourself in another relationship, it is very important that you never bring in past issues that you believe to be resolved. This can be just as dangerous, if not more so, than holding on to issues from your past. When an argument has subsided and peace has been reached, whatever the disagreement, it should be truly over for you. Be careful not to dwell on any mistakes made by either party or to compare this new relationship to an old one. Even I find myself having flashbacks from my past, wanting to punish the man who loves me now for the sins of the man that never did. It's easy to make someone your whipping boy, especially if it seems like he's willing to endure it, but that doesn't make it right. Eventually, he will leave you, too, and you'll find yourself back in the same abandoned boat. I often have to talk myself out of this way of thinking and rationalize my way through it. Reason and logic are the only way. If you truly love the man you are with and respect yourself, you'll accept his faults, and yours, and move forward together, learning from each other's mistakes and not punishing each other for things that happened in the past.

It's natural for people in relationships to argue and disagree, and even though it's usually uncomfortable, it can be very necessary. What we as women need to remember is that with our emotional currency intact, we have the power to change the direction of an argument from bad to better. We need to remember to fight with love, acceptance, and intelligence. Of course, I would never suggest going through the motions of an argument without speaking your mind and making your point, but after a while you have to just let it go, even if the two of you are still at odds. You may be able to come back to the subject at a different time, a time when thoughts and reasoning may have changed and cooled in the process. Whatever you do, if you remain in control of your emotions, you should be able to steer the discussion in a positive direction toward resolution.

Nevertheless, none of this means that you should be an emotionless woman. No man wants an android—not a real man, anyway. You were designed with emotions for a reason. Use them to your advantage, ladies, instead of allowing them to dominate you. An emotionally secure woman could never be empty and uncaring, anyway. This is about being in control of those thoughts and feelings that have the potential to take you to a dark place. You possess the ability to redirect those emotions to a place of productivity. It takes practice, but believe me, the respect you'll gain will be its own reward.

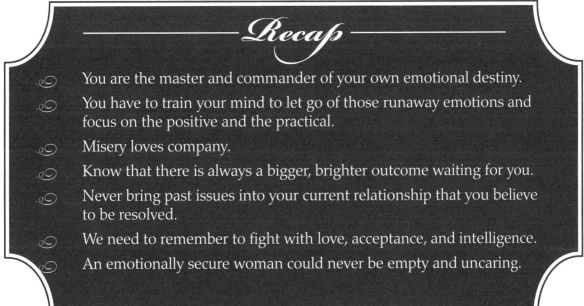

Recap

- You are the master and commander of your own emotional destiny.
- You have to train your mind to let go of those runaway emotions and focus on the positive and the practical.
- Misery loves company.
- Know that there is always a bigger, brighter outcome waiting for you.
- Never bring past issues into your current relationship that you believe to be resolved.
- We need to remember to fight with love, acceptance, and intelligence.
- An emotionally secure woman could never be empty and uncaring.

Chapter Nineteen

Asset

Every woman needs to assess whether or not she is an asset or a liability to her lover and family. First, we need to be clear about what an asset is. *Merriam-Webster's Dictionary* defines it as an "advantage," a "resource." Is that what you consider yourself? If not, then you make sure that's what you are before you attempt to pursue a romantic relationship. And you shouldn't just be doing this to get a man. It is crucial that you become an asset to yourself.

A woman who is an asset, by definition, provides herself and her man with significant advantage. She is a resource. She contributes more than she takes away, and in return is contributed to by others who are eager to meet the needs of someone so dynamic. Her man can't imagine his life without her and does everything in his power to ensure that she is happy. She is the opposite of a woman who is a liability (which we will discuss in detail in the following chapter). This kind of woman depletes. She can suck the life out of the person she is with, offering nothing substantial toward the growth and betterment of the relationship and of the future. This includes financial, educational, and emotional growth.

If you are, or will be, someone who's considered an asset, you must be a woman of goals and of principles, knowing what you want and what you stand for. You should take every step possible and each available opportunity to meet the goals that you have set for yourself, no matter how big or small. It's important to have a life plan, and although you should be mindful of compromise in your relationships, you should never compromise your goals and principles for the sake of someone else's comfort. You shouldn't give up on your career in order to bear children, especially if that wasn't your dream, or cancel your education in order to emotionally support your man and his career goals, if you have career goals of your own.

People in relationships make compromises all the time, especially if both are just starting out together in the world, trying to establish a solid foundation upon which to establish a family. One partner may agree to defer his or her objectives in order to assist the other in attaining position and, ultimately, financial security for the relationship. Once that is accomplished, the other partner can then be supported in pursuing his or her career goals. This is a very common occurrence in relationships and there's nothing wrong with this kind of arrangement. Just make sure your dreams aren't constantly being deferred and relegated to secondary importance, or you may wake up one day to find that your man is very accomplished, and you're just a cute little ornament hanging on his elbow with not much more to offer. You owe it to yourself to be just as whole and multifaceted as your mate. It will serve you well in the long run, on many levels.

A woman who is an asset has great resilience, able to weather and recover from even the most challenging of adversities. She's built of tough stuff and knows it, which is why she has taken the time to establish her own identity, be resolute about her principles and self-defined moral compass, and has pursued her own dreams, not merely supported the dreams of others. Even though she may have the primal need for family and not feel fulfilled unless she's in a relationship, she never sacrifices herself for the sake of her family and her man. To do so would be doing them a terrible disservice.

We get it so wrong sometimes, ladies. We believe that we must give up ourselves for the betterment of our man, our relationship, or our children. Nothing could be more wrong. The best way for us to serve those we love is to make sure we are living within our fullest potential. Only then can we meet their needs on an optimum level. Only then can we be the true assets that they, and we, deserve.

In the long run, it is you who will be the first teacher and primary example for your children and, in many ways, for your spouse. They are constantly watching you and the way you conduct your life, taking their lead from you, even though it may not seem that way. If they see that you are a quitter, quick to abandon goals at the first hint of resistance, if they find that you are easily persuaded from ideals and values, two things will happen: their respect for you will diminish, and, more important when it comes to your children, they may pick up this same type of quitter's mind-set. How can you convince your children to pursue a higher education if they know you dropped out of college and never went back? How can you convince them that they can be anything they want in life if they watch you toil and sweat in a miserable low-paying job as though you have no options? If those around you see that you will settle for less yourself, that is what they will give you and that might be who they become as well.

Throughout the first twenty-six years of my life, all of my relationships were built on the obvious fact that I was never for one moment a woman who valued herself enough to realize and activate her assets. A man can smell a liability from miles away. I found myself doing what other women in my family had done for years—waiting for a man to save my life, all the while feeding off the assets of others. I don't just mean financial assets, either, but their sense of pride and confidence. I felt good being around people who, seemingly, had their lives together, especially since mine was not. It seemed like the perfect plan, as if I could somehow, by osmosis, absorb some of their self-esteem just from being near them. From the time I was in high school, I was impressed by important careers and titles. The more powerful the person, the more I wanted to be around them.

This grand plan of mine to be around impressive, dynamic people all the time was faulty from the start. What would happen once those people had other things to do, things I couldn't participate in? I was setting myself up for becoming a person who didn't know how to be alone.

This was a major factor in my relationship with my son's father and the reason why, even though he was physically, verbally, emotionally, and financially abusive, I stayed. If I had been more of an asset to myself, I would have never wound up in such a relationship in the first place. Even if he had been charming enough to fool me into getting into a relationship with him, the moment his true intentions were unveiled, I would have been able to leave. My principles and values would have guided me to do so. It took two weeks after the day we met for him to slap me. It took four years for me to walk away. Now, more than ten years later, no one can even look at me crossly without me walking out the door and never looking back. That reaction may seem extreme, but with your assets in hand—whether it is your education, the ability to work and support yourself, or just the ambition it takes to dare to pursue your dreams—you'll know you can always make do without a man, especially a man who doesn't deserve you.

I finally realized I needed to have all of the things those successful men in my life had. While it was important for me to be a part of their worlds, watching how they went about things, I didn't have the epiphany that I needed to become accomplished in my own right until *after* I started a family with a man who owned everything around me. I had nothing of my own. I was just the humble recipient of his generosity. He paid for the house, the car, and everything I wore and ate. I contributed nothing substantial. This would turn out to be one of the biggest mistakes of my young life. Luckily, I was just seventeen and had plenty of time to learn and move on. The question is, how much time do *you* have?

When you are an asset to yourself and to those around you, it will be in part because you've accomplished, and are still accomplishing, all you have planned for yourself, whether before or after creating a family. You should see to it that you are educated and able to stand on your own. It is easy to be dominated by others when they feel as if you need them. Many women make the mistake of waiting for a man to come along that will take care of them and give them a more acceptable social status. This plan, as I personally discovered, is terribly outdated, full of holes and traps. In this millennium, you must make your own way and focus upon your goals as early in life as possible. There is nothing more attractive to a secure, successful man than a woman who shares those same traits. A woman who shares these same characteristics with her man is more likely to make it through the long haul, but in the event that she does not, she'll be more than efficient as a single woman and/or mother, able to stand on her own and continue to succeed.

What you represent in your relationships is exactly what you represent to the world around you. If you are strong-willed, determined, and capable in your role as a wife, a mother, and a woman, those around you will take notice and respect you as such. It is important that you are an asset to yourself first and that you are unwavering in your definition of who you are and who you will one day be. You will feel respected not only by your mate but also by your peers. Most importantly, you will respect yourself.

Vixen Tip

I always recommend that women write a list of things detailing who they are and a list of things they want to be, then post those lists in places where they can see and read them each day. It is important to define yourself. If you don't, others will try to do it for you. This is an exercise that I have used to remind myself of who I really am, especially when others would try to redefine me. Knowing who you are, having a plan for your present and future life, being in charge, and taking full responsibility for yourself makes you both invincible and irreplaceable. My list includes: *I am a mother. I am a friend. I am an author. I will earn my degree in psychology. I will run a successful publishing company.* Make your own list. Claim all that you are and all that you will be. It will help you identify who you are again and give you goals to work toward.

When you are an asset to yourself and to those around you, you'll walk through life with purpose and intent as an achiever and a model whom other women will want to emulate. You'll find yourself happier and more focused. More harmonious and compatible relationships will come your way because you'll be satisfied with yourself and, therefore, happier with your life, your partner, and your family.

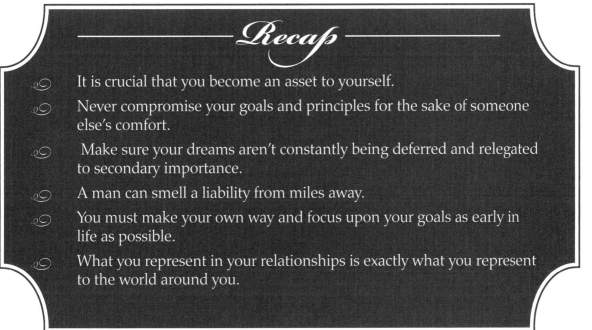

Recap

- It is crucial that you become an asset to yourself.

- Never compromise your goals and principles for the sake of someone else's comfort.

- Make sure your dreams aren't constantly being deferred and relegated to secondary importance.

- A man can smell a liability from miles away.

- You must make your own way and focus upon your goals as early in life as possible.

- What you represent in your relationships is exactly what you represent to the world around you.

Chapter Twenty

Liability

You should never want to be a woman who has made herself a liability. A woman who is a liability cannot offer anything of substance to her man and their relationship. She has very little of value monetarily, emotionally, or intellectually and offers even less to those with whom she interacts. If supported by her spouse or mate, the amount of money and energy that it takes for her upkeep are considerably more than she contributes to their home and lives together. In most cases, this is a woman who doesn't have goals that are substantial to herself or the relationship. Perhaps she has suppressed them, having mistakenly been taught that she should put the needs of others before her own. Whatever the case, her poor planning has left her with a tremendous deficit on multiple levels. A woman like this tends to have wavering principles, and her moral compass is easily manipulated. She's often overly dependent upon her man and the generosity of others.

It's mind-boggling to me how, especially in my generation, so many bright young women are still unable to pull their own weight. So many of us want to be taken care of, believing that's the only way to live successful, fulfilling lives. The irony is that being taken care of can have the opposite effect. It requires the abandonment of certain freedoms, particularly the ability to speak one's mind without some form of penalty and knowing that should something happen to your mate and he doesn't leave you anything to fall back on, you have the wherewithal to fend for yourself. An educated, worldly man would find it nearly impossible to showcase a woman if she were unable to contribute to an intelligent conversation with his peers and colleagues. He would always be concerned that maybe she would say or do something to embarrass him and herself, thereby threatening his position in the world. Smart, successful men tend to be practical about how they choose a mate, often electing to go with one that will prove beneficial to him on every level. They make decisions of the mind, not just the heart, and no man in his right mind—not one who is upwardly mobile, anyway—would choose to be with a woman who might drag him down or potentially sabotage everything he's working hard to accomplish.

Many women have no social lives of their own outside of their romantic relationship. Some of you either don't have to work or don't want to, yet find yourselves resentful and envious of your partner happily and aggressively pursuing his career and life purpose. You may feel threatened by his relationships outside of the home, afraid that these relationships might make him realize that he can do better than you. This can be a time bomb waiting to erupt within a relationship. Create a life, no matter how big or small, outside of the one you and your mate have built together. Whether it be volunteer work, a seasonal job, or your own career, you should have something of your own, something that makes you feel as though you're living and moving in your purpose.

Vixen Tip

Everyone has a talent. Use yours as either a hobby or for financial gain. That way, you're doing something you love and are good at. If you can manage to do the majority of this from home, then you've hit the jackpot!

And find a network of people who enjoy the same things you do, either locally or on the Internet. You can even start your own network of friends who are interested in the same hobbies!

Many of you are just biding your time until your knight rides up on his white stallion and swoops you up onto his saddle, and the two of you ride off into the sunset. Has that ever really happened for anybody? Seriously? The one time we thought it did, with Prince Charles and Princess Diana, the most watched and anticipated wedding in the world, well, look what happened. Proof positive that even fairy tales can go horribly awry. Truth be told, if you've ever read fairy tales, they all go horribly awry at some point. They are typically frightening, murderous tales of babies being stolen, innocent people being killed, folks being turned into animals, and kingdoms being pillaged and overtaken—all the more reason why we shouldn't be using fairy tales as guides for our love life. But I digress…

Back to why you shouldn't be waiting for a man to save you and allow your life to truly begin. Take it from me…I've tried living life that way. It's never a good idea, not even under the best of circumstances with the most successful man. Even though you're in a relationship, you should always have your own thing. If you don't, you may find that the very same man who came along and swooped you up and promised you heaven and earth might eventually begin to view you as so much dead weight, not nearly as exciting and vivacious as that smart little cookie in his office who's such a go-getter and is able to converse with him about everything under the sun. Men compare what they have at home to what they see out in the world. If you're not competitive enough, if you can't make him believe he's got a real treasure on his hands (and that starts with how *you* feel about you and the steps you take to expand your own life), he may begin to think of you as just a liability and a taker. You may not even be fully aware of it.

How do you know you're a liability? Do you have any power in your household? No? Hmmm. Can you make important decisions that are adhered to? No? Wow, this looks bad. Okay, how about standing your ground in debates with your mate—can you do that? That's three nos, ladies. This is not looking good at all. (If you've answered *yes* to at least one of these questions, then you're on the right track.) When you cannot do any of these things, your stability decreases exponentially. Your life could very easily be uprooted at any time. What's to stop your man from asking you to leave home because you have not contributed to its upkeep, financially or physically? More than likely, your name is not on either the house or automobile titles, and your bank account is dependant upon an allowance. Under any or all of these circumstances, your man is in complete control and this can be potentially dangerous to you and your quality of life.

You should be aware that some men are insecure and *need* to have a woman of liability in their lives. This gives him power over you and, in short order, you may find yourself made subservient and dominated. Don't be lured into this type of arrangement even if the man is wealthy and promises to take care of you. Financial abuse is a very real form of abuse; it is one of the most subtle, and easiest, ways to gain power over another person, whether the relationship is business or personal. If you are a woman of liability, you'll lend yourself readily to this form of abuse. A woman who is an asset, however, will always have the resources necessary to stand on her own.

Again, I would never tell you something that I didn't know for sure. Everything I believe in has come from experience. Financially relying on a man was, at one point, my life plan. I couldn't see past the immediate gratification of a shopping spree or a night on the town. I must have done this with every man I dated from high school until I was about twenty-five. I know that while a man is taking care of you, it feels as if you'll be set for life and that nothing can go wrong. But in a world riddled with divorce and single parents, the chances of you and your partner being together the rest of your lives are less than fifty-fifty. Relationships are tough enough without compounding them with liability. You have to be able to bring as much of yourself as possible into your relationship, with the condition that the man you have chosen is worthy of having all of you.

We live in an age of entitlement where many women seem to feel as if men owe us something. Many of us want the world handed to us without doing anything to earn it. We want our men to work and make enough money to give us all the things we want. In turn, we do little to help support him, the relationship, and the family's goals. Some of our priorities are all wrong; we look to material objects to define us. We are becoming less and less concerned with education and having goals we can accomplish ourselves. If you wait for someone else to save you, you have already made yourself a liability. Save yourself. You're perfectly equipped to do so.

Ladies, there's nothing wrong with wanting a partner in life who can support you and your children, a man who has enough money and resources to allow you to live well under normal conditions and in the event of an emergency. I prefer having a man who can support me, my son, himself, and his own family (such as his parents as they get older). I also prefer, however, to be able to be the exact same thing myself. I want a man who can take over in a crisis, financial or otherwise, but what if something happens to him and his assets? Then I need to be able to take care of us and keep up the standards of the life to which we have grown accustomed. If I am a liability, I cannot do that. My whole life will be dependent upon him. When he suffers. then so do we all.

Vixen Tip

If you are in a situation where you are feeling trapped and disrespected because you have not contributed to your household in a way that demands respect, it is time to decide what and who you are. It is very possible to have other interests and still be an effective wife and mother. Women do it all the time. The biggest part of being and doing it all is the organization of your thoughts. What have you always been interested in? Are there classes that can help you get the education you'll need to start or continue your career? There are countless online college courses than can be accessed from your home. With a bit of organization, you can easily set aside time to focus on that goal. Once you have decided what field you are interested in, research people who have done what you wish to do. It sounds simple. That's because it is. Find motivation in the stories of those who have come before you. Don't be afraid to follow in their footsteps. There is a world of information out there for you. You can find anything you need to know on the Internet with just a few keywords typed into any search engine. If you don't have access to the Internet at home, use a friend's computer, or head over to your local library and use one of theirs for free. Teach yourself things that you have never thought of learning. Keep abreast of current events and trends by subscribing to a national newspaper or other types of periodicals. If you can't afford a subscription, most newspapers are online for free. If you can access the Internet, you can read the news of almost every newspaper in the world daily, ensuring you're knowledgeable about current events and constantly expanding your mind. Read books on anything and everything that interests you. The information is out there, right at your fingertips. You're just a few keystrokes, books, and articles away from learning how to create the life and the lifestyle you wish.

When I realized that I wanted a better quality of life, I paid close attention to what other successful people did to get where they are. I wanted to know what they knew, especially those who created something out of dreams and pure ambition. I spent hours on end watching lifestyle shows that depicted the places these people would go and the homes they lived in. Maybe I would never be able to live the extravagant lives they live, I reasoned, but then again… maybe I would. I just wanted to know what was out there and do my best to work toward achieving it for myself. Even if I didn't get close to having a summer home in San Tropez and a winter cabin in Aspen, at least I'd get far enough away from where I started. Dream big, set goals, and stick with them. Learn continuously and as much as you can regarding the matters of the world, business, home, and relationships. Learn about yourself. That way, no one can come along and change you, telling you who you are and how to feel. You will have so much to offer those around you, making yourself the ultimate asset in their lives.

As a woman, you are responsible for so much and so many. Like it or not, it is an expectation that comes with our sex. You only do yourself an injustice if you are not completely self-sufficient and reliable. A man loves to know he has a woman who can take care of herself and him and their family. A worthy man wants to be supported at times, not always leaned upon. Even a man needs an occasional crutch and wants to know that the woman he has chosen not only carries her own weight in their relationship, but can also carry his, if necessary.

As a liability, the only thing you can carry is a child and, in the event the relationship with the father ends, those children will be the only tangibles with your name on them.

Recap

- A woman who is a liability cannot offer anything of substance to her man and their relationship.

- No matter how big or small, create a life outside of the one you and your mate have built together.

- Men compare what they have at home to what they see out in the world.

- Financial abuse is a very real form of abuse.

- Relationships are tough enough without compounding them with liability.

- If you wait for someone else to save you, you have already made yourself a liability.

- Dream big, set goals, and stick with them.

- A man loves to know he has a woman who can take care of herself and him and their family.

Chapter Twenty-one

Pretty vs. Smart

We've all heard the old adage, "Beauty is in the eye of the beholder." While I'm sure this is true, there seems to be a bit of confusion about who the beholder is. Everyone has an opinion when it comes to women, and one of the first to be expressed is usually based on our outward appearance. There have been countless studies on the art and effects of beauty in an attempt to define it and, ultimately, understand our attraction to this ideal.

One study showed that babies are more attracted to symmetrical faces. Another concluded that the average person doesn't think of beautiful women as smart. This same study also showed that the average person participating in the study did not believe that a sexy woman, nor a woman who is overtly sexual in nature, could be intelligent. And just based on my own personal experience, I have noticed that many people, men especially, are shocked to find that a woman who looks like me not only reads and collects books, but also writes them. Since I live in Los Angeles, a place notorious for its emphasis on the superficial, the basic assumption is that I am a model or an actress. No one ever assumes that maybe I'm a schoolteacher or a medical student. Only when I reveal I am a *New York Times* best-selling author does the conversation become intellectual—after their initial shock, of course—whereas, when the individual assumed I was just another pretty girl, he spoke to me as if I were three years old. All right, maybe not three, but so severely limited in scope he assumed I couldn't carry on a halfway decent conversation.

Knowing how demeaning it can be to be treated this way, I wonder why so many of us feel the need to dumb down when in the presence of men or those we feel subordinate to. So many women in my generation, and generations before, are waiting for a man to make them. We focus on our outward appearances and neglect education or pretend as if we have none. We find ourselves desperate for companionship and feel as if intelligence will only challenge a man and his bravado, encouraging him to find someone more apt to following his lead without question or input.

Again, as we've already discussed, there are lots of men out there who are very superficially focused. They only want a woman with a pretty face and a perfectly sculpted body. They have no desire to be with a woman who can hold a conversation about world events, politics, and literature, as well as fashion, beauty, and the weather. This could prove a threat to their own intellect, revealing what they consider chinks in their well-crafted armor that might have gone unnoticed had some annoying broad not pointed them out by bringing up subjects they were unable to discuss. This type of man would prefer that his woman just shut up and look good. I can't tell you how many times I've dated one of these men. They are legion, ladies, so beware. To some women, this is a dream come true. Some women have been raised to just be pretty and at their man's beck and call. But for those of you who want more out of life, those who know your worth and have established your life goals and desire an equal position next to their mates, this will never suffice. Not ever.

In one of my past relationships, I realized that the highly intelligent, wealthy man I was dating was more interested in my body and way of dress than my intellect and life experience. There were times, while getting dressed for a night out, when he would ask why I didn't wear more provocative clothing, such as miniskirts and shorter tops with more plunging necklines, even in the winter months. When we were in crowds or with his friends, he often didn't introduce me but would ask someone's opinion on how I looked that evening. Eventually, the introductions were made, and I carried my own in conversations and, in turn, impressed his friends. Once, during a fight, he said to me out of anger, "All my friends think you're stupid." That's what he wanted me to think. After dating porn stars, Playmates, and hookers with no intellectual capacity, he wished I were like them—pretty, sexy, and sexual, with nothing else to offer. He couldn't handle anything more. It was easier for him to choose to attempt to break my spirit at that moment, by insisting all his friends thought I was stupid, than for him to accept and deal with me as someone who was intellectual as well as sexy.

Somehow, somewhere along the way, someone told us that we can't have it all, and for some reason we believed it. This doesn't just apply to women classified by others as beautiful, but to smart women, as well. Since entering the world of publishing, I have met a number of women who are incredibly talented and learned, women who have followed the smart-girl blueprint. They were the model students in high school and found their ways into some of the most prestigious universities in the nation. These are women who have earned respectable degrees and have gone on to work in a well-respected industry and make names for themselves. Some of these same women also wish they were more physically alluring to the opposite sex.

Many of us are so focused on our careers and education, so set upon being the smart girl and being taken seriously for our minds and not our bodies, that we neglect our bodies altogether. As is the case with many women I have come across, one day they find themselves in their forties and emotionally unfulfilled, because they forgot, or never stopped, to take the time for a social life or a family of their own. It's okay to pursue a social life while you're building your career. Life doesn't mandate that we be all of one thing and none of the other. You don't have to be either pretty or smart. You can be both! It's perfectly fine. Women do it all the time. You can and should be one of them!

It's okay to come out of your trousers once in a while and show a little leg in a business skirt at work, or something even shorter on casual days. It's okay to buy clothes that actually fit and don't hang on your frame like a burlap sack. More than anything, it's okay to be smart when the rest of the world expects you to be only pretty, and to be pretty when the rest of the world expects you to be only smart.

Vixen Tip

No matter how you look or how far you have gone in your education and career, there are a few things I think everyone should do, men and women alike. When I was dating one of the smartest men anyone could have the pleasure of meeting, he taught me the importance of periodicals. Newspapers and magazines are tried-and-true methods of exercising the brain and gaining information. It is important for women especially to get our noses out of fashion and beauty magazines once in a while and subscribe to magazines such as *Time* and *Newsweek*, weekly news periodicals that will keep you abreast of what's happening in the world around you. Read the newspaper, and not just your local paper. As I mentioned in the last chapter, if you have access to a computer, you can read almost any paper in the world for free online. All that's required is that you register at their site, an easy step that usually means providing nothing more than your name and e-mail address, no credit cards or anything complicated. Start with the *New York Times*, at www.nytimes.com. Follow what's going on in politics by reading the *Washington Post* at www.washingtonpost.com. These are inexpensive ways to remain completely abreast of what's happening in the world. The same concept goes for the news we watch on television. When you're finished watching your local edition of the evening news, switch over to the national news for a bit, then cable news programs on CNN and MSNBC, and then to BBC News. To go even further, look online for news programs being streamed from other countries. Get as much information as possible from different sources to allow you to develop an informed opinion about what you have read; blog about it, if you can find the time, and share your opinion with others, starting a conversation or debate.

Beauty and intelligence may be relative terms, but their concepts are universal. You should strive to be all that you can and not just rely solely upon your looks or your education to open all the doors in your life. There is no bigger turnoff than a pretty woman who has nothing else to offer, one who cannot contribute anything past her physical attributes. At the same time, it is equally as unattractive to be the woman who can only offer her intellectual side when the man in your life needs you to find the vixen within, to be vivacious and uninhibited, charming and funny. Maybe he just wants you to let your hair down and wear something formfitting during your times together, perhaps wear a little makeup, get dolled up, and be his fantasy. Whether single or in a relationship, don't be afraid to bring your brain to the party, even as you're wearing that little black dress that lets everyone in the room know just how sexy you are!

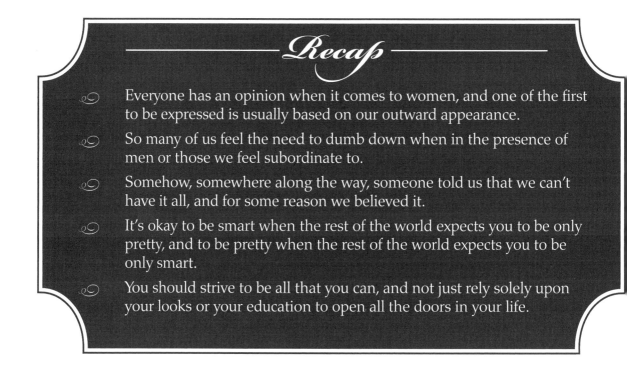

Recap

- Everyone has an opinion when it comes to women, and one of the first to be expressed is usually based on our outward appearance.

- So many of us feel the need to dumb down when in the presence of men or those we feel subordinate to.

- Somehow, somewhere along the way, someone told us that we can't have it all, and for some reason we believed it.

- It's okay to be smart when the rest of the world expects you to be only pretty, and to be pretty when the rest of the world expects you to be only smart.

- You should strive to be all that you can, and not just rely solely upon your looks or your education to open all the doors in your life.

Chapter Twenty-two

Being One of the Boys

Boys and girls tend to be socialized separately from birth. Boys are taught to conquer and are often encouraged to experience as much variety as possible before choosing a life mate. Girls, conversely, are taught to preen, prepare, and wait—wait for the right man who will come along and then their lives can officially begin. A famous line from an old Bette Davis movie, *Mr. Skeffington*, says, "A woman is beautiful only when she is loved." With lines like this, it's no wonder each gender has such difficulty understanding the other.

Exactly whom are these boys supposed to be conquering while the girls are waiting to be loved? Who's showing them the way? From childhood on, girls lean toward other girls and boys convene with other boys, each gender debating about the other with friends who, for the most part, are equally naïve. And while it's a great idea to bond with the same sex, there's definitely something to be said for hanging with the boys (and vice versa). Plenty of us girls are, and have been, slipping through the cracks and mingling with the opposite sex as platonic friends, allowing us to gain valuable experience and readiness for a relationship. We actively interact with a sufficient number of boys so that we, too, can make educated determinations about life mates.

Vixen Tip

Yes, it is very romantic to sit in a fine dining establishment with their best bottle of Chianti and make puppy-dog eyes at one another over flickering candlelight, but once in a while, do it his way. Suggest that the two of you go to Hooters on game night. Order a pitcher of beer, a platter of wings, and get into the game. Need a little more excitement? Visit your local strip club, preferably one that serves dinner, and enjoy a little exotic entertainment with your meal before going home and ravishing your man. Fishing, four-wheeling, or just lying in bed watching reruns—it doesn't matter. Just be with him, listen, and learn.

Women who socialize with men, preferably those with whom they do not share an intimate relationship, have a tremendous advantage over women who don't. Because of the way our society has historically defined male and female roles, however, a young woman who befriends mostly men is usually labeled a "tomboy" or "fast" (and occasionally worse). This assumption often comes from other women who envy or resent the camaraderie between that woman and the men who gather around her. Since women are taught to believe that men and women, outside of the professional world, can communicate only on an intimate level, the assumption is that a woman spending time with several men is surely doing so for sexual purposes. This kind of social stereotyping often keeps women away from men in casual, friendly environments, as the women do not want to appear easy or available, both to onlookers or the men in question.

This archaic thinking serves only to keep us divided and continually mystified by each other. As progressive as society seems to have become, some women are still reluctant to see men as viable friends and confidants. This is arguably one of the main reasons for our startling national divorce rate. Perhaps if more women and men were friends first before dating and marrying, a stronger level of understanding and willingness to fight for, instead of opting out of, marriages and relationships would be achieved.

Ever since I could remember, I have always been more comfortable around males. As a preteen, I would borrow clothes from the boys I climbed trees with and dress like them at school. We hung out on backstreets and in the alley behind our neighborhood KMart, experimenting with cigarettes and graffiti. It was one of my male friends who taught me how to ride a bike by pushing me down a hill on his ten-speed. My first fight, in the fifth grade, was with a boy. Yep, sure was. After he cut in front of me in the lunch line, I coldcocked his ass. He, his black eye, and I promptly ended up in the principal's office. After he told the principal it was an accident, we were best friends!

None of the girls in school understood my relationships with the neighborhood boys, why I was the only girl hanging out with them, or why they all paid attention to me and not the more feminine girls. As a result of them being unable to understand why I preferred being around boys instead of girls, from a very young age, probably around ten years old, I became accustomed to being called a slut and having vicious rumors spread about me. Now, some twenty years later, it's pretty much the same. Some little girls never really grow up, choosing instead to maintain the same fixed opinions formed in childhood, instead of engaging someone like me in dialogue, exploring my motivations and what I could possibly glean from being in the company of the opposite sex. It's easy to judge from the safety of one's corner, but in doing so you limit yourself. So many women still fail to understand the dynamics of the male species. Many also fail to understand a woman who relates well to men and can earnestly share in their lives during work or play.

A woman who spends more time around men has a better chance of learning not just about the opposite sex but also about the characteristics that drive men. Many of these traits are missing from our general makeup, as many women have been raised to be worker bees instead of the queen bee. Don't misunderstand what this means, ladies. There is nothing wrong with being a worker. Indeed, there are those of us who make diligent and excellent supports, playing a necessary and vital part in keeping things together. But there are some women who, because of their drive and hunger for leadership, are clearly cut out to be bosses. But all too often, as we are growing from girls to women, we are not provided with the strong, leading female role models we crave. This is where the appropriate male role models can come into play.

Vixen Tip

Where personal relationships are concerned, it is vital that you find a way to make your man's hobbies and interests your own, even if just for a moment. Interact with your male friends and family members more often and indulge in things you wouldn't usually. Sports are a surefire way for women to participate, even if you don't fully understand what's happening. Just be there and get involved. Talk to the men in your life about the women in theirs. Find out their likes and dislikes about their women, ask about the experiences that made them laugh and those that made them angry—and listen, really listen. Don't interject with opinions or suggestions, just empathize and understand. Interjecting can be cute once in a while, but when trying to relate in a man's world, it's often better to watch and learn before speaking. You'd hate to come across as annoying when trying to bond with your man. No matter what the men in your life are interested in, give it a try. You have no reason to be intimidated by any of it.

Vixen Say What?
It's better to be thought a fool than to open your mouth and remove all doubt.

Though it is true that men and women are wired differently, it is also true that with sufficient time and consideration, each sex can begin to understand the other. Every woman has a masculine side and every man, a feminine. Each should learn to tap in to the side less utilized and take note as to how much more smoothly their relationships and life will run. Make yourself available to the men in your life, whether family, platonic, or intimate. Learn as much about the opposite sex as you can.

You will find yourself becoming more open and understanding of your mate, and he will enjoy your company so much more. When you learn as much as you can about what it means to be a man, he will open up more of his life to you and respond accordingly, allowing *you* to feel all that it means to truly be a woman.

Recap

- From childhood on, girls lean toward other girls and boys convene with other boys.

- There's definitely something to be said for hanging with the boys.

- A young woman who befriends mostly men is usually labeled a "tomboy" or "fast."

- A woman who spends more time around men has a better chance of learning not just about the opposite sex, but about the characteristics that drive men.

- Every woman has a masculine side and every man, a feminine.

- When you learn as much as you can about what it means to be a man, he will open up more of his life to you.

Chapter Twenty-three

Wooing Your Man

Unlike what most of you probably think, attracting a man has very little to do with feminine wiles. It's as if we truly think that men are stupid, not paying attention to every single detail about us, and can be lured by something as simple as a cartoonish Betty Boop gesture. If this is what you believe, then you need to reprogram your thinking, pronto! Not only are our men paying attention to us, they are taking plenty of mental notes along the way.

A man will observe all the little things about you, focusing particularly on those that annoy or frustrate him. Many times, he won't say a word, even as you are doing that very annoying thing. Then one day, he'll up and leave. You'll have no idea why because you weren't paying attention to all the things you do and all the things you don't. Sure, he should have given you a heads-up. That would have been the fair thing to do. But life isn't always fair, and men aren't always quick to complain. They aren't nearly as complicated as we are, and often go out of their way to avoid what they feel might turn into drama. In many instances, they look to us to be vigilant about what concerns them in the relationship, just as we look to them to be problem solvers. Men may be simple creatures, but they are far from stupid. This is the reason why the previous chapters focus on you, the total woman, from the inside out. Pay very close attention to who you are as an individual before trying to become part of a couple.

Once you become part of a couple, however, your desire to remain attractive to your mate should not diminish. If anything, it should be heightened. In this desire to attract him, you must cater to all his senses: touch, taste, sight, smell, and hearing. Titillate your mate from the top of his head to the bottom of his feet. Generate sensations he has never experienced before. Don't be afraid to push your own limits as well as his. Get into his head first before you get into his bed. Some say romance is dead and that courting has gone out of style, but both are still alive and well, as long as you have a plan and know what you're doing.

Contrary to what many women may believe, men love to be courted just as much as we do. They appreciate the little things like notes and thoughtful trinkets that may not hold monetary value but mean a lot sentimentally. It is vital to your relationship to tap into your man's feminine side once in a while without attempting to emasculate him. Sending little notes like these once a day is fine, but I would not recommend you say or do more than this in the very beginning, when both of you are still learning about one another. Ease into the relationship. There's no need to put all your cards on the table with long, drawn-out letters about your innermost hopes and dreams. Don't overwhelm him with a flurry of feelings after the first, second, or even fifteenth date. Moderate yourself. Give him something to look forward to by unveiling the mystery of your self one facet at a time. Sometimes a little is just enough.

Vixen Tip

Massages are fun. Pouring hot wax on your man is fun. Combining the two is exhilarating! But actual wax can be dangerous and it can't be massaged into the skin. Solution? One hundred percent soy candles! The secret of soy is that it is extremely moisturizing to the skin, burns warm (not hot) to the touch, and with the right fragrance you have an erotic night on your hands. Enjoy!

As a woman, you should always be concerned with scents. Everything around you should always smell good. Human beings are highly attuned to and affected by odors. Men in particular, when falling for a woman, are very impacted by her scent and the smell of her environment. Every room in your home can benefit from the aroma of a scented candle or incense, especially bathrooms. Your bedroom linens should have that straight-out-of-the-dryer smell when you're expecting company. Most important, you should always smell

Vixen Say What?
Foreplay begins way before you take your clothes off and, many times, before you have even met.

nice. From your hair to your ankles, there are countless places on the body that wouldn't suffer from the application of a little body spray or a dab of perfume. Your man will take notice and his senses will be further titillated.

Vixen Tip

After an oily massage, the perfect end to an evening would be a hot bath. Given you have a spacious, presentable tub, a hot bath with the appropriate accoutrements can further relax him, maybe even putting him in the mood for love. More than anything, however, it demonstrates your ability to nurture while presenting your sexy, alluring side. Bath salts and oils, loofahs and scrubs, all of these should be used to heighten the experience. Fill your tub with what you'll need to get clean while pampering one another. The mood in the bathroom should mirror that of dinner and the bedroom, with the soft music and lowered lighting or candlelight.

Whether using your bed for simply cuddling and sleeping or for lovemaking, it is imperative that your bed is a place where both you and he want to be. This is fairly easy and very inexpensive. You can give your bed the look and feel of luxury and elegance for very little money, making it a place your man wouldn't mind spending all his time on a lazy Sunday afternoon. You may think men don't

Vixen Tip

Try a bath made of milk. Using powdered milk will be cheaper but just as effective. For dramatic effect, scatter red rose petals on top of this white bath and indulge.

113

particularly care about these sorts of girly things, but you would be very wrong. Though a single man may not be so dainty and detail-oriented in his life and home, he will love and appreciate it in yours. The way you keep up your home and yourself will be key in your attempts to attract him, both initially and over time.

Vixen Tip

Spray freshly washed sheets with a dab of fabric softener and water or linen spray, which can be found at any body, bed, or bath store. My favorite line of linen sprays is the one by Bath and Body Works, with aromatherapy scents such as Eucalyptus Spearmint. Crisp, white linens are alluring, more so than colorful, large patterns. Try your best to stay away from floral prints when you're spending time in bed with your man. Though it may only be a subconscious notion, it may be tough for a man to lay naked among a field of daisies. White sheets are simple and cater to both of you. You should have a clean sheet set with at least two pillows for each of you, and a light blanket under a heavier down comforter covered by a duvet, all white. I recommend duvet covers versus owning several comforters, which only tend to take up space. Make your bed plush and inviting. Make your man want to stay there all night and into the next day.

Men tend to have fantasies that the average woman thinks she cannot live up to; nothing could be further from the truth. If the local gentlemen's club intrigues your man, then don't try to stop him from going. Go with him! During those times when you wish he would just stay home with you instead of chasing his fantasy, turn things around. *Become* his fantasy. Bring the gentlemen's club to him. Romantic music and lighting will set the mood. After a trip to the lingerie or costume store, you'll have everything you need to become his private dancer. We all know about Victoria's Secret, and although it is an outstanding source for everything lingerie, sometimes a man wants to see something a little more risqué. If you don't know of any place in your area that sells fantasy wear, call the local gentlemen's club—disguise your voice and block your phone number, if you're uncomfortable about calling—and ask someone there where you would go to get costumes if you were a dancer. I'm sure you'll find someone eager to provide that information. As you prepare to become your man's fantasy, don't forget to put on your body scents. It never hurts to use cocoa butter instead of regular lotion. Cocoa butter gives off a soft, sensual scent and complements most perfumes nicely. Make sure you've had a recent pedicure and manicure, and that your hair is freshly done and smells clean. Imagine him noticing a chipped or broken nail in the midst of your carefully orchestrated affair. Nothing should distract him from you. Everything should be perfection. That's what fantasy is all about!

Vixen Tip

You don't have to be a professional dancer to be enticing to your man. Just be yourself and do the things you know he likes.

1. Sit him on the sofa and make full contact with his body.

2. Straddle him face-to-face.

3. Begin by nibbling on his ear and neck.

4. Whisper in his ear. Tell him how much you love him and missed him while he was away, or how turned on you are just by the sight of him.

5. Place his face between your breasts and manipulate your nipples in, out, and around his lips.

6. Continuously gyrate, slowly and gently grinding your body against his.

7. Slowly and carefully switch positions, sitting on him with your back to him.

8. Place your feet on the floor between his legs.

9. Slowly stand while simultaneously pulling off your bottoms.

10. Tease him with your bottoms, pulling them up and down, on and off, while moving your body like a snake to the music.

11. When you have removed your bottoms, sit on his lap with your back to him and bring your legs up onto the sofa to straddle him.

12. Once you are propped up on your knees, bend down and touch the floor with your hands. This will place your bottom half directly in his face.

13. Slide onto the floor, carefully, slowly.

14. Lie on your side, raise one leg and bend the other inward.

15. Showcase your extended leg and your perineum.

16. Rock back and forth on your bottom. Switch legs and repeat.

17. Get creative, have a good time, and visit the gentlemen's club once in a while, either with your mate or with girlfriends, just to pick up some pointers. No doubt about it, these few tips will lead to more excitement in your relationship. And, lucky for you, there are more tips and diagrams ahead. Read on!

These are tricks out of my own bag, tried-and-true methods that work every single time. Though I have lived the kind of life most people would dare to judge, there is a lot I have learned that has been useful in many aspects of my life, even as I evolve. Look at the span of my life thus far, from being an exotic dancer at the age of sixteen, to being a wife at seventeen, a mother at nineteen, a divorcee at twenty, a Video Vixen at twenty-one, and realizing my dream, at twenty-five, of becoming a *New York Times* best-selling author. What a transformation! What a long and winding road! Along the way, I've learned a lot about life, lust, love, sex, and human nature. A lifetime's worth, more than most people might ever experience. Know that as I give you this information, I give it to you as I practice it. There isn't a halftime during Sunday and Monday night football that doesn't warrant a lap dance at my house!

Recap

- Not only are our men paying attention to us, they are taking plenty of mental notes along the way.

- Men may be simple creatures, but they are far from stupid.

- Pay very close attention to who you are as an individual before trying to become part of a couple.

- Get into his head first before you get into his bed.

- Sometimes a little is just enough.

- Though a single man may not be so dainty and detail-oriented in his own life and home, he will love and appreciate it in yours.

- Men tend to have fantasies that the average woman thinks she cannot live up to; nothing could be further from the truth.

Section 3

How to Engage Him

Okay, now that you have captured his attention, what do you plan on doing in order to keep him? The thrill of the chase is only a small portion of the adventure. You have to keep him motivated and intrigued, wrapped up in you, unable to flinch or glance away.

Chapter Twenty-four

Love

Once you've found a man you can trust, then you're free to love. Sounds great, doesn't it? Unfortunately, it's not always that easy. Love is an emotion that's often involuntary, independent of choice and practical decision making. Wouldn't it be wonderful if we could control how it happened, when it happened, and with whom? Of course, those objectives can be negotiated up front, as many cultures throughout the world have proven, by way of prearranged marriages predicated on social status, financial stability, business relationships between families…in other words, everything *but* love. The hope is that love will follow. In many cases, it does not.

Vixen Say What? There is nothing harder to obtain or maintain in life than true love.

The reality remains, however, that when the L-word does come into play, so does its inseparable partner-in-crime—unpredictability. Love itself has a way of appearing when least expected. Sometimes, from the very moment you lay eyes on a particular man and before you're able to establish any foundations, you realize in that moment that you are his, wholly, fully, no question. You've had that feeling before, haven't you? (And if you haven't, brace yourself for the day you do!) It is a knowing, something so big, so irresistible, so all-consuming, you can't fight against it. And you don't want to. You meet a man and you instantly fall in love with him, and with that feeling you're willing to accept whatever baggage comes along. From a practical standpoint, this sounds crazy, but when the emotion hits you with gale-force intensity, it's as real as it gets.

If this sounds like you that means you are a lover, in the truest sense of the word. You love love and all that it stands for. You embrace it. Love is the means, the end, the everything. Because of this, you give yourself over completely to your man, without terms or conditions. For many, this can be a frightening prospect, but not for the true lover. Even when your man has failed you, your feelings remain fixed, not *despite* his faults, but *because* of them. This type of love, what the Greeks called *Agape*—signifying a love that is self-sacrificing, unconditional, active, thoughtful, even divine—is considered the purest form, able to withstand the passage of time, even after it's no longer romantic.

That all sounds lovely, doesn't it? Still, you should know that just because you love your man and your love is rock strong and rock steady, this is not a sufficient reason to endure a painful relationship. Because love's natural mate is unpredictability, it is not uncommon to find ourselves wanting to be with someone who is simply wrong for us. That doesn't mean you can't give yourself over to the feeling, which we've just addressed is a native instinct for the true lover, but you must know when to leave for the sake of your heart, health, mind, and spirit. Love is in great abundance. The world is awash in it. Know and understand that you can never run dry of this emotion as long as you are willing to share it. But thanks to tons of books about soul mates, twin flames, and transcendent love, women have found themselves fixated on the idea of that one person who will walk through the door or bump into them at the supermarket or gym, perfectly matched and suited on every level, the cosmic answer and salve to every bad date and broken heart ever endured. Really, ladies, that is a lot of pressure to put on one man, don't you think? That's a lot of pressure for anybody. The truth is you will probably love many people in your lifetime, some of whom will stay, some of whom will go. Appreciate each experience. It was brought into your life for a reason. Savor these moments. Every man that passes through your world comes bearing gifts, indelible experiences whose value you might not recognize at the time, that ultimately play a critical role in your personal growth. Our instinct is to interpret a short-lived affair as failure and fall into despair as a result, but it is often through experiencing what we don't want in a relationship that we are able to focus our intention and attract a better match.

> **Vixen Say What?**
> Be sure no man can ever say you have been or done worse once he has left.

Ideally, to reduce the likelihood of disappointment, a woman should give her body only when love is mutual and her man is as invested on all levels as she. When that kind of commitment is present, passion takes on an almost supernatural form where you and your man are so exquisitely in tune that all worries, fears, and inhibitions fall away. You'll find yourself willing to try almost anything with the man you want to share your life with. Those are the moments when sex transcends. There is a unity of mind, body, and spirit between you as you both aim for the same objectives, of which bonding sexually is an important component. Sex is nothing without love. In its absence, you have flailing bodies connecting based on artificial hype. The hype may be strong, but the results are fleeting. Only in presence of love can the real benefits of sex endure.

We often mistake love for a romantic emotion, but, in the case of true *Agape*, we should love despite the romantic feelings we have for someone, even if that person doesn't love us the way we had hoped. In order to do this, you must exist on a strong foundation of self-love. We've all heard the saying, "Before you can love anyone else, you have to first love yourself," but most of us don't. Most of us just don't know how. Take the time to fall in love with *you*. You're the most important love you will ever know.

Vixen Tip

Undress and stand in front of a full-length mirror, no makeup, no fancy hair. Look at every inch of your body, everything that sags, ripples, and stretches. Know that though there are ways to improve certain imperfections, but also know that when you love yourself, you will never see any physical traits as imperfections. You will love it all! Treat yourself with love. Indulge in the little things that make you happy. Learn to be comfortable in your own skin, to take yourself out to lunch and enjoy your own company. Do things for yourself that make you feel special and loved instead of waiting for someone else to do them for you. Treat yourself the way you would want your mate to treat you. Uplift yourself with positive affirmations and feel secure in knowing you are loved with or without a lover.

Men can always sense if and how much you love yourself. Women who are happy with themselves give off a glow that is both infectious and magnetic to virtually everyone they encounter. Conversely, if you are self-loathing and insecure, people can spot this straightaway, especially a man who is in the market for such a woman. Such men will draw you in with kind words, then turn the tables, quick to accentuate your negatives and treat you as you have treated yourself. Remember, you will get only what you believe you deserve. When in love, be sure you are doing so selflessly and not with ulterior, self-serving motives. Speak to him with kindness and understanding; listen with intent and empathy. Even when you're upset, be so lovingly, not with harsh words.

Vixen Say What?
If you wish to ever find true love, you must truly love yourself.

As I enter my thirties, I realize that I'm still learning a lot about love and its true definition, purposes, and effects. After living most of my life not knowing love, I am more sensitive to and aware of it than most. I appreciate the feeling of loving and being loved by my mate, my family, my friends, and myself. What I have learned is that in life, there is nothing more important than this. Love is everything because it is in everything.

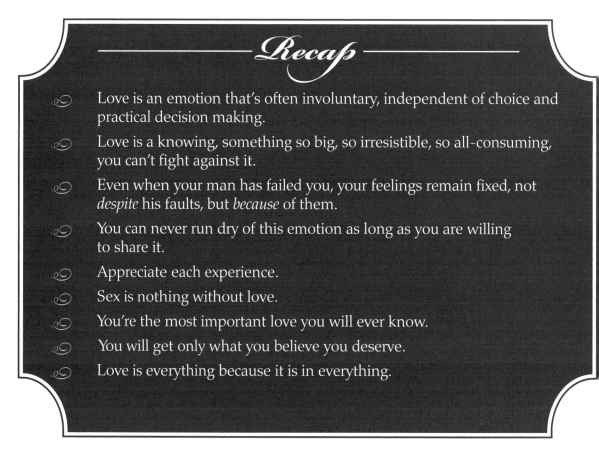

Recap

- Love is an emotion that's often involuntary, independent of choice and practical decision making.

- Love is a knowing, something so big, so irresistible, so all-consuming, you can't fight against it.

- Even when your man has failed you, your feelings remain fixed, not *despite* his faults, but *because* of them.

- You can never run dry of this emotion as long as you are willing to share it.

- Appreciate each experience.

- Sex is nothing without love.

- You're the most important love you will ever know.

- You will get only what you believe you deserve.

- Love is everything because it is in everything.

Chapter Twenty-five

Trust

The surest, most effective way to begin any relationship is to lay a solid foundation of trust. However, trust can be a tricky word, as many people have differing definitions. For some, the meaning is ironclad and literal. You believe your man will never lie or cheat on you, and if he does, all trust—and the relationship—is forfeited. That sounds great in theory, but it's about as pie-in-the-sky as it gets.

We must be fair about trust and what exactly the word encompasses. Every human being is fallible, subject to the weaknesses of time, moment, and space. Whether we fall prey to those weaknesses are testaments to how strong we are as individuals. The objective in a committed relationship is for you and your man to stand strong against weaknesses, even in the face of great temptation. Lying, however, is another issue. Every day most of us tell what we believe is a small, insignificant untruth, even to those we love wholeheartedly, in an effort to save face, encourage others, buy time, and so on. How often have we asked our mate, "How do I look?" in the hopes that he'll tell us we're the most desirable creature that ever walked the earth? Your man knows you need that affirmation, so even if you're in the most jacked up of outfits and your hair isn't exactly flattering, he might just tell you a little white untruth to keep the peace and make you feel good about yourself, because he knows you worked extra hard to look good for him.

There. Your man just lied to you. Does that mean he's not trustworthy? Is he a dog? Is it time to let this dishonest jerk go?

Of course not! It means he loves you and wants to make you feel loved. Most people lie without the intent of causing harm. Now, your girlfriend might have told you, "Take that mess off, you look awful," but your man knows his words have the potential to wound you more deeply, so he treads carefully. We all tread carefully in love. We do so because we care. That doesn't mean you don't want your man to tell you the truth when you do, indeed, looked jacked up. It means you want him to do so with care. Just know that care might involve a little lying on his part. And yours.

I mean, come on, ladies. We've all told the occasional little white untruth in bed to make our man feel like more of a sexual warrior than he actually is. We do this because we want him to feel good about himself and us. We do it with the hope that he will actually *become* that sexual warrior, if given enough encouragement. After all, "as a man thinketh, so he is."

Trust goes much deeper than demanding someone not tell lies or cheat. It should be built upon the knowledge that your mate absolutely means you no harm and has only your best interests at heart. You should feel the same way about him. This means you each consider how your actions will impact the other, opting to avoid behavior that may prove problematic. This is the foundation upon which you should build. Without real trust, you cannot establish a healthy relationship.

Back to those little white relationship untruths: this doesn't apply to being honest about your feelings and thoughts. A woman or man who is worthy of trust is straightforward and direct. Neither of you should have to bite your tongue for the other, but you should operate with a certain level of grace and finesse. There are positive ways to deliver even the most hurtful information. If you and your man have truly built a relationship where you know that you mean each other no harm, then truth will have no choice but to live among you. Be as forthright as possible. At the end of the day, the pain of truth is dull compared to the pain of the untruth.

> **Vixen Say What?**
> Allow no one to take you off your square.

Most important, trust yourself. Be aware of and follow the guidelines you have set for yourself. Once you've defined your moral, spiritual, and emotional compasses, resolve to never behave to the contrary. Your man will follow your lead when it comes to how he should treat you, and only when you trust yourself can you be assured of the treatment you deserve. It naturally follows that when you trust yourself and your own instincts, you'll be much more inclined toward healthy interaction with others and open to trusting them. Even if that trust is somehow breached, you will always be composed by the trust you have in yourself.

Vixen Tip

We often find ourselves suspicious of our mates, wondering if they have lied or have been unfaithful. We sometimes take it upon ourselves to spy and root out the answers for ourselves, thus breaking the trust in our relationships. If you ask your mate if he has been unfaithful or untruthful and the answer is no, then you should be willing to accept that as the truth. As a woman, you have natural instincts that are clear and definitive about what is true and what is not. Follow those instincts. If your man breaches your trust or cannot disprove your suspicions, let him stand on his lies. He'll have no choice but to face them. Do not compound the matter by losing your cool and giving him something to blame you for. Do not retaliate by breaking his trust in you. There's something to be said for the old adage, "Two wrongs don't make a right." Let that be your wisdom.

If the two of you are able to create an environment of open communication—something that eludes many relationships today when most people are hiding IMs and secretly texting—you will find that your relationship will thrive. Even in the worst situations, you'll be able to trust each other to tell the truth and to do so with compassion. Trust has always been a difficult thing for me. After being hurt and let down so many times, almost constantly, it seemed almost impossible for me to let down my guard. I'd reached a point where I *expected* to be let down. What I've learned, however, is that you get what you expect, and if you don't take a chance, none will be given. How can I get what I want out of life if I'm not willing to open the door and receive it? That takes trust.

Trust is the only way.

> **Vixen Say What?** Trust yourself enough to trust others.

Recap

- The objective in a committed relationship is for you and your man to stand strong against weaknesses, even in the face of great temptation.
- Most people lie without the intent of causing harm.
- Trust goes much deeper than demanding someone not tell lies or cheat.
- Without real trust, you cannot establish a healthy relationship.
- There are positive ways to deliver even the most hurtful information.
- Trust yourself.
- You get what you expect.
- If you don't take a chance, none will be given.

Chapter Twenty-six

Sex

Sex, when performed effectively and with mutual enthusiasm, can be a sublime experience that carries the couple away—physically, spiritually, and emotionally—to a place where only those two can go. And just as no two individuals are alike, the sexual connection between two partners is unique to them and cannot be re-created with anyone else. Approached correctly, with all the proper conditions in place—trust, love, friendship, respect—the ride can be binding as these two bodies move together in hot, passionate unison. It is not the lust, the thrill of the chase, or the electricity of the moment that binds them. It is all the things that have led up to this moment, things that have encouraged security and stability. The physical act of sex by itself has very little to do with what makes a truly emotional and satisfying sexual experience.

That's right. The physical act is a minor part of what's most important about a true sexual union. Once you've reached a heightened, successfully functional relationship with your partner, all manner of freedoms will begin to take place. You both will feel uninhibited during sex, free to express your desires, fantasies, and needs. You will breathe in and devour each other, becoming one in mind, body, and soul. As cosmic as that may sound, it is very real, and those who have experienced this kind of connection know the Vixen speaks the truth. Once you truly love and trust one another, there is no room for prudence and barriers in sex. You should be able to give your man what he wishes because you know he only has the best intentions for you. He, in turn, should be willing to fulfill your every fantasy because he understands your intentions for him. In this state of pure mutuality, there is a certain power that arises from each sexual encounter with your mate. Because of the open communication that exists between you, you are able to meet his needs and calm the uproar of testosterone normally raging beneath his surface, thereby creating a willingly domesticated man. A man is only a man among other men, but to his woman he is all things. (Even a shivering, surrendering shell, once she has performed her magic.)

Vixen Tip

Invest in toys and learn as many new tricks as it takes to keep your love life fresh and fun. Anal and vaginal beads and probes are easily found at any adult store or, for maximum privacy, online. Be very careful as you're poking and prodding. You don't want to hurt one another! Lubricant is essential, and the tried-and-true KY brand has never let me down.

1. One of you stands on all fours (the Top).

2. The other lays beneath in a sixty-nine position (the Bottom).

3. The Bottom enters the Top with a probe, either anally or vaginally.

4. The Bottom orally stimulates the Top, simultaneously.

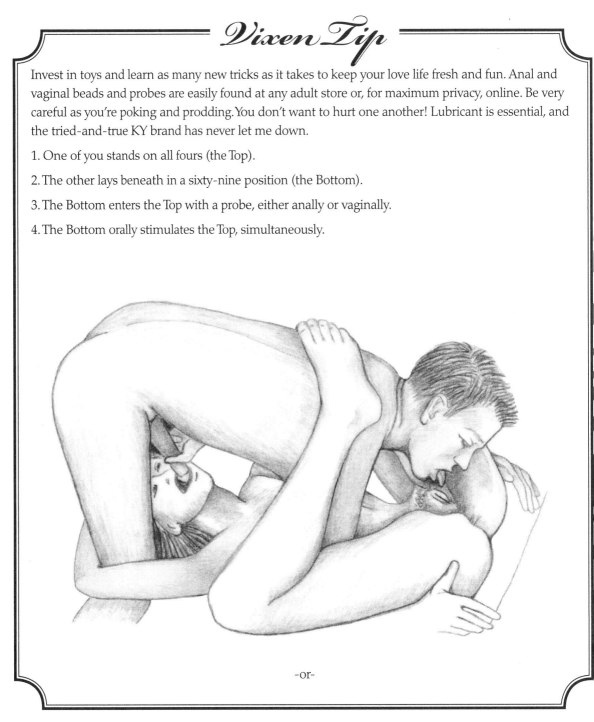

-or-

Vixen Tip

FOR THE ADVANCED COUPLE

1. Lie on your back and bring your legs up and around, over your head.

2. Your partner sits on your face for oral copulation.

3. Your partner enters you with a probe, either anally or vaginally.

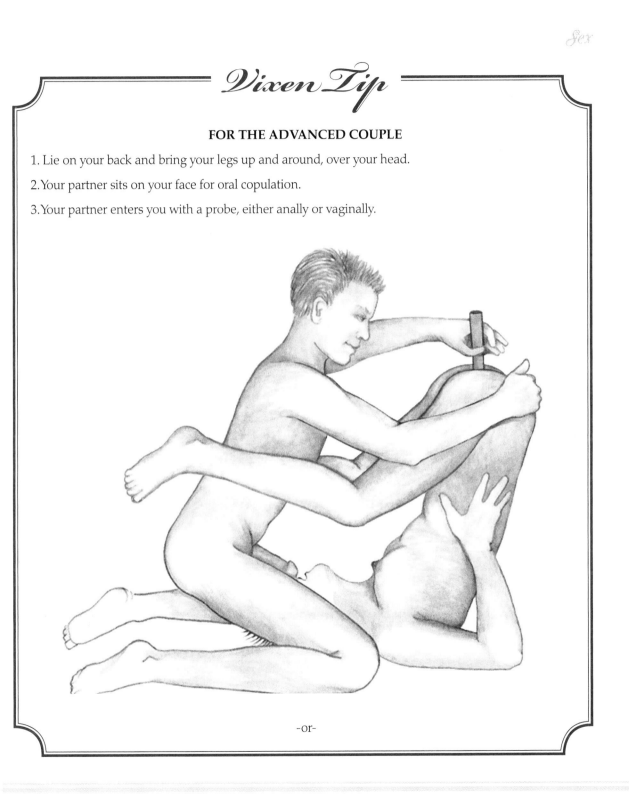

-or-

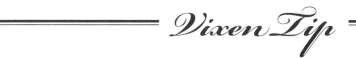

Vixen Tip

FOR THE ADVENTUROUS COUPLE

1. Your partner lies on his back with his legs hanging off the bed and his feet on the floor.

2. Lie on top of your partner in a sixty-nine position.

3. After a little fun in this traditional position, your mate holds on to you tightly and stands up with you.

4. Once you're certain it's safe, you can both continue orally stimulating the other while standing up or even walking around. Since you will be upside down in the position, I like to call this the *Upside-Down Pineapple Cake*. Enjoy!

Everyone knows that sex can be a form of power, but what many people, especially women, don't often realize is that female sexual power, when properly applied, has the ability to over-power and lead the male. Once you understand the range and complexity of your sexuality and are free to utilize it without shame, you become intriguingly powerful. Single women are then free to have sex with whomever they wish, whenever they choose. But wait…just because you can doesn't mean that you should. The most important thing about sex is having the ability to control it. Like most forms of energy, sex is most powerful when it is harnessed. It is your genie in a bottle. Sex should work at *your* command, not the other way around.

Vixen Tip

Keep a secret stash of lingerie and add to it often. He'll be wowed by your devotion to pleasing him, as well as your imagination and gusto. I have found that thigh-high boots with five-inch heels and fishnet thigh-high stockings work well. They're impossible to walk in, but I have a feeling you won't be doing much walking! There are countless types of outfits to choose from—a bustier; waist cinchers; thongs; Brazilian-cut bottoms with side ties. The list goes on. Then there are costumes that represent a certain fantasy. My favorite costume company is Trashy Lingerie, a Los Angeles landmark and the best designers of imagination-charged intimate apparel. Visit them at www.Trashy.com and fulfill your fantasy tonight!

We're just getting started. Now, take the last two tips, combine them and apply them to the following.

Vixen Tip

Enjoy being submissive in the missionary position, but revel being in the power position as well. She will handle him with both delicate care and domineering strength. When in the power position, which is on top of him, face-to-face:

1. Place your hands around his neck gently, and, ever so slowly, apply pressure.

2. Caress his hair, then begin to tug at its roots.

3. Speak into his ear, saying all the things he needs to hear. Coax him on, even tear him down to build him back up. "Is that all? Is that it? Give me more! Do it better than that! Yeah. That's it. Like that…"

4. Take the time to understand the way his body works, every muscle, small and large.

5. Place your hands on his chest for support.

6. Ride him up and down, front to back, and side to side.

7. Shift from sitting on your knees to straddling while on your feet.

-or-

Vixen Tip

FOR THE ADVANCED COUPLE

1. Without disconnecting, turn your body around and ride him backward.

2. Spread his legs and run your hands up his thigh while riding.

3. Gently cuff his scrotum.

4. Slowly and carefully, run your fingers across his "no fly zone," the perineum between his scrotum and rectum.

5. If he's adventurous enough, visit his rectum…maybe even with a probe!

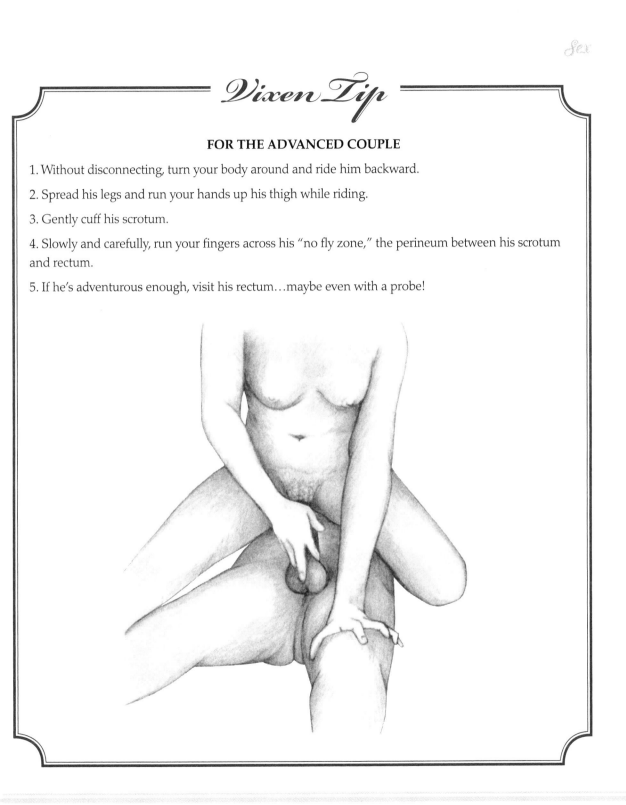

Many couples suffer a disconnect when it comes to porn. Usually, it's the man who wants to watch, which may trigger the woman in his life to feel a bit insecure, as if she is not adequate enough. Perhaps, she surmises, he'd prefer to be with someone who looks and performs like the women on-screen. While that may be true—there are many men who get caught up in an unrealistic ideal—it doesn't matter. He's with you, and if you know how, you can meet that ideal for him…rather, alter it so that *you* become the ideal.

Take the initiative to be more present in your love life. Investigate what these women on-screen are doing. If you're not comfortable watching porn with him, watch it alone. Study, study, study. Dare to take on the things you feel comfortable with. As you grow bolder, watch porn with him, paying careful attention to the parts he responds to. Emulate those acts, if you're physically able and feel so inspired. Instead of shunning the women in pornography, you might want to pay attention. You'll expand your horizons and, soon enough, he won't need as much porn because he'll be busy watching you!

Vixen Tip

If you are having a difficult time participating with your man while he's watching porn, take a different approach to the situation. Set up your own video recorder and make a date with your man to *tape your own sexual encounter!* Bring your best outfits and stilettos to the party. Bring toys and all the tricks in your bag. Be adventurous and try new things. Make up things as you go along! Tape this session and every one after that and watch them together later. Turn your man on all over again. Give him oral sex while he watches, or share in a dual masturbation session—or have sex all over again! You may begin to feel differently about porn if you're the woman in it.

A major issue in relationships can be the frequency of sexual activity. If I had my druthers, I'd have sex five times a day. My partner, however, isn't always up to this, nor do we always have time. In those instances, I'll settle for just once a day, every day…and I do mean "settle." But even that is too much for some women, especially those in committed and marital relationships. Sometimes we don't feel pretty or sexy enough. We blame it on our children and careers and a lack of time to focus on ourselves. While these things do affect how we feel about ourselves, that doesn't mean you can't do something about it.

Just one day a week, pamper yourself in the bathroom. Soak in a long, hot bubble bath with plenty of scented candles. Make time for you. Take an hour and do all those little things that make you feel like a woman, then take those good feelings and share them that night with your man.

Not everyone can find the time and stamina to have sex every day. If this sounds like you and your mate, try setting aside a particular night for just the two of you. Call it Date Night, if you have to give it a name. Before you get to your special night, be aware that everything you do leading up to that night can be considered as foreplay: dinners, massages, cuddling, kisses, and kind, loving words. All of it counts. Just because you're not having sex today doesn't mean that you can't appeal to all his senses and make him feel special, loved, and very wanted. These things are the very building blocks of intimacy, which will, ultimately lead to spectacular sex.

Based on what many of you may think you know about me, you might not exactly consider me the poster child for monogamy…but I should be. I wholeheartedly subscribe to everything monogamy stands for. There is nothing more fulfilling to me than being with one person and being able to make it work. It's easy to make it work when you're juggling several people. When one gets on your nerves, you just move to the next. Each one of them may have some characteristic you absolutely adore. You find yourself thinking that if you could just put together the best traits of all the men you're juggling, they'd make the perfect man. Sounds great, doesn't it? But check this out: there is no perfect man. We're all imperfect, but in spite of those imperfections, it's still possible to find our ideal in one man.

While I do believe you should date several people when deciding upon whom to spend your time and possibly your life with, once you have made the decision, stick with it. After all the people I've had relationships with throughout my life, and after believing I never wanted to be in another serious relationship again, I've found that monogamy is what truly makes me happy. If this is your feeling, then accept nothing less. Monogamy isn't for everyone, but for those who prefer it as a way of life it can be very fulfilling.

Sex can be amazing when it's just you and a man you know loves you and only you. There is nothing more exciting than a man and a woman who are free to do anything and everything with each other because they're exclusively committed. Monogamy, in these times of diseases and death, is like an insurance policy. Yes, it can be challenging to be limited to just one person. It requires being vigilant and aware of ways to keep the relationship from growing stale and yourself from becoming complacent. And while being with several people on a regular basis can seem like fun, in the long run monogamy can prove to be a lot less heartache. Take it from the Vixen…I know! Eventually, one or more of the guys you're juggling will start to get serious and ultimatums will inevitably follow. Feelings will get hurt. The more people involved, the greater the potential for pain. I've come a long way from those days of needing to be with more than one person, so exclusivity works best for me. Whatever works for you, live by it. As long as you understand yourself and your partner(s) sexually, you should be able to create an enjoyable experience.

All right, now—I hate to go here but I must, because whether we want to admit it or not, *anal sex* exists. A lot of us are having it and even more of us would like to and just can't muster the courage. Well, surprisingly I'm sure, I have a bit to say about anal sex.

First of all, anal sex is a huge commitment and something I feel should be saved for your husband. I mean seriously, do you really want a bunch of guys running around telling people they fucked you in the butt? I wish we all felt the same way about vaginal and oral sex but, hey, one cause at a time, I guess. So, for those of you who have not been anally entered but would consider trying it, please wait until you're sure the man who pops your backdoor cherry is the man who is committed to you.

Now, at first, anal sex hurts—bad. And not only that, it has the potential to be messy and bacterially hazardous. It's like running through a minefield; the chances of a gruesome, painful encounter are damn near assured. But if it's what you want to do, how can you make it as pleasant as unnaturally possible?

Vixen Tip

To avoid an ultramessy experience, you may want to empty your bowels before anal intercourse, either naturally or with an enema.

Vixen Tip

Here are a few tips on preparing for your big backdoor day.

1. When you're alone, take some time to practice on your own with anal probes and dildos.

2. Begin with smaller instruments and gradually move up to larger ones.

3. Be sure to use lots of lubrication.

4. Try a little bit every day until you feel you are able to take your man.

Okay, now after lots of practice, you'll have to get suited for game day. Put this next tip in your playbook!

Vixen Tip

Here are a few tips on making your first anal experience bearable.

1. Warm up first with anal probes and dildos.

2. Engage in vaginal sex first in order to get your libido and adrenaline going.

3. While having sex in a doggie-style position, have your man loosen your anal cavity with the toys and/or his fingers.

4. Once hot and wet, decide which position will be best for you to be entered. Try letting him in from behind while lying on your side to avoid your body tensing.

5. Upon feeling the pressure of his manhood against your sphincter, push outward as if having a bowel movement. This will help you not to clench your sphincter muscle instead.

6. Lube, lube, lube, but be wary of numbing lubricants, which can prove dangerous by not allowing you to feel if you're being hurt or even torn. And for unprotected couples, numbing lubricants will obviously affect you and your partner.

7. Keep antibacterial wipes by the bedside to clean his genitals and yours, should you decide to switch to vaginal sex.

8. Clean and disinfect all sex toys after use with either cleansing products sold at sex stores or simply by dropping in boiling hot water and antibacterial soap or solution.

Well, now that we've tried that let's tackle something that should be a lot simpler: *oral sex*. I say, "should be," because from what I am hearing, women aren't as good at it as either sex would like. That's right, I could be talking about you—you may give terrible head! How do you think your husband feels about that? Just imagine your man going down on you and licking around like you're some sort of melting ice-cream cone. Damn it, we want suction, we want it fast, we want it slow, we want it up, down, and sideways, too!

Guess what, girls? Men want the same thing, and we (and when I say "we," I mean "you") are just not giving him what he wants! First rule of the gift of oral sex is: you have to love it. There is nothing worse for a man than feeling as if he's forcing you or you're forcing yourself to do it. No, gagging with disgust during the act is not a turn-on.

Vixen Tip

Spend some real time with the penis in your life, and make up your mind whether you really love and respect this muscle of love and oh-so-much-pleasure. When you and your man are laying in bed or on the couch, instead of laying on his chest, lay your head on his crotch and smell him, feel him, live among his genitalia for a while. Does his bare essence, or pheromones, turn you on? Or do you wince and throw up in your mouth a little at the very thought of being "down there"? Wait a minute…do you actually call it "down there"? If so, get away from him and never go to his happy place again! Or, at least, not until you learn to love his penis and everything it does and represents. Only then can you welcome it into the orifice that receives your food and puckers to kiss your children. And that's how much you should love this instrument—as much as you love food and your kids. If not, don't fake it; he will only resent you for it, and you will resent him and his body if either of you forces the issue.

I can hear some of you now asking, "Well, how do I learn to love the damn thing?" I know, ladies, it's not the prettiest thing you've ever seen and maybe he hasn't maintained it or the area around it very well. Hmmm…so what can you do to make this thing more appealing? Maybe the following tips will help.

Making the penis appealing.

1. *Clean it!* If you have to get into the shower with your man and do it for him, then fine; just call it pampering and he won't know the difference. If he is uncircumcised, you're going to have to pull that skin back and get the crusties out. Use a soap that you like, something you'd love to smell on him or even on yourself.

2. *Clean around it!* With a pair of mustache trimmers, trim his pubic hair using the one-inch guard. Be very careful not to nick his sensitive skin, especially around his scrotum. This is why the guard is crucial.

3. *Make it smell yummy!* Baby powder isn't only for babies, honey. Powder his hairy areas and in between those ass cheeks! If he won't let you go there, then let him do it himself. Either way, get that sucker powdered up. This will keep odor away throughout his day.

4. *Remove and trim as much hair as possible.* This means his armpits, chest, and his rear. Trimmers are great for most areas, but that crack is going to give you some trouble. If he lies very still and lets you get in between there, Nair works wonders in this crevice, however, the makers of Nair DO NOT recommend this and so I can't, either. If you try this, you may need to protect his anus with a cotton ball. But again, I can't recommend it, officially.

Now that you've gotten it all clean and smelling good, what do you do with it? Technique is important but in this case, it's a difficult thing to teach. Every man is different and will like different things. Some want more suction; some want less or none and prefer to just feel your mouth and tongue glide up, down, and around their penises. So, when you're with your guy, pay close attention to what makes him squirm and moan—but if your mate isn't doing either of those two things, you'll need to brush up on your skills a bit.

Vixen Tip

The beginning of a successful oral experience.

1. First, remove all jewelry before beginning.Get yourself in a stress-free position that will help support your neck and back during the exercise. While in bed, the most comfy position is pretty basic. With him on his back, lay on your stomach between his legs with your nonoperative arm wrapped around his thigh, and grab hold of his upper leg for leverage.

2. Place his penis in your mouth, being aware of teeth and tongue placement. You want to be very careful not to scrape his sensitive skin with your razor-sharp fangs. You also want to be adventurous with your tongue, allowing it to explore the instrument. Up, down, and circular movements are helpful as well as interchangeable fast and slow speeds.

3. Suction is crucial. Switch between no suction to heavy suction, gauging which range of pressure your man likes best. Apply different amounts of pressure at different times, while alternating the movement of your tongue.

4. Incorporate your entire face in the process. Use the outside of your mouth and the side of your face as well.

5. Get creative and find your rhythm. If it helps, use music to help you create a rhythmic flow to your blowjob.

6. Don't be afraid to use your hands, but pay close attention to your partner's reaction. This can make the head of his penis too sensitive and move him further away from orgasm. Use one hand or two; move them up, down, and in a circular motion. Underhand and overhand positions are both pleasurable.

I can just hear it now: "That's it? That's all you're gonna give us?" Yes, girls, that's all I can give you, and here's a great example as to why. I am no layman when it comes to the art of pleasing a man, whether it is with my witty repartee or with my legendary mouth. When I began one of my more long-standing relationships, I just knew I had this one in the bag, sexually speaking. I was sure I would knock his socks off, rock his world, give him jungle fever, *and* the fever for the flavor. All jokes and clichéd phrases aside, let me not be shy here, honey—I knew I could suck a dick and make it splash in three minutes or less. Period. So there I was, poised and positioned to change this man's life, forever. I was certain that I would become, for him, the standard by which all dick sucking that came after me, if any, would be measured. I did all the things I've told you to do, but I made one crucial mistake: I treated his cock like it was someone else's. Basically, I performed the same old tricks with my new man.

Accustomed to roughing it and manhandling penises, I grabbed that thing, shoved it in my mouth, applied pressure, and incorporated my hands, my lips, and all my usual techniques. Within seconds, he was screaming…and it was not out of ecstasy. That man was screaming for his life! All I heard was, *"Ouch!"* and *"No!"* and before I knew it, I was being pushed off his injured member. Imagine that! *Me*, pushed away from a penis! Are you as shocked as I was?

Come to find out, this man had a sensitive penis (who knew they even existed?) and needed only a light rubbing of the lips to arouse him. No hands, no suction, no bells, no whistles. I'd never met a man like this before in my life—a man who actually *wanted* a lazy blowjob! Yes, it made my life a lot easier; still, I missed the experience of ravishing a man and eating him up. But this was a different man, different in every way, and everything I'd known before was thrown out the window. My point is this: what works for one man most likely won't work for another. When it comes to fellatio, men and their penises are like fingerprints. No combination is the same. So if you're looking for me to tell you the exact, perfect way to give head, stop being lazy. Throw your man on his back, rip his bottoms off, and figure out what *he* likes.

What I have offered you are just basic tips; it'll be up to you to get in the game and find a position that's right for you. Everyone's technique is different, and the act of giving a man oral sex is such a personal one, there is almost no way to ensure what's good for one couple will be just as good for another. Take your time, explore, take notes, and pleasure him orally as often as humanly possible, if that's what he likes. Allow yourself to be turned on by turning him on, and don't be afraid to listen to criticism and instruction.

Some of you will be good, some of you will be great, and a few of you may even be super. But as long as you and your mate are comfortable with your skill level, it doesn't matter what other couples are doing and what other women know. Just be open to him and to learning more and even to inventing your own tricks. Don't just change positions, change locations; make it exciting every time, and your love life will never be the same. Besides, a good man will return the favor, and that's always an added bonus.

Vixen Tip

Ummm…I know you may have a hard time believing this, but some men don't care much for oral sex at all! So, first, find out how your man feels about it, and if he's all for it, ask him how he likes it.

In the event that you hit a home run and your man is brought to the brink of orgasm, what do you do? There is always the option of him placing his semen somewhere, anywhere, on your body. If you decide to allow him to relieve himself on your face, be careful not to get his bountiful load in your eyes, especially if you wear contact lenses. The burning is excruciating, and it's murder cleaning the enzymes from your contacts. In the event you decide to allow him to blow a fuse in your mouth but wish not to swallow, try not to look disgusted in the moments before spitting it out. A man does not want to feel as if he or his essence is vile, though many times the goopy liquid is! When you're finished collecting the flow, smile a bit and slowly walk to the restroom and over to the sink, and quietly spit it out. Don't do some sort of spit take and then gargle with bleach water! Stay calm and be sure to protect his feelings. Now, if you're determined to swallow his spunk, be a trouper and do so without negative comments like "Ooh that was thick" or "Yuck!" Even if it is the most despicable jizz ever, smile and respond with a resounding, "Mmmm!"

Sure, sometimes it's thick and sour, sometimes it's smooth and sweet, sometimes it's just a squirt and sometimes—watch out! There are tons of old wives' tales that promise to make it more pleasant for us like feeding him pineapples. Bad habits like smoking and drinking can make the taste of his dickspit unbearable, as well as not drinking enough water or certain medications. No matter what you decide to do—spit, swallow, or gently place it somewhere neutral—do it with a smile or don't do it at all. None of us want to feel unwanted, especially not in *that* way. Enjoy!

Now, for the men reading along, this may be a good time to either skip ahead or let your woman continue without you. This next bit will have you, literally, seeing red. For some of us girls, the topic may be a sensitive subject as well, but we must put it out there and talk about it: having sex on your period. That's right, ladies, a good old-fashioned Bloody Mary. For some couples, this will be against your religion or social customs, as are quite a few things in this book. For the rest of us who are adventurous and completely uninhibited, having sex on our periods can be a comfortable, clean, and even erotic experience, if using the right tips. And even in the messiest of Bloody Mary situations, your man can enjoy being caught red-handed! For men who are not squeamish, the sight of blood can be an absolute turn-on, a sign that he is, as we say, "beating it up" or "punishing that pussy." Whatever his mannish, gory fantasies, the sight of blood only propels a warrior forward, not makes him retreat.

Vixen Tip

Here's to a better Blood Mary happy hour.

1. If you wear a tampon, it is best to leave it in until right before crawling into bed with your lover.

2. A long bath before intercourse also helps to clean your vaginal cavity directly before having sex on your period.

3. A popular old wives' tale claims that adding Epsom salts to your bath helps not only to clean the existing blood but also to slow your flow and tighten the vaginal walls. Who knows whether that's true or not? Who cares? Try it anyway! If nothing else, it'll relax the hell out of your aching muscles.

4. Cover your bed in a dark-colored absorbent towel, sheet, or blanket—black, brown, blue, or my personal favorite, red. There is something primitively ritualistic about having a special cover just for that time of the month, especially if it's red.

5. For a less messy situation, if that's your major concern, enjoy your Blood Mary doggie-style, letting gravity assist you.

6. Be sure to lubricate; you'll be a bit dry after removing your tampon or sitting in a hot, salty bath. Besides, blood isn't the best lubricant.

7. Relax. As long as you and your partner are safe and comfortable with the idea of being together during your "lady's days," don't worry about squirts and gushes. Just stay on your special blanket and let your warrior go to battle. Be sure to give him a good fight!

For some of you, having sex on your period will not be planned but an embarrassing moment filled with apologies, followed by hot towels and a mad rush to the washing machine. Personally, I'm obsessed with planning, scheduling, and knowing exactly what's going to happen and at what time. Yeah, there's a touch of OCD there, I'll be the first to admit it. But because of this little quirk, I am always right on top of my menstrual schedule and it never, ever surprises me.

After discussing this with my girlfriends, I discovered I was the only one in the group who actually tracks her period! What? Well, no wonder there are all these women on *Maury*, bringing ten, fifteen, or

Vixen Tip

Got blood on your sheets? Remove that damn spot with hydrogen peroxide. On white linens, there may still be a twinge of color after using peroxide. Treat the stain with Clorox's Ultimate Care Bleach. It's safe enough to put right on your fabrics.

even twenty men onto the stage for DNA testing! Ladies, if you educate yourself on the way your body works, when you ovulate, and when you get your period, it'll be almost impossible to think you slept with twenty men during the limited window of time when you're mostly likely to get pregnant, nor will you experience the accidental Bloody Mary on your new 950-thread-count Pima cotton sheets. For those of you who actually *don't* want to scream Bloody Murder every month, plan around those visits from Aunt Flow.

Vixen Tip

Here's a fun Web site that'll help you track your periods and ovulation, and even send you e-mails to remind you of those breast exams and everything! Visit www.MyMonthlyCycles.com.

So, after all this sex with your man, what about sex with yourself? Masturbation is awesome, but be warned—too much of a good thing can be ultradisastrous. Be careful with your vibrators and dildos. Overstimulating your clitoris can render you unable to be pleasured by anything that isn't battery powered, pulsating, or supercharged. Ladies, there is a reason God didn't make men with a battery pack in their loins, a vibrating wand, and a switch. It just ain't natural! Still, by all means, a woman's gotta do what a woman's gotta do. Just don't use powered equipment too much, too fast, too hard, or too often. The old-fashioned finger method works just fine and may spare you a bit of nerve damage. Think about it before you end up too numb to be satisfied by anything or anybody.

Recap

- The physical act of sex by itself has very little to do with what makes a truly emotional and satisfying sexual experience.
- Once you truly love and trust one another, there is no room for prudence and barriers in sex.
- A man is only a man among other men, but to his woman he is all things.
- Sex is most powerful when it is harnessed.
- Just because you're not having sex today doesn't mean that you can't appeal to all his senses and make him feel special, loved, and very wanted.
- We're all imperfect; in spite of those imperfections, it's still possible to find our ideal in one man.
- Whatever works for you, live by it.

Chapter Twenty-seven

Keeping a Home

I sometimes wonder if we realize how much our men pay attention. It is not uncommon for women to underestimate men's intelligence and attention to detail. It's not in their nature to be as chatty as us, to comment on everything they see. They observe, take note of things in passing, and make decisions based on what they've noted. We may never be aware of what's going on in their heads as they observe us until it's too late.

How many of us have been cozied up with a man, content, oblivious, when he suddenly announces, "I can't do this anymore."

"Do what anymore?" you ask. "What are you talking about?"

"This messy house," he says. "The way you look. You don't care about your body."

It could be anything. You wonder why he didn't tell you before this moment. But men are ruminators, contemplators. They wait to see if things will change even though you have no idea the waiting is taking place. You're being graded. Yes, you! Graded! And you might be flunking and not even know it. Your man may drop little hints— "Is that dust on the TV?" "Is this all we're having for dinner?"—that you miss altogether because you don't even recognize these are things that matter. If there's no open line of communication between you, you're at an even greater disadvantage.

Because of this, we have to be vigilant of even the minutest details as they relate to our bodies, our selves, and the environment in which we live. Do this not just to impress a man, but also to impress and uplift yourself. Your appearance and your home are direct extensions of who you are. To believe otherwise is to be deluded. An impeccably attired woman whose living conditions are in complete disarray is living a lie that's waiting to be unearthed. A man will recognize that lie that moment you invite him over. I can't tell you how many male friends I have who, when asked about a particular woman they've been dating, casually say, "Oh, I could never get serious with her. Her house is too dirty and she can't cook for shit." Sex can go only so far, ladies. Sooner or later, your man is going to have to get out of bed and eat. He wants to know you'll wash the sheets and make the bed! He needs to know you'll be able to feed him, and that doesn't mean just pick up the phone and order takeout.

Even if your man isn't the neatest bachelor around, when he walks into your home, he is looking for proof that you are equipped to be his partner, part of that proof being evident in the way you keep your living space. As archaic as it sounds, men are socialized to protect and provide for the family, and women are socialized to nurture and take care of the home. Sure, times have changed. Yes, there are plenty of instances of those roles being reversed, especially since women now work just as hard outside of the home as men. But the male-provider/female-nurturer archetype is the foundation upon which relationships and the family have historically been built. If you are a woman who wants a solid relationship with a strong, leading man, then you must be willing to be a strong, supportive woman, one he's proud to have by his side. Keeping a nasty home won't cut it, ladies. And if you're so busy with other obligations that you don't have time to keep up the house, don't allow your home to become disheveled. Get a maid if you have to, but whatever you do…keep a clean home.

I wasn't aware of men's domestic concerns until just a few years ago. I invited a few guys over for dinner and conversation during the NBA play-offs. Upon serving my gentlemen callers on my new Mikasa china, I was surprised by the flurry of compliments on my brand-new dinner service and flatware. I glanced around my dining table at these towering, burly, ultramasculine men as they marveled at my home and all its immaculate details. That's when I realized men are not as oblivious as we may believe, and all these seemingly inconsequential things—fine china, cleanliness, a good home-cooked meal—set the terms by which every woman is defined.

Most men have memories of growing up and watching their mothers buzz around the house accomplishing many things simultaneously: laundry, cooking, cleaning, tidying up, all the while doling out hugs, kisses, and encouragement. Most men, though they may never admit it, are looking for a little—or a lot—of their mothers in their mates.

Vixen Tip

Total and complete cleanliness is the most important aspect of keeping a home. Floors and walls should be cleaned; pay close attention to baseboards and light switches. Clean kitchens and bathrooms are a must. Keep your sink empty of dirty dishes and your garbage disposal clear of waste. Every so often, grind a lemon in your disposal to freshen it. It's always a plus when your dishes, utensils, pots, service, and glassware are matching sets. Keep your counters and the rest of your home free of clutter. Dust your furniture top to bottom. Dust above, below, and underneath objects. Keep wood furniture polished. Finally, keep dirty laundry to a minimum, obscurely stored in hampers and not strewn about. While this probably sounds like advice from your mother, keep in mind…it probably is. There's a lot to be said about a woman who takes pride in her home and family, and even more to be said about the old-school mothers and grandmothers who carried on these traditions. Men love that!

Vixen Say What? Everything has its place. Put it there!

Speaking of old-school mothers and grandmothers, I find it amazingly rewarding to spend time with women older than I am, especially those who have the wisdom and experience that comes with the passage of time and are willing to share that knowledge to benefit others. If you are fortunate enough to have women like this in your life, learn from them. Ask questions. Don't consider yourself so wise that you don't know how to listen to your elders. You and your mate will appreciate them for it.

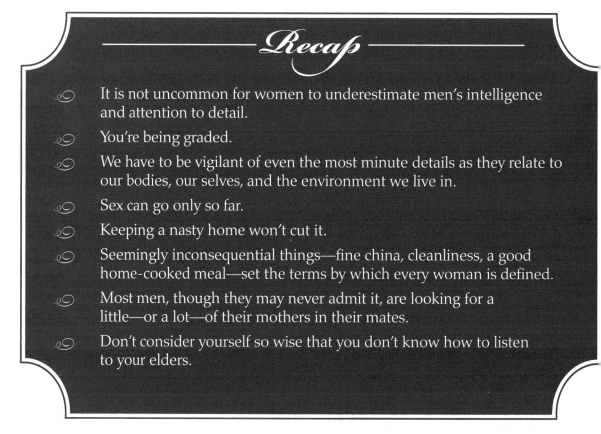

Recap

- It is not uncommon for women to underestimate men's intelligence and attention to detail.

- You're being graded.

- We have to be vigilant of even the most minute details as they relate to our bodies, our selves, and the environment we live in.

- Sex can go only so far.

- Keeping a nasty home won't cut it.

- Seemingly inconsequential things—fine china, cleanliness, a good home-cooked meal—set the terms by which every woman is defined.

- Most men, though they may never admit it, are looking for a little—or a lot—of their mothers in their mates.

- Don't consider yourself so wise that you don't know how to listen to your elders.

Chapter Twenty-eight

Give Him What He Wants

('Til He Don't Want It No More)

Let's be real. We've all heard the same rhetoric—"Relationships are fifty-fifty," "It's all about give and take"—the usual schlock, most of which evolved during the rise of feminism, when women wanted assurance of being equal partners. But let's harken back for a moment to the simple advice our grandmothers have always been quick to dish out: *Please your man. Give him what he wants.* While that may sound like an outrageous suggestion in an age where we as women pride ourselves on independence and "getting ours," there's something to be said about the fine art of submission. If you really want to get yours, make sure, first and foremost, your man gets his.

"Getting his" can mean a number of things, including, but not exclusively, sex.

Think about it. Seriously. Has there ever been a moment when your mate asked for something that you found either alarming or absurd—like space, for instance—and you had no idea where the request came from or what to do with it? Our typical response to things that seem counter to what we want in the relationship is to fight, but do you even know why you're fighting? On the surface, it's because he's asking for something that seems to threaten the order of your universe, something that somehow might mean he no longer wants to be with you. That could be true, but more than likely it's not. You wouldn't know that, though, because you haven't taken the time to find out. You immediately went into fight mode and everything fell apart.

Vixen Say What? You cannot hold relationships together by falling apart.

Most of the time, we fight because we are selfish. We're making it about us. Step outside yourself for just a moment. Consider his feelings. Be your man, if you can imagine that. It might be hard because we're so conditioned to react instead of sympathizing in moments like this. He's trying to take away the goods. You've invested your time, your emotions, and perhaps a great deal of your money in being with him. How dare he want space! The nerve!

Let's rethink this, though. There's a new strategy to be had in all this.

He just told you he wants some space. Okay. Then space it is! Don't be mean or sarcastic about it. Give your man what he asked for, no matter how hard it may be, but before he goes, let him know how much you love him. Then love him. HARD. Give him the full monty (inclusive of, but not exclusive to, sex). Then set that little birdie free and watch what happens.

He'll appreciate you for understanding him as a man. He'll appreciate you for understanding him as a human being. Appreciation is a major cornerstone of successful relationships. A woman who is appreciated always, ultimately, gets hers. This is a different kind of fighting. One that's much more effective for getting what you want.

His need for breathing room (or whatever seemingly irrational thing he has asked for) might have nothing to do with you. There could be other issues at play that you're completely unaware of—stress, work and family, or something in his past unexpectedly rearing its head. Men are notorious for going inward when it comes to problem solving. The last thing your man needs is you leaping into hostile cling mode when he's trying to sort his thoughts and regain his footing.

So you give him his space happily, unconditionally. But what if he doesn't return? Then what?

But I listened to you, Vixen, you might say, *and look what happened!!!*

Sometimes the hardest thing in the world to do is to let someone go, but the truth is, if he loves you—if he really loves you—he *will* come back. Maybe not in the capacity you're wishing for, but that's okay. You may be better off as friends, at least for now. Just don't fight him about it. There are ways of fighting for a relationship without fighting the man who's in it with you. When we do that, our fears make us run our mouths so much, we end up talking ourselves out of everything we want.

Don't trip. Breathe in. Breathe out. We all know men have a habit of asking for things that they really believe they want. In that moment, you should give him whatever he asks for—within reason, of course. (You should never do anything that violates your moral and ethical code in order to keep a man; you'll only resent him, and yourself, in the end.) Somewhere along the way, we as women became increasingly combative and argumentative. This new woman works well among her counterparts in commerce but fares less successfully when it comes to building intimacy in personal relationships. It's time for us to go back to what worked for our grandmothers and their grandmothers and the grandmothers before them. Give a man what he asks for if it's something he needs for himself, be it space, time, a night out with the boys, or maybe a few nights at his mother's house. Stop fighting your man and learn to stand down. Submit to his will and you'll end up bending it back toward your own.

The word *submission* carries an uneasy stigma, thanks in part to the feminist movement. Submission is not a sign of weakness but of respect for the one you love and, mostly, for yourself.

By submitting to your man, it shows that you're in control of your emotions and are willing to exercise selflessness. That's not to say that you should be expected to agree with everything he says and does, but sometimes the battle is better won with silence and compliance.

If he doesn't feel like he's getting enough sex, don't counter with how busy your day is with school, work, kids, and errands. Don't bring up cramps. Cramps have never done anything to advance a relationship.

Bite him with his own dog. Buck up, gird your loins, eat your Wheaties, then sex him—and don't just go through the motions, either. Put your whole heart into it like it's the Sexual Olympics. Like sex is oxygen and he's a set of lungs. Pump him up! Give it to him for breakfast, lunch, and dinner. And snacks. You've got to give him snacks. Give him so much sex, he waves the white flag. Eventually moderation will come into play and everyone will end up getting what he or she wants. (And you just might set free your inner freak along the way!)

In my experience, when you give a man what he asks for and do so without questioning, you allow him room to come to his own conclusion that in many instances is the opposite of his first thought, but he needs the latitude to figure that out. Men often operate according to the Law of Diffusion, moving from an area of high concentration to an area of low concentration. Translation: if the air is thick where you are, you can best believe he's going to start hanging out in a place where he can breathe—*away from you.*

Vixen Tip

So your man thinks he needs to roam the streets a little; he feels as if you've been smothering or nagging him and he needs space to breathe. A woman's first reaction is usually, "No, don't go. Stay here and talk to me about this." Well, it may be difficult but you have to fight against this and simply say, "Okay." You'll probably shock him and impress yourself when you do this, but it won't make you feel any better. Yet, instead of holding him captive for hours, trying to make him hear and understand you, call a friend, a relative, someone you can really trust and share your pangs with. Be sure it's someone you can trust, though, or this may backfire on you. Never share your personal affairs with someone who is known to gossip or has shown they cannot be trusted. Remember, there's always someone who wants your life. It could even be his own mother (more on that later). As for you, you need a safe place to land; you need someone who loves you and is rooting for you and the health of your relationship. By the time your man returns, you will have released your frustrations and be better prepared to talk things over with him more calmly, and he will come back because you didn't push him away by trying to make him stay.

For this very reason, you should never dump shit on your man. Save your shit for your girlfriends. That's what they're for! Rant to them about the fact that he had the audacity to ask you for _____ (insert whatever crazy thing he asked for here), but once the rant is through, hang up the phone and give your man what he was asking for—over and over and over again. By maximizing the role of your girlfriends as emotional outlets, you're freed up to "yes" your man to death. In due time, all that "Yes! Yes! Yes!" from you will make him say, "Wait! Wait! Wait, baby…I feel full."

Vixen Say What? Warning: Pseudofriends will wish you well, but never too well.

A full man is a happy man. And we like happy men, don't we, ladies—because then *we* get served.

Recap

- Please your man. Give him what he wants.
- We fight because we are selfish.
- Our fears make us run our mouths so much, we end up talking ourselves out of everything we want.
- Stop fighting your man and learn to stand down.
- Submission is not a sign of weakness but of respect for the one you love and, mostly, for yourself.
- Bite him with his own dog.
- Save your shit for your girlfriends.

Chapter Twenty-nine

Consistency

Under ideal circumstances, change is a good thing, if done in the spirit of moving forward. But life is inconsistent, and we're not always operating within the ideal. The world comes at us aggressively from the moment we step out the front door, which is why it's imperative that when your man is at home, it should be a place of consistency, a comforting and comfortable haven where he knows the lay of the land. There should be no booby traps, minefields, or sudden shifts of the wind. When a man walks through the door, he wants to know what's waiting for him, and he expects it to be as it was when he left, unless he or the two of you jointly initiated further change. There's no place like home, so the saying goes, and for a man—if the conditions are right—there's no place he'd rather be.

"Home," of course, is a metaphor in this instance. I'm not talking about your hair or perfume, the position of the furniture, new fabric softener, or the thread count of your sheets. Those are adjustments hopefully meant to improve things for you and your man. When I say "home," ladies, I mean *you.*

In the beginning of a relationship, we tend to present a perfect version of ourselves. We answer the phone on the first ring and allow him to call us very late at night, eager to appear upbeat and available. We are pleasant and nonabrasive, avoiding conflict and resistance at all cost. Some of you are not pretending. This is actually how you are and how you remain throughout the relationship.

Most women, however, can only keep up this act for so long before the veneer begins to crumble. There's an old saying about familiarity breeding contempt, and while you might not become all-out contemptuous once you settle into what you now feel is a secure relationship, the likelihood for you to become less tolerant and accommodating is prone to increase. That's just human nature, although it's one of the key reasons why relationships fail.

The more we know our mate and the more we begin to believe that he's not going anywhere, the more our façade—and yes, it *is* a façade—falls away. These changes can be behavioral, physical, emotional, and/or sexual. You might start taking your time getting to the phone when he rings you up, perhaps even rushing him off because you've got one of your girlfriends on the line. Once upon a time, you may have put off your girlfriends for him, but now it's the other way around. Don't think your man won't notice that.

Perhaps you're cranky if he calls when you're sleeping. Or your mate, inexplicably excited by the sight of you as you vacuum, wants to do it on the living room floor right then and there, but you refuse. You're busy, you protest, and dirty. In the early days, you might have leapt upon him without question, but not now. Practicality intervenes instead. You've now settled into texting or e-mailing your feelings more than you verbally and physically express them. Or you don't make as much of an effort to look sexy for him or bother to cook elaborate meals the way you did in the beginning. Why should you? you say. You've got him. He's sprung.

Are you sure? We've already discussed in prior chapters how stealthy our mates can be about what they observe. Men notice the slightest nuance of difference, especially as it relates to how they're being treated. Every time you reject your man sexually, he will make a mental note of it. When he comes home to more takeout rather than cooked meals—especially when it used to be the other way around—that will be filed away, too. Uncombed hair and sweats? Check. More attention to your friends than him? Duly noted. Quick to argue about the slightest things? All-right-y, then. All these things quietly erode your relationship to the breaking point, and by that time it's usually too late for recovery.

Vixen Tip

Progressive change is good! Instead of surprising him with matted hair and your old, bleach-spotted college sweatshirt, surprise him with a new negligee, or a different hairstyle or hair color. Hell, find a sexy red nail polish and come out of those bland nudes you always wear. Are you a fullback panty girl? Visit the thong section of your local Victoria's Secret and go nuts! Do anything, do everything, be it all, honey. That's what you were built for.

One of the strongest maxims delivered by our mothers and grandmothers is something most of us have heard many times before: whatever you do in the beginning to get a man is what it will take to keep him. Statistics say it takes twenty-one days to form a habit. Odds are, after the first twenty-one days of your relationship, your man has become quite accustomed to being treated well and will find any sudden, or gradual, change in behavior from you both shocking or disappointing. Eventually, he will begin to feel duped and might go looking for that faux earlier version of you elsewhere.

This is not to say that your man is exempt from how he treats you. Critical to the success of any relationship is the idea that both partners should never take each other for granted and should work hard to assure each other's happiness and well-being. But you must play an active role. We often allow our relationships to set to autopilot, focusing our attention on places we believe deserve more effort, such as work, children, or school, if we're pursuing higher education. Your man requires just as much attention or his affection will atrophy and ultimately fail. Consider his emotions as muscles, which need to be exercised. Active, positively reinforced muscle grows strong, able to uplift, support, and resist. Unexercised muscle can weaken to the point of being unable to support the slightest weight or withstand any form of resistance. You must "exercise" your man consistently, with proactive love and care, enlisting the same intensity, which encouraged him to commit to the relationship. Your man will grow strong in his love for you, more able to resist attempts to break him down or lure him away.

Just think, ladies, if that twenty-one-day habit-forming rule holds true as applied to you, then you should have no problem treating your man the way you did in the beginning. Just do so long enough and it'll become a natural part of your behavior. Consistency is the one habit you should never break.

Recap

- When your man is at home, it should be a place of consistency.
- "Home" means *you*.
- In the beginning of a relationship, we tend to present a perfect version of ourselves.
- Most women, however, can keep up this act for only so long, then the veneer begins to crumble.
- These changes can be behavioral, physical, emotional, and/or sexual.
- Men notice the slightest nuance of difference, especially as it relates to how they're being treated.
- Whatever you do in the beginning to get a man is what it will take to keep him.
- Consistency is the one habit you should never break.

Chapter Thirty

Being a Helpmate

Many of you spend so much time wondering why your man won't act right, get serious, or sometimes even come home, but have you ever considered the obvious: why should he want to? To paraphrase an old popular song, "What have you done for him lately?" A man wants to know that he can depend on you to be there when he needs you, no matter how great or small that need may be. It can be something as trivial as picking up after him as he rushes out the door on his way to work, tossing the boxers and socks he left on the bathroom floor into the hamper. It can be as significant as making sure his mother gets to her doctor's appointment, or that the checks for the bills are already written and in their stamped envelopes by the time he remembers they're due. Being a helpmate comes in many forms, but not many women understand the importance of this role.

Some of us are so self-absorbed and focused on not getting "played" that we end up henpecking a man to death. This includes everything from challenging his every request to refusing to step outside of your comfort zone to assure him of your support. Many of us have been socialized in recent generations to bitch and moan every time our man forgets to pick up after himself or leaves a dish in the sink. We've heard our mothers say, "I ain't your damn maid"—and then one day, we hear ourselves saying the same thing. Well, the day I said it, I said it to a man who wasn't having it. His response? "Well, if you're not going to be my helpmate, then what good are you?" He had a valid point. From that day forward, I was a laundry-washing, dinner-cooking machine. There wasn't a thing needing to be done in his home that wasn't, even though I was only visiting. Even though we lived in two different states, when I was at his place, you can bet I was helping.

Now, this man wasn't worth the sweat equity I put into him or his damn laundry, but I learned a valuable lesson. A man who has a lot to offer, the right man, wants and needs a woman who is not just arm candy but a true partner and teammate. No man wants to shoulder every single responsibility. In that case, there'd be no reason to ever seriously commit. Building a family, for a man, first starts with finding the proper woman who is worthy of all he brings to the table. Men—real men—enjoy working hard to provide for and bring pleasure to a woman who appreciates him. This is one of the most important ways in which a man shows his love. The more participatory and accommodating his woman, the easier it becomes for him to offer himself and all that he comes with. A worthy man deserves a worthy helpmate.

Vixen Tip

Nike said it best—just do it! If you have a man that is worth his weight in gold and would do most anything to assure your happiness, then why not pick up behind him, remember the things he's forgotten or take out the trash for him. When it's time for his shower, grab him a new towel and washcloth and hand them to him when he's finished. Every once in a while, when you're in the shower with him, wash his entire body for him. Make him feel like the king he is and he'll know you are his queen.

This requires major rewiring on the part of a lot of women in terms of how we think. In this post–sexual revolution age of empowerment and level playing fields, many of us view words like *helpmate* as indicating indentured servitude. Servitude, however, typically entails subjugation, where only one party benefits and the other suffers humiliation and a lowered standard of living. What I'm suggesting is the opposite of that. I'm talking about being "of service," as we are in any role we undertake that requires our commitment and expertise. You are of service in your career, as a parent, or as a friend, so why wouldn't you be the same in your relationship with your man? A man chooses you based on your ability to be of service in areas where he needs support. He, in turn, hopes to be of service to you by meeting your needs. This isn't difficult to understand when you look at it this way. Men and women choose partners to meet each other's needs. When a woman can surrender her resistance and pride and work for the general benefit of the relationship, knowing that her man is doing the same, everyone thrives.

This is how successful businesses are run, and creating an effective relationship is, in many ways, like running a business. Every effort that is put in must be done with the objective of overall success in mind. You forego complaining about picking up after him because you realize he's out there making money to take care of you. This is quid pro quo—this for that—at its best. If your man is happy and well taken care of, you will be, too.

As I write this, I can hear women flinging this book to the floor, shouting, "I ain't no damn servant!" See? This is where the retraining starts. Let's look at the definition of *servant*. According to Merriam-Webster's Dictionary, it means "one that serves others." That's it, pure and simple.

It has nothing to do with you losing your freedom or sense of self. In fact, helping others can be quite empowering. This is a part of your description as a woman, a wife, and a mother. That means you've been given the greatest responsibility on Earth: caring for others. Teachers, doctors, nurses, firefighters, and police officers—all-powerful positions, all considered public servants. Servants! Imagine that. As a woman, you are built to do, be, and have it all because of your natural ability to be of service. That service does not go unrewarded. Men are proud to uplift a woman who staunchly, humbly, and selflessly supports them. The accolades will rain down upon you.

None of this is to say that you don't deserve to have your feet rubbed, your bathwater run every night, or your dinner cooked and served to you in bed, if you so desire. But do you honestly think you'll get any of that if you're of no help to your mate? There's nothing wrong with giving, ladies, because when you do so with a generous heart, you will get, get, get! This rule doesn't apply only to women. Men need to get their asses in gear, as well, pitching in around the house and becoming more involved in the lives of their girlfriends, wives, and children. But this book isn't for your man (though we all know he's going to sneak in and read it as soon as you're done). At the end of the day, what your man and your kids need to know is that nothing would run as smoothly as it does if it weren't for you taking care of and serving them. Being a helpmate represents the height of partnership. And the best way to have a great partner is to be one!

Recap

- Being a helpmate comes in many forms, but not many women understand the importance of this role.
- A worthy man deserves a worthy helpmate.
- Men and women choose partners to meet each other's needs.
- If your man is happy and well taken care of, you will be, too.
- As a woman, you are built to do, be, and have it all.
- The best way to have a great partner is to be one.

Chapter Thirty-one

Giving Him Space

Here's an idea: leave him alone! (Insert applause from every man in the universe here.) Yes, believe it or not, as much as your man might love you, need you, and want to spend the rest of his living days with you, he needs you to back the hell up every once in a while. But why, you ask. Who knows? Who cares! If you've done your homework and spent your time developing friendship, love, open communication, trust, and all the other aspects I've recommended in prior chapters, you should already know that he wants to be with you and has no plans to disrespect you in any way. These very things may be a part of the reasons why he needs his space.

When a man has found what he wants and has chosen to be there for the long haul, it is the space and time between you that will help make your relationship last. Forever is a long time. So is fifty, twenty, or even five years for some people. The prospect of this, if given heavy contemplation, can make a man nervous or make him panic. Having the same person around you every day and every night can become frustrating and claustrophobic, even under the best circumstances. Every once in a while, it's good for him to get away.

Vixen Tip

I'm not saying that he's the only one entitled to a "Get Out of Jail Free" card. You're allowed to have one, too! Let your man care for the house and kids while you take a day to yourself and do the things that make you happy. Or the two of you can venture out with your respective friends on the same night…separately. Either way, go somewhere! Do something! Even if you two are holed up in the house and don't feel like going out, you can still inhabit your own separate spaces. Choose neutral corners for the evening. You can catch up on your reading or all the gossip with your closest girlfriends, while he's in another room watching the game or catching up with his friends and family. Just a few hours of quiet time or time spent away from one another a few times a week can do wonders.

Space is critical for him, even if you're living together. He has to feel like he has breathing room and is still clearly defined as an individual, even though he has committed to joining his life with yours. Insisting on constant time together or demanding to know where and what he's doing every second of the day can be strangling. The worst thing you can do is make a man feel trapped or backed into a corner. This is when he'll come out fighting and will more than likely retaliate against you.

But how can you be sure he's not cheating if you're giving him all this time to go off and do what he wants? Honestly? You can't be sure. How can any of us be certain of what anyone is doing at any given time? That's why trust is such an important element when forging your relationship. This works both ways. Once your partner realizes that you trust him to come and go, you just might find that he comes and goes even less, opting to bask in your presence instead. The irony of freedom often lies in the fact that the more you have, the less you exercise it. Sometimes just him knowing he can come and go at his leisure without getting grief from you is sufficient enough. Encourage him to do so, but make sure you don't come across as trying to get rid of him.

That's definitely not what you want. He might think you're up to some dirt of your own. The key is letting him know you're genuinely concerned about his mental well-being, and showing him that you understand his having time alone is a big part of that. And when he gets back, make sure to show him what he was missing. He'll have a healthier attitude because of it, and so will you.

> ## Vixen Tip
>
> Give him his space without him asking for it and he won't mind the times you insist on being close.

Recap

- He needs you to back the hell up every once in a while.
- It's good for him to get away.
- The worst thing you can do is make a man feel trapped or backed into a corner.
- Once your partner realizes that you trust him to come and go, you just might find that he comes and goes even less.
- When he gets back, make sure to show him what he was missing.

Chapter Thirty-two

Encouraging His Manhood
(aka Stroking His Ego)

Baby talk. Sexy coaxing. You know what I'm talking about. We've all done it before. After enlisting your man's help to rearrange the furniture, you stand back and watch, cheering him on with such lines as, "Daddy, you're so strong. I love your body." Or after watching him answer number Forty-two Down on the notoriously difficult *New York Times* Sunday crossword, you pipe in with a rousing, "You're so smart, baby! I would have never guessed that." The truth is, you could've moved that furniture all by yourself, and number Forty-two Down wasn't really that hard. But a man needs encouragement and praise, especially from the woman he loves. Your man needs to feel needed and it's your job to make that happen.

Saying these things doesn't require you to be disingenuous. You don't have to feel like you're lying in order to make your man feel good. It's been proven time and again that words have power, and positive reinforcement can bring forth positive results. Tell a man he's strong enough times for him to believe it, and you'll have a man eager to show you his strength in every way. Repetition is how we come to believe the things we believe, for better or for worse. If you repeatedly tell a man he's worthless, hoping it will result in him manning up and becoming a winner, you're going to be sorely disappointed. His confidence will become so eroded under your hurtful words it will diminish to the point of nothing, or he'll become so fed up with you being a constant source of negativity, he'll leave. Remember the Law of Diffusion. He will head for an area of low concentration, away from the stress—and away from you.

It's always easier for us to encourage our men when things are going well, but what happens when you hit a rough patch in the relationship? What if one (or both) of you suddenly comes under enormous stress? Suppose your man loses his job? A man's sense of worth is often tied to how he makes his living. He can be at his most fragile emotionally when he finds himself unemployed. The worst thing you can do is attack him at this time. This is when he needs you most. Choose your words carefully. Deliver them in a way to show support without diminishing his manhood. "Don't worry, babe, we have enough money coming in to take care of things until we find something new and even better" is much more desirable than saying, "I'm prepared to carry the household until you find another job." Sure, they both mean the same thing, but the first statement allows him to still feel empowered, employing the word *we* repeatedly to show that you are with him during this difficult time. The second statement sounds like *you've* become the man ("I'm prepared to carry the household") and will handle it until he can be a man again ("until you find another job"). Of course, that's not what you're saying, but that's what he'll hear.

A man needs to feel encouraged especially when he perceives himself as a failure. He should be reminded that you still see him as the strong, desirable figure that made him attractive to you in the first place. Do not emasculate him by reminding him that you're the one who has to pick up his slack in instances like these. He will only resent you for it.

Vixen Tip

Every chance you get, reassure your mate that he is the most wonderful man you've ever known. Comment on even the most simple of gestures or articles; tell him how great those jeans look on him or how turned on you are by the way the corners of his mouth turn up when he smiles. Stand or lay very close to him and slowly bring your nose to his neck and chest, then whisper, "I love the way you smell." Let him know that every part of his body is desirable to you. Laugh at all his jokes, especially the ones that aren't funny. When he speaks, listen intently, even if you couldn't care less about the topic. He is wonderful and wondrous, and there is no one manlier, sexier, or more perfect for you. Make sure he knows that.

A lot of this might sound silly to most women, but remember, we're not socialized the way men are. Most men are taught to conquer and provide, and when circumstances prevent them from doing so, they can often feel inadequate and unworthy. Because many men are trained from childhood to not cry and to man up, they internalize their stress and disappointment, making them apt to fall into depression if not afforded the proper outlet and support. That outlet is you. Your job is to stroke his ego. It might feel like an emotional handjob—jacking him off, if you will. This doesn't mean you're turning him into some mollycoddled whiner who'll become comfortable relying on you to take the lead in the relationship. This is merely another form of support to get his ego back up to speed. Just as in sex, it is equally as necessary to offer a bit of gentle stroking to encourage him as a man.

And why shouldn't you? They do it for us all the time! If you've taken the time and gone through the proper processes to select a man—the right man—he'll know when you're in need of a little pick-me-up. How many times has your man heaped compliments and reassurances upon you, right when you needed them most? If your mate is as attuned to you as he should be, and vice versa, you will both be a comfort to each other during times of crisis and calm. He will shower you with loving words as if he's only just discovered how incredible you are, and he'll do it on a day when you're most distressed, even though you haven't told him how upset you are. In turn, during the times that he's most doubting himself, you'll wrap him in your arms, tell him how much you love him, and proceed in giving him all the reassurance he needs. And you'll do it without him having to ask. It's called relationship sixth sense. The stronger your bond, the more heightened your sensitivity to each other's needs. Encourage your man. Lift him up before the world. The more uplifted he feels, the higher he will raise you.

Recap

- Your man needs to feel needed, and it's your job to make that happen.
- Repetition is how we come to believe the things we believe, for better or for worse.
- A man's sense of worth is often tied to how he makes his living.
- Do not emasculate him.
- It is equally as necessary to offer a bit of gentle stroking to encourage him as a man.
- The stronger your bond, the more heightened your sensitivity to each other's needs.
- The more uplifted he feels, the higher he will raise you.

Section 4

How to Release Him

How do you know when you've had enough?

There are certain things no woman can ignore; some are his fault and,

believe it or not, some are yours. Either way, a woman must know

when enough is enough and just how to release her catch.

Chapter Thirty-three

When a Woman's Fed Up

So let me get this straight: you've done all you can, you're one hell of a woman with all your ducks in a row, and you've done nothing but right by your man. And even with all this, he *still* continues to act up? Is he coming home in the wee hours of the morning? Getting strange late-night calls? Has he become caught up in a web of elaborate lies, unable to explain his strange behavior? Maybe he never quite recovered from losing his job and has become a permanent fixture on your couch. Or every time you come home from a hard day's work, the only thing he's done right is guess the baby daddy on *Maury*. Have you officially had enough of his ass? Well, I get it, girl. It's time to turn this joker a-loose! That's right, I said it—*a-loose!*

But let's be methodical about this whole thing. Once we realize we can no longer bear a relationship, we must act with our heads and not solely from our emotions. First off, through no fault of their own, men aren't always that smart when it comes to women. As we've discussed already, men and women are socialized separately and differently from the time they are born. We interact with our own during our formative years much more than we do with males. The same is true for men. Then you reach a certain age and are expected to know what to do when faced with the prospect of dating and marrying one of "the others." And they are, indeed, the others. They're like aliens to us, as we are to them, so naturally it takes a lot of reprogramming and flexibility to begin to understand the opposite sex. Add to this major disadvantage my theory that men can be slow learners, and the likelihood of situations arising where a man is perplexed, tempted, or tricked by a woman other than his mate increases exponentially.

Vixen Say What?
Dear Men: Just because you've slept with a bunch of women doesn't mean you know anything about women.

One of the most significant aspects about us—an aspect that men often fail to fully understand—is that, by nature, women have a very high threshold for pain. We have to. We are the bearers of children, and that event alone can be excruciating beyond description, capable of inducing a pain so great, the average man would probably black out if he had to endure it. That ability to tolerate pain for an extended period of time also applies to our emotional tolerance.

This is why we can take on so much, from having a career, to running a household, carrying children in our bodies for nearly a year, bearing and raising those children, and caring for our men in all the ways that they require. It's a lot.

Just because we're built for such burden and pain, however, doesn't mean we're unbreakable. It might take a long time for it to happen, but we're more likely to become overwhelmed if we tolerate more than we could, and should, bear. You might wake up one day, after years and years of entertaining your man's foolishness, only to realize your feelings for him have done a complete about-face. There were no major signs or warnings from you to indicate this change was taking place. Instead, there was a quiet, consistent erosion that finally broke through your tolerance threshold. It is on this day of epiphany and reckoning that all hell finally breaks loose, and you, a fed-up woman, become determined to break free.

Another major thing about women that men still fail to realize is that when we've had enough, that's it. Show's over, move along folks, there's nothing here to see. Because men don't always grasp this truth about us, they often pile on the pressure, compounding our already heavy burdens with even more weight, such as their insecurities and shortcomings. On the day you finally break, he'll most likely have no idea where it came from. Having watched you endure so much for so long, he'll be convinced you're indestructible, unlimited in your capacity to take bullshit. Because of this, if your break is severe and disruptive, he'll probably label you "that crazy bitch." *She just flipped,* he'll say to his momma, his boys, and anyone whom he believes will commiserate. *It just came out of nowhere. I don't even understand.* Even though you'd be well within your rights to act this way, let's make an informed decision, ladies, to do our best to avoid it. *That* girl—that crazy bitch who just snaps—typically gets no respect. She's perceived as the unstable variable, even though the opposite might be the case.

> **Vixen Say What?**
> If you and the fool are arguing, from a distance how are we to tell which one is which?

Vixen Tip

Here are five ways to remain calm once you've become fed up.

1. The good old-fashioned ten count.

2. The tried-and-true "turn the other cheek" (walk away).

3. The girls. Rant and rave to your buddies before talking to him.

4. The letter. Save your breath and write it all down.

5. All of the above!

If you're in a relationship where things are becoming increasingly unbearable, don't just let the load get heavier and heavier. Make your man aware along the way, as issues arise. The two of you should have open and active communication. Perhaps you can defuse these issues. You should feel comfortable enough with him to breach both important and minimal concerns that affect you. It shouldn't come as a huge surprise to your man should you call it quits. He should have had some warning, along with the chance to adjust his behavior. Otherwise, he will remain clueless as to why things failed, and you'll be guilty of passing the buck, sending this none-the-wiser man on to the next woman so he can possibly repeat the same mistakes. We owe it to ourselves to be forthright with our men and we owe it to other women to be responsible for the men we date. If you must leave a relationship, try to do so having imparted, and gained, some wisdom from the experience. When you unleash an ignorant man on the world, everyone suffers.

Vixen Say What? One woman's trash is another woman's used trash.

If you're leaving, be sure to treat him with the same respect you would want for yourself. Most importantly, depart with your dignity. Show him that not only is he losing his woman but he's also losing one hell of a lady.

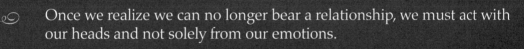

Recap

- Once we realize we can no longer bear a relationship, we must act with our heads and not solely from our emotions.

- By nature, women have a very high threshold for pain.

- When we've had enough, that's it.

- Make your man aware along the way, as issues arise.

- If you must leave a relationship, try to do so having imparted, and gained, some wisdom from the experience.

Chapter Thirty-four

Lying

I'm not very good at lying. It's not my strong suit. For better or worse, however, I have met lots of people who are quite good at it. Unfortunately for me, most of them were men I ended up dating. In my opinion, there is nothing more despicable than a bald-faced, no-good, down-and-dirty liar! *Ooooh,* I get chills just writing about it. Seriously, ladies, if we don't accept this type of behavior from our children, why do we allow it from our men?

> **Vixen Say What?**
> One of the best ways I heard someone called out for being untruthful was the phrase, "You're a liar and you don't love the Lord!" Ha! (Picked that one up at church!)

We're quick to dole out all sorts of punishment and ass whoopings when our kids look us square in the face and tell us a lie. But the minute a man tells a tall tale we suddenly go dumb. Don't act like you don't know he's lying. We're women, damn it, born with an internal truth gauge so strong, so powerful, they gave it a name all its own—*women's intuition.* That means you know when that sorry, no-good SOB is lying to you. So why are you acting as if you don't? Toucan Sam, that clever, colorful cartoon bird from those Fruit Loops commercials, told us years ago to "follow your nose," and I'm telling you the same thing now. If it waddles like a duck and quacks like a duck, you can best believe it's probably a damn duck, and that lying man better hope it's not duck-hunting season!

You've been gullible for far too long. We all have, and it's time we started paying attention to

> **Vixen Say What?**
> Your first thought is always the truth, every thought that follows is you talking yourself out of the truth.

our first feeling, our God-given women's intuition. What better time to start calling out the liars in your life than now? You're on the road to empowering yourself, establishing a solid foundation of self-esteem and position. If the big liar in your life happens to be your man, don't let that deter you. Just as he's stood nose to nose with you and told some Grade-A stinkers, stand square-shouldered before him and expose him for the fraud that he is! Let him know you're no dummy and you're certainly no pushover. And, while you're at it, ask him why he's starting to look a lot like a duck.

It is impossible to build a relationship based on untruths. Lies are the subtle cracks that ultimately destroy the dam, causing it to break. Even those that seem the most insignificant, compounded over time, can be crushing to the trust between two people. That's why it's crucial that the minute you become aware of your mate lying, you have to put the kibosh on it, just as you would with a child. You must alter or stop the behavior before it has the opportunity to become the accepted norm.

As undesirable as it is to have a man who lies, there is a form of fabrication that's even more abominable than having a lover or a child deceive you. It's when you lie to yourself. If you're not honest enough with yourself to acknowledge when lies are being fed to you by your man, if you'd rather be mired in delusion than face the hard truth that there is deceit in your relationship, then you're doomed, and so is your self-esteem. Eventually, your relationship will fail as well, but it was already chock-full of lies, so it couldn't have been much of a relationship to begin with, anyway.

We lie to ourselves about so much in our lives, creating alternate universes in which we take refuge to avoid facing the truth of our circumstances. We do everything possible to maintain appearances and try to keep up with the Joneses, while the Joneses are busy trying to keep up with the Smiths. It's a lie, all of it. Everyone's creating an illusion to compete with everyone else's illusion!

Vixen Tip

Try being honest about everything with everyone, even if just for one day, and experience how freeing it is. There is one simple thing we all do, every day, that if changed can alter the way the rest of our day goes. How many times today has someone asked, "How are you?" and you've said, "I'm fine!" Now, how many times was your answer a lie? We say these sorts of things without even thinking about what the real answer should be. We're all so busy thinking about what we have to do next that we fire off quick lies to get out of conversations, not realizing we've just gotten caught up in the perpetuation of another piece of fiction. The next time someone asks how you're doing, tell him or her the truth—I dare you! Look them in the eye and say, "I'm not so well today. My man's getting on my nerves, the kids are driving me crazy, I hate my job, I'm having a bad hair day, my mother-in-law's a moron, and, on top of it all, these shoes are killing my corns!" Let it all out, whatever it is, and then ask them, "So, how are *you* doing?" Even if they clam up because they're jarred by your response, you'll be surprised to learn how much lighter you'll feel by answering just that one simple question honestly.

It's important that you stop the lies before they become habit. You do yourself a tremendous disservice when you deceive yourself and refuse to face facts. If this is a behavior you indulge, do yourself a favor and put an end to it now. As for your man, it's up to you to check him. Even if he had a habit of lying to past girlfriends, make it known that such behavior will never be acceptable to you. As I've stressed throughout this book, people look to you for direction on how to treat you. Allowing a man to lie without penalty is a recipe for disaster. When you refuse to accept bullshit, you set a bar that only the most worthy men will dare to reach.

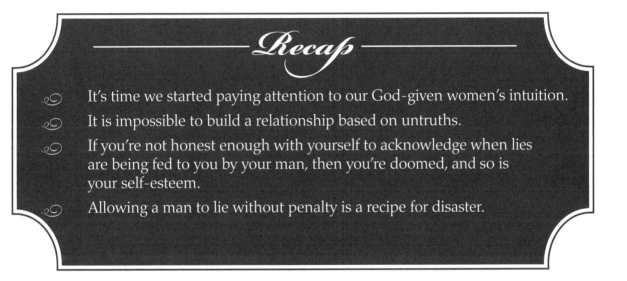

Recap

- It's time we started paying attention to our God-given women's intuition.
- It is impossible to build a relationship based on untruths.
- If you're not honest enough with yourself to acknowledge when lies are being fed to you by your man, then you're doomed, and so is your self-esteem.
- Allowing a man to lie without penalty is a recipe for disaster.

Chapter Thirty-five

Flirting

There are always signs, many of them obvious, that a man is not the one for you. Whether you face those signs head-on or choose to ignore them makes all the difference in whether you will breeze past this guy and wait for more suitable options or end up in a situation that causes you considerable emotional distress. One of the most notable clues that a man is not exactly going to show you the respect you deserve is flirtation.

I'm not talking about mild flirtation. We all do that in some way or another, even when we're not aware that we're doing it. What I'm referring to is the blatant kind, like when you're out having dinner with your man and he can't even keep his focus on your conversation because he's so busy eyeing every other woman in the room. I'm talking about the guy who won't hold your hand in public or walks a few paces ahead of or behind you because he doesn't want other women to know he's off the market. If he does hold your hand, he still winks and ogles passersby, to your alarming embarrassment and humiliation. Or he's texting, always texting, every five minutes. Who the hell is he talking to? Do you even know? Of course, you don't. Interestingly enough, when you first met, he was always texting you just the way he's texting now.

Ladies, you know who I'm talking about. *That* guy. The perpetual attention seeker. If this describes the man you're dating right now, you might want to face some obvious facts, one of which is that your chances of him being in for the long haul are very, very slim.

We've all encountered the pathological flirt. He has an insatiable need to be the center of attention. You must always be focused on him, even though he's hardly ever focused on you, not the way you deserve. This kind of man is always "on," with his Las Vegas personality and his ten-thousand-watt smile. You can't do or go anywhere with him without his stopping other women under the guise of making small talk about some seemingly insignificant thing. While this may seem like a harmless act and he may protest that he's just being friendly, don't go for it, ladies. This type of behavior is dangerous to even the most confident and strong-minded of women. It is a constant erosion that will, if allowed to continue, make you doubt yourself and wonder why you aren't enough to keep his attention. Don't be mistaken. His behavior has nothing to do with you. There will never be room for anyone else with a man like this. He—and he alone—is the center of his universe.

On the surface, this man appears to be ultraconfident and sure of himself, but nothing could be further from the truth. This is the classic insecure man, an infantile attention whore moving throughout his adult life screaming "Me! Me! Me!" in an attempt to overcompensate for some void from childhood or a humiliating slight in his past, neither of which can ever be rectified without seeking professional help. But wait—this man would never seek professional help. Therapy is for suckers and punks, he says. Besides, there are women to be flirted with. Lots of them. Being admired and having his desirability constantly validated is much more important to him than getting to the root of why he behaves this way.

One of the worst things you can do is try to fix this man. We often get caught up in playing the role of rehabilitator, trying to repair a man who doesn't want our help. People like the flirter choose to be the way they are, whether out of fear, habit, or ignorance. When you attempt to alter his behavior, you will only be met with resistance and, perhaps, more of the same behavior. As women, we are predisposed to trying to make things better. It's the nurturer in us. This, however, is not your fight. This man knows who he is. He revels in it. If he doesn't want to rehabilitate his behavior, the best thing you can do is get out…and fast! If you stay, you do so at your peril.

Dating this kind of man means finding yourself in constant conflict with him. It will happen every time you see his eyes wander away from yours. You'll wonder at whom he's glancing, just over your shoulder. You will become angry, then sad, then fed up. What you do after that determines how much more your esteem suffers. If you leave him, you can get away with minimal injury. If you stay, your confidence will continue to diminish—unless, of course, you're impervious to this kind of constant distraction. If you are, my hat's off to you.

What's interesting about the flirter is that he doesn't just flirt with women. You'll find there's also a strange kind of man-on-man thing that happens as well—a sort of "peacocking," if you will—a ritualistic exhibition that flirters go through to acknowledge and be acknowledged by each other. When you and your flirter walk into the room, he will make sure other men are checking out his woman and how fierce he must be to get a woman like that. He'll strut his stuff and give a head nod here and there, as if to say, "Yeah, I'm the man." Once he has their admiration, he'll then proceed to get it from the women in the room. More power to you if you are up for this. Men like this are often incredibly charming, having honed their skills, especially the gift of gab, into sharp, alluring weapons that always capture prey. How do you think he got you? Right. Knowing this, what makes you think he's done hunting? Exactly. He's not.

There comes a time when a man has just got to stop talking to strangers. When you interact with another individual, you take on their energies, bringing them into your space. Imagine the energies—negative and positive—that a pathological flirter absorbs every time he kicks game to someone throughout the course of the day. Then he brings those random energies home to you. And you wonder why you suddenly felt burdened and depressed after he walked through the door. Aside from the obvious, who knows what kind of negativity he's deflecting onto you?

If you're dating someone like this, you have to be very thick-skinned, or you'll become so bothered by it your resentment will be insurmountable. Someone who flirts all the time with every living thing is suffering from a major psychological issue and is not capable of being in a healthy relationship. It's as if everyone has to love him, down to the infant who doesn't even know him (flirters are baby kissers) and the dog on the street that he absolutely must pet (especially if there's an attractive woman holding on to the leash!).

Mr. Look At Me will be very unhappy, and will tell you so, if you're busy with things that take your focus off of him, like your job, children, family, and friends. He can't stand to be alone and not looked at. As a result of you taking your attention off of him, there'll be an opening for him to cheat, because that's the next logical step for a flirter. Naturally, he'll blame you for his infidelity. You never should have left him alone, he'll say. If you can't stroke him all day, he will definitely find someone who can.

Run away from this man as fast as you can, ladies. You deserve to be adored by a man who loves you. There should be a mutuality of appreciation and regard between you. Most importantly, there should be respect. Flirtation on this level is extremely disrespectful. Refuse to accept it. Remember, you set the bar for how you're treated and unhealthy flirtation should never be an acceptable element in a relationship.

Recap

- One of the most notable clues that a man is not going to show you the respect you deserve is flirtation.

- This type of behavior is dangerous to even the most confident and strong-minded of women.

- His behavior has nothing to do with you.

- The classic insecure man is an infantile attention whore moving throughout his adult life screaming, "Me! Me! Me!"

- If you find yourself with a serial flirter, the best thing you can do is get out...and fast!

- Men like this are often incredibly charming, having honed their skills, especially the gift of gab, into sharp, alluring weapons that always capture prey.

- Someone who flirts all the time with every living thing is suffering from a major psychological issue and is not capable of being in a healthy relationship.

Chapter Thirty-six

Cheating

Cheating. It's the one word every woman seeking a healthy, long-term relationship hopes to avoid, especially if you've ever dated a cheating man before. You know the pain that comes with betrayal. You know how it feels to learn you've been lied to and misled, maybe even shamelessly used by some man who convinced you that his heart and intentions were pure when, all along, they were anything but.

The subject of cheating has always been a difficult one for me because of my own experiences. If you've read my prior works, you know this already. I've been very frank and forthcoming about what I've endured in my personal journey. There was a lot of pain, some of which was brought on by my own gullibility. But, as they say, you don't know until you know. Still, just as in the case with pathological flirters, men who are inclined to cheat give off signs. It's up to you to listen and be aware. In my particular situation, every time I was cheated on, I could trace the behavior back to something the man said or did, maybe even in passing, that gave him away. Cheaters say things early on that give them away. Things like, "I can't see myself settling down" or "I used to cheat a lot." The first statement is an indirect way of saying, "I won't be here for long" and "I like variety." The second one, which is much more deceptive, suggests infidelity was a thing of the past and that the behavior no longer exists. Be warned, ladies. This is yet another way of ensnaring you.

It's up to you to dig deeper by asking questions, meeting past girlfriends, as well as female friends and family members (mother, sisters, aunts, cousins) in order to find out if this man has healthy relationships with women. Cheaters are, at their core, disrespectful, self-centered, and unconcerned about the hurt they cause. People like this will have plenty of evidence surrounding them to indicate who they are. Don't just accept a man's word for who he is, especially if you hear rumors of his past behavior or he already has a reputation for being unfaithful. We often ignore blatant signs and the warnings of friends and family. Seek evidence on your own before you invest your time. It can end up saving you a considerable amount of heartache, emotional scarring, and possibly money, especially if the man is a lazy, no-good loser all around.

It's not attractive to be nosy and snoop through a man's things in order to find evidence of cheating. After all, you would just be giving him leverage against you if you do. Instead, simply ask to see his telephone and e-mail records and offer to show him yours as well. Be honest and up front by telling him you have suspicions and are having a difficult time trusting him. If he is not willing to discuss this issue with you and put your suspicions at ease, you've pretty much gotten your answer. It's better that you be unjustifiably distrusting than for your man to prove your feelings are correct.

Whatever you do, once you see evidence of your man cheating, don't accept this behavior. It will only increase. If you allow it, it will become the norm. Don't take him back just because he promised to never do it again. Part of the cycle of cheaters is convincing you that this is an isolated act that will not be repeated. The trick of that argument, however, is that if you accept it and stay, you'll have made an unwritten agreement to stay if it happens again. You will have defined how you'll handle that particular issue when it comes up. *Cheating can be negotiated,* your action says. *As long as you explain yourself and make me feel better, everything's cool.* Everything's not cool. You've just set yourself up for more to come.

That's not to say people can't make mistakes, because they do. His cheating might truly be an isolated incident. Look at the circumstances and decide if you're willing to live with them. Just know that when it comes to cheating, acceptance can be the equivalent of a green light. By sticking around, you've essentially given him permission to rake you over the coals.

As I've already mentioned, the possibility of this can be minimized by doing your homework before getting involved with a man. Meet his friends. Watch how he interacts with them. Pay attention to the things he talks about with his male friends. Do they like to brag about their conquests? Are his buddies cheating on their girlfriends? Does your potential man allow himself to be an alibi for their whereabouts? If so, that might mean his friends do the same thing for him. There's truth in the saying "Birds of a feather flock together." What kind of relationship does he have with his exes? Are there legions of women around town who can't stand him and think he's a dog? Ask him to let you talk to one or more of them. If he balks, do a little investigating on your own. If you are able to find one of his ex-girlfriends, introduce yourself. See if you can find out, from her perspective, what kind of person he is. You don't have to take her word as gospel. She might very well be the reason they broke up, or she may have her own reasons for cutting him down to you, including that she wants that cheater back in her life. Still, it doesn't hurt to ask questions.

A good man is not usually a bad breaker-upper. He should have healthy friendships with former girlfriends and wholesome friendships with his closest friends that don't include condoning cheating. If he learns that one of his boys is being disrespectful to his woman, he's usually the voice of reason, trying to encourage his friend to do right. This is the kind of man you want. You definitely don't want the kind of man who'll provide an alibi for a cheating buddy.

Don't ignore the warning signs. Set the bar high. Decide early on that cheating will never be acceptable for either of you in your relationship. And that doesn't apply to just sex. There is emotional infidelity, the kind where your man confides in a female friend about issues in your relationship, thus building a bond with her that should rightfully be yours. Emotional infidelity can be even more damaging and far-reaching than sexual infidelity. Men are capable of having sex with someone and having it prove meaningless. We don't always understand how they can do this, but it happens with them all the time. They're socialized that way. When they make an emotional connection with someone else, however, it involves a transference of feelings that divides his interests and drives a wedge between you. Make it clear from the beginning that this is a no-no, both for you and for him.

Once you've found a good man, make sure you have open dialogue about your expectations of each other. Be sure your man agrees with you not just about physical infidelity, but about how dangerous emotional infidelity can be to your relationship. This is critical, because if he doesn't—or, even worse, if he insists that it's harmless to confide in women friends outside your relationship—he'll ultimately find himself on a path that leads to cheating, whether he's aware of it or not.

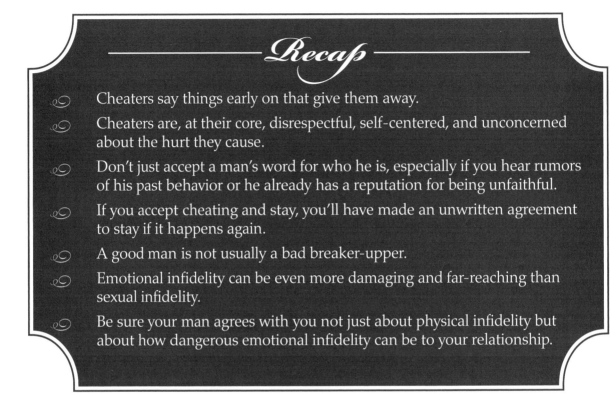

Recap

- Cheaters say things early on that give them away.

- Cheaters are, at their core, disrespectful, self-centered, and unconcerned about the hurt they cause.

- Don't just accept a man's word for who he is, especially if you hear rumors of his past behavior or he already has a reputation for being unfaithful.

- If you accept cheating and stay, you'll have made an unwritten agreement to stay if it happens again.

- A good man is not usually a bad breaker-upper.

- Emotional infidelity can be even more damaging and far-reaching than sexual infidelity.

- Be sure your man agrees with you not just about physical infidelity but about how dangerous emotional infidelity can be to your relationship.

Chapter Thirty-seven

If All Men Are Dogs. . .
(. . . Then All Women Are Bitches)

We've all been out with a group of women when the subject of men comes up and, suddenly, we find ourselves agreeing along with everyone else that, "All men are dogs!" This refrain is usually accompanied by much neck popping, eye rolling, and finger snapping, with more than one or two people in the group chiming in with a resounding *mmm-hmmm* as confirmation. As a part of this communal gender bonding, each woman, one by one, reveals her latest "I'm dating a dog" story, and every story ends with a combination man-demeaning declaration followed by high fives all around. Strangers in the group may hug, laugh, and cry with each other and perhaps even establish friendships on this common ground of misdirected, blanket-assessment negativity. Sure, we've all seen and participated in this, and while it may feel like a "'Kumbaya' meets girl power" moment, it's actually anything but that. All men are not dogs, and if this is what you believe as you are reading this book, you are surely destined to watch that statement become a self-fulfilling prophecy.

This may come as news to some women who prefer to blame their dating woes—and countless other issues—on men, but as the old saying goes, "It takes two to tango." First, let's refer back to the updated version of the Golden Rule that I've been emphasizing throughout this manual: you teach people how to treat you. Others will do to you only what you allow them to. They take their lead from you. If you find yourself constantly attracting these so-called dogs who treat you like dirt, odds are it's because they've spotted an opening, something inside of you that says, "Come on…take advantage of me." Dogs are attracted to bitches. It is an irresistible, instinctive, visceral urge more overpowering than sense and reasoning. A "bitch," in this instance, would be someone who just assumes the position and takes whatever is thrust upon her without protest.

That statement may have strong sexual overtones, but it is not exclusive to sex. It applies to every aspect of your life. If you're willing to be someone else's bitch, then you're willing to lie down and be a doormat, a victim, a punching bag, and the perennial whipping girl who has accepted that this is her lot in life because she never learned or accepted her worth. If this is you—a woman a man feels that he can hump on with no regard for your feelings and with no interest in developing solidarity—then you can forget about monogamy, respect, and all those other things most of us want out of a man. You get dogs, honey, and all the assorted fleas and drama that come with them.

A man will treat you like a bitch until you show him you are a lady. Men will not respect you if you're interested in financial gain strictly by way of whom you date. I know this from personal experience. Men will not respect you if you do not respect yourself, if you're needy and incomplete, or if you're unsure of yourself and your future, personal goals, and principles. Simply put, if you don't have your shit together, men will treat you like shit.

We each attract a certain type of man, depending on how we carry ourselves. Don't expect to have a respectful man if you, for instance, curse like a sailor. Such behavior always reflects more negatively upon you than it does to those you're cursing. As for other important aspects of your life, if you don't have any goals, principles, power, or worth, then what makes you believe you can attract a man who has any of those qualities? You are what you attract, whether you like it or not.

Vixen Tip

Take a long, hard look at the type of men you have been attracting, and make a list of all the reasons why these men weren't right for you. The answers you come up with will probably be a mirror image of what is wrong or missing with you. Now, take a long, hard look at yourself and ask, *What is it about me that makes me allow these type of people into my life? Don't I think I am worth the best? Don't I know how special I am?* Dig into your past, as far back as your childhood. How is your relationship with your father? Do you even know him? It may sound like something out of Freud's handbook, but our behavior with men can be directly traced to our relationships with our fathers. Little girls who have good daddies grow up to make better choices with men. Ask yourself if you are desperate, lonely, gullible, or naïve. If so, honestly examine what you believe to be the reasons for this. And what about your mother and other female role models in your family? What has been their record with men? Behavior among generations of women in the same family is often duplicated, based on the examples those women have had to guide them. Also, since so many of us have a hard time being honest with ourselves, I recommend you consult a good friend, someone who's known you for a considerable amount of time, and ask for her honest opinion of you. There can be so many reasons why we allow ourselves to be mistreated. You should turn to yourself for the answers, not blame men, individually or collectively, for your misfortunes with the opposite sex.

Contrary to what you may believe, we are not designed to follow the lead of men. They are made to follow us, at least when it comes to male and female relations. In the days before the sexual revolution, a man could never hope to lay with a self-respecting woman unless he first made her his wife. But then things changed. During the bra-burning "free love" period of the sixties and the "I am woman, hear me roar" days of the seventies, these ideals changed drastically. Women who were sexually liberated were seen as hip and progressive, in charge of their lives, able to bed as many men as they chose without fear of being frowned upon. Men followed along because we set the rules, not them. Once the rules changed for women, the expectations of marriage, monogamy, and fidelity did as well. Men have been following us all this time and we have led them to what they, in general, have now become. As a gender, we set the tone. If none of us ever fell for bad boys, there would be no bad-boy stories to tell. It's my personal belief that even though men go through so-called bad-boy periods, they really want to be respectful to women. They want to be loved and cared for, just like us. But why doesn't that happen? you ask. Because *we* get in the way. If we don't know how to demand respect, love, appreciation, and care, then even the most well-meaning man will be unable to meet those needs for us.

How many of you have dated a man only to watch him treat you—and the other women he's simultaneously dating—badly, without remorse or regard for the impact of his behavior? Then, miraculously it seems, that same no-good man suddenly turns his life around, settles down with one woman, and becomes the model husband. How can it be? This is the part where most clueless women will say, "He cheated on me, so he'll cheat on her, too." But what if he doesn't? The truth is, most men only do what they want to and you can never make them be or do something that makes no sense to them. The extended truth is that some women, based on how little they value themselves, are only good for having sex with. Some are just good for living with. Some are the kind you come close to marrying, but not quite. But when a man meets a woman who has it all together, both for himself and herself, then he can make a life-changing decision in what might seem like the blink of an eye. *This is the one*, he says to himself. *No one else compares to her.* If this makes him a dog, then it most certainly puts you in the category of one of his bitches if he has merely sexed you or consumed years of your life with cohabitation but no permanent commitment, and then moved on.

There were plenty of men in my life who have treated me horribly, but they would have never had the chance to do so if I hadn't let them. Those same men who treated me poorly were kind and respectful to others, because that's what those others demanded of them. A man will treat you according to what he sees you'll allow. What you need to understand is that it is never too late or too early to change; even if you've been mistreated, you can still do something about it.

Trust me, ladies, I understand that you're human and in need of affection and intimacy. But what I also understand is that in this sexually adventurous age, we spend most of our sexual life on people who do not truly love us. The act of loving is so much deeper than most of us realize or ever experience. It is not just an emotion but also a way of being. It is a decision, a vow. If you don't make a decision about the value you place on yourself and your emotions, you can and will probably be violated somehow. I'm not trying to make it sound like you're the reason for the bad behavior of the men in your life. That is certainly not true. Some people just aren't good people, no matter what you do or who you are. But if you pay attention and are thinking clearly, you'll be able to spot a person like this a mile away. If you are not so desperate, so lacking in self-confidence, empowerment, and worth, then you should be able to sift through the men who do not mean you well. Even the most duplicitous people cannot hide their intentions for long. There are always some indications, if your awareness is heightened. It's up to you to vet the men who come into your life. Don't be afraid to ask honest questions. If he runs off as a result of being interrogated, then he probably has something to hide. Ask about his past relationships. Pay close attention to how he deals with his mother, sisters, ex-girlfriend, ex-wife, and his children. Does he keep his word? What kind of reputation does he have? All these things speak to the character of an individual. Make sure your eyes are open. Heed all the signs. So many of us carry youthful gullibility into adulthood, leaving room for gross misjudgments and titanic mistakes that can easily set us back years.

When I became fed up with the way my personal life was going, I sat myself down and figured out why I was not getting the results that I so desperately wanted—not just from the men in my life but from myself. I made the lists I've spoken of throughout this book, plus a few other lists of what I wanted from my future. I organized my thoughts and pulled back from dating for almost a year. I elected celibacy during this period. I had to so that I could stay focused and keep a clear sight of my goals. It's possible that if you find your vision for yourself blurred by all the chaos in your life brought on from ill planning and unsuitable mates, this strategy can work for you. Back away from dating, including sex. Spend more time getting to know yourself. Demand respect by respecting yourself first. This is a tried-and-true method of finding what you truly want out of life and from a man.

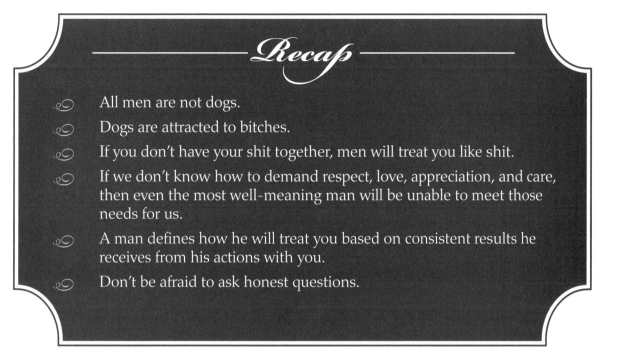

Recap

- All men are not dogs.

- Dogs are attracted to bitches.

- If you don't have your shit together, men will treat you like shit.

- If we don't know how to demand respect, love, appreciation, and care, then even the most well-meaning man will be unable to meet those needs for us.

- A man defines how he will treat you based on consistent results he receives from his actions with you.

- Don't be afraid to ask honest questions.

Chapter Thirty-eight

The Other Woman

The smell of a perfume you don't own, the strand of hair that's a different color from yours, the smudged lipstick on his collar in a shade you would never wear—you know the signs, so unmistakable they're practically a cliché. There's another woman in the picture and your man has been with her. You feel as if you've been sucker-punched in the throat, and once you recover, your first instinct is to go for blood. You are officially a woman scorned. Okay. Now what?

You cry, you scream, you throw and smash things (your things!) around the house. You drive around the city looking for this hooker who had the bald-faced nerve to snag your man. Your pulse is racing, your face is hot, your eyes are tear-streaked—ooh, you're going to show her a thing or ten when you finally catch up with her! But in all that driving and racing around with vengeance on your mind, there's one thing you've failed to realize: this man you're so furious about—he was never *your* man! That's right. He was never your man.

Unlike family, we choose our mates; they are not assigned to us. The man who chose you can unchoose you (and vice versa, of course). People change their minds all the time, and sometimes there's absolutely nothing you can do about it. You might believe you're still in a functioning relationship because, in your mind, he's still the one, but that doesn't mean all is well with him. Did you see the signs? Were you even paying attention? There are always clues, whether you want to acknowledge them or not. Is it honorable of him to begin consorting with another woman before ending his relationship with you? Of course not. Is it honorable of you to stay? Only if you believe you're of little worth. Any self-respecting woman who knows her value would send him and all his perfumed, lipstick-stained clothes packing. As I've continually stated throughout this book, a woman of worth refuses to settle for less than she deserves.

When there is another woman involved, the foundations of trust and love between you and your (now ex) man, if they were ever there to begin with, are no longer stable. Everything he says to you becomes suspect because he's already told you at least one very big lie. It is very difficult to rebuild trust once it has been breached on this level. The potential is high for your esteem to suffer as a result of such a blow, which can affect other areas of your life outside of the relationship. During this time, it's critical that you take care of you. This person you thought of as your man has already shown that he's thinking only of himself. Enlist the aid of family and your closest friends to provide emotional support to help you keep it together in the face of what can be one of the most crushing situations a woman can experience.

As for this duplicitous man, there is nothing you can do to him that will make matters any better. The more adversely you react, the more likely you are to help him justify his behavior. He'll say, "See, this is why I can't be around you anymore. You're crazy!" Duplicitous men love using the "crazy" clause as a reason for their lies and infidelity. Let your silence be your sword. Say nothing so that he'll have nothing to defend. Leave him looking like a jerk. Your friends will surround you with love, practically making you a martyr. He will be perceived as a no-good cheat. Yes, that's an extreme simplification of things and may not be totally accurate, but it does help when it comes to getting over him. If you were anywhere near the sort of partner I've been suggesting in prior chapters—one who has goals, dignity, power, and position—you will be able to stand in confidence, knowing that while you were in the relationship, you did your best and treated him with honesty and respect.

Our natural instinct, when injured, is to close ourselves off to future experiences, but don't take this course. It's the express route to bitterness and will set you on a path of nothing but failed expectation after failed expectation. Draw near to those you trust. Open your heart to them; cry, purge, air your grievances. If they are smart, evolved women like yourself, they will comfort and reassure you that this is all a part of the human journey, but it's not reason enough to never again open your heart to a man. Whatever you do, don't vent all this with your ex. Don't give him that kind of power. He doesn't deserve it and may very well mock or betray your trust even more. A man who cannot stand by his word and commitments isn't worth your time and emotions. He should never be able to say he's seen you lose your composure.

Vixen Tip

Whatever you do, do not go out and get yourself another man in order to show your cheating ex that you can do what he does, as I always say, ten times faster and a hundred times better. Just because you can doesn't mean you should. Be the bigger, better person here and, by all means, remain the victim—in theory, of course. Now is not the time for tit-for-tat behavior and one-upmanship. Your feelings, after all, are in play. Trying to salve them through artificial means, such as immediately dating and/or bedding another man, will only leave you more confused and emotionally injured. Now is the time for you to face what has happened head-on. Take the necessary amount of time to lick your wounds and heal your heart, then move forward with your life, wiser, stronger, and more alert to the signs that allowed this to happen.

Every man comes with a cost, whether it's financially, emotionally, or physically. Every man withdraws from your reserves and, in many ways, can never give back what he has taken. That is the give-and-take of relationships, but there has to be a balance. If a man is draining your reserves without replenishing them, you have to decide if you can live with that. Most women can't, not without a cost, whether it is to their dignity, their bank account, their health, or their dreams. Being in a relationship with a man who has another woman on the side is not an ideal scenario for you, not if you are seeking a wholesome, fulfilling partnership. Put this trash out on the curb where it belongs and never look back. If the other woman still wants him, so be it. If she's the kind of woman who's willing to dine off the trash from your Dumpster, then let her. Chances are she'll end up with the same tummyache you suffer from now.

Vixen Say What? The only way to get over something is to go through it.

Don't be afraid to go through the hurt and pain. He's not worth a woman like you, but allow yourself to miss him, even though he broke your heart. This is all part of the process of mourning a loss and moving on. Once you've gone through this and feel more stable emotionally, you'll be able to face him and—this is a big one— forgive him. Perhaps he's gone through his own emotional journey in the time you were apart and has seen the error of his ways. There's always the remote chance that there is still love between you, although you shouldn't place your hopes on it. If it is to be, that will reveal itself in time. Many relationships and marriages have seemed irretrievably broken then somehow managed to find their footing and flourish again.

What matters most, however, is that this won't be the death of you. Finding out about the other woman and dealing with it accordingly can be a major teachable moment on your journey, allowing you to learn more about yourself, your expectations, and your boundaries when it comes to men.

Recap

- The same way that the man you were with chose you, he can un-choose you (and vice versa, of course).
- It is very difficult to rebuilt trust once it has been breached on this level.
- Enlist the aid of family and your closest friends to provide emotional support to help you keep it together.
- Let your silence be your sword.
- A man who cannot stand by his word and commitments isn't worth your time and emotions.

Chapter Thirty-nine

Never Let Him See You Sweat

So you're upset. I'm talking *really* upset. Let it out, girl, let it out! Sob uncontrollably, scream obscenities to the heavens, go ahead and break that lamp your grandmother gave you for a wedding present (you've always hated it, anyway). Trash your place, refuse to take a shower, lie in bed every day for weeks. It's okay, really. Through it all, however, it's important that you remember this one thing: whatever you do, don't let your man see any of it! When your phone rings, let it. You can't be bothered right now, anyway, because you're depressed and pissed off. According to the cheery message on your voice mail, "*We* can't get to the phone right now." The truth is, *we* have broken up, *we* are not on speaking terms, or maybe *we* just found out our man is a closet homosexual. Whatever the reason, this is the season for shit storms and you're upwind, getting hit full-on. He's calling and coming by, trying to connect so he can fix what just might be unfixable. Don't do it, ladies. Don't pick up the phone. Don't answer that door. Not now, not when your emotions are surging out of control. Never, ever, let a man see you at your worst.

There are people out there who will tell you it is unhealthy to close yourself off from the world. I'm no doctor, but as a woman, I know that there are times when blocking out the noise of the outside world is the only way to heal from a breakup, even if it was all your idea. In the last chapter I recommended that you lean on those closest to you and cry your eyes out to help cope with the pain, but sometimes you just don't want anyone to see you like this. You want the freedom that comes from solitude, where you can scream as much as you want and question why this has happened to you. It's okay to grieve in private, just as it's equally acceptable to call up your best girlfriend and ask her to bring lunch into your den of sorrow. There'll be days when you will want to be alone. On the days when you don't, call someone you trust who loves you unconditionally. Whatever you do, don't call *him!* Not even in your weakest moment. You'll immediately regret it and you'll never be able to take the moment back.

Vixen Tip

In times like these you'll have to take your life one day at a time. Don't think too far ahead and definitely don't think too far behind. Keep your brain in the here and now, focusing solely on what you can do to pass the time right this minute. Whether it's staying on the phone with your friends or watching reruns of *The Golden Girls*, find your comfort zone and stay there until it all blows over.

At first, it will feel as if the sky is falling. Let it. Better to get it all out of the way in the beginning.

Vixen Say What? No man is an android.

The beauty of having the sky fall is that one day you'll wake up and notice the sun is shining brightly again. You got through what you believed was a dark, never-ending moment that ultimately did pass. These moments always pass. You just have to be fair with yourself and allow a sufficient amount of time to go through it. No one can tell you when to get better or to not be affected by disappointments in relationships. You're human, after all, and only you can determine how much time is right for you.

That's not to say the only emotion women feel is sadness or defeat. We can be volatile, angry, even hateful creatures when we feel we have been betrayed. In this instance, it is most important to do what you can to prove yourself worthy of respect by keeping it together and not letting the outside world see you as a broken woman. You are not broken; you've just gone through some bumps. If the person the world sees when you finally do step out the door is someone who's teary, bitter, reckless, or vengeful, it will reflect poorly upon you, not the man who was probably the reason you feel this way. The world doesn't see the man. It sees you. Strive to always present the best that you can, even in times of distress. Hold your head up. Make sure your hair, makeup, nails, and clothes are as impeccable as they would be when you are at your happiest. Restraint is a far more skillful exercise than an eruption of emotion, especially during times of great stress or anxiety.

Remember the ten-count rule? The one where you count to ten while taking deep, slow breaths? It works. If you've never tried it, you should. Do it when your rage, panic, or sadness seems as if it's so overwhelming you are unable to contain it. A slow count, coupled with slow breaths, will allow you to calm down and put the moment into perspective.

Remember how your grandfather talked about turning the other cheek and walking away from a fight? Guess what? He was right! These clichés are clichés because they have been proven true and will continue to be so until the end of time. There is a lot to be said for a woman who knows how to think before she speaks, especially when she's upset. It's a trait we should all practice until it becomes second nature. When you measure your words carefully, you are in control. When you act on impulse, driven by your emotions, you place yourself in a position of vulnerability, open to attack.

Guard your image, especially when it comes to an ex. Your image is your brand. It is the thing everyone sees and by which they define you. By learning to master your emotions, you build a stronger you, one who is able to weather even the roughest of times and emerge triumphant.

Recap

- Never, ever, let a man see you at your worst. You'll immediately regret it and you'll never be able to take the moment back.

- Strive to always present the best that you can, even in times of distress.

- When you measure your words carefully, you are in control.

- Your image is your brand.

Chapter Forty

Get Yourself Some Real Girlfriends

My mother always said, "Everyone ain't your friend" and "Learn to live without friends." The latter may not have been the best advice—no man is an island, after all—but there was a point she was trying to emphasize as it relates to *who* you make your friend. As a young girl, I never understood what these sayings meant because at ten years old, hell, everyone's your friend! Then one day you're thirty and, as you look back on your life, you remember the people you once called friend, individuals with whom you shared common bonds and treasured secrets, but now they are nowhere to be found. You'd probably have just as hard a time locating the friends you had when you were ten, or even the friends you had when you were twenty, twenty-five, or maybe even last year. What happened to all of these people? Where did they go?

As we get older, life and people disappoint us. Sometimes we become jaded by personal experiences and consequently end up hurting the ones to whom we are closest. Someone may betray our trust, like stealing or spreading false rumors. No matter what the reason, as we grow we tend to outgrow certain people, places, and things we once revered. As our definitions of ourselves evolve, we naturally shed the earlier versions, much like animals shed their skin as their bodies require bigger accommodations. That doesn't mean some of our friends can't come along, but those who don't grow with us, who are more conditional about their relationships with us, or who are on markedly different courses than the ones we are charting for ourselves are inevitably shed like so much skin. Seemingly overnight, we can go from having tens of friends to just a few, if even that.

Along the way, we learn the difference between acquaintances and friends. We often make the mistake of referring to acquaintances—meaning someone we know only in passing or on a surface level—as friends. If you find yourself with a revolving door of so-called friends coming in and out of your life, this could be where your trouble lies. Real friends are people who know you on your most dynamic level, not just the surface. They've seen you up, they've seen you down, and their opinion of you is never diminished. A friend is there for you in good times and bad, providing sage advice or just an available ear and shoulder when you need to vent. If you find yourself trying to access these benefits with mere acquaintances, don't be surprised if you're met with odd stares, unreturned phone calls, or are accused of offering TMI—too much information—because this person doesn't have you on the same par as you've placed him or her.

As a rule, I've found that the best guyfriends are the ones who *aren't* trying to have sex with you, and the best girlfriends are the ones who aren't trying to be you. It may seem hard to find men and women who fit these parameters; when you do, keep them close. Be there for them the way they are there for you. The best way to have a true friend is to be one.

It's better to have girlfriends who are not embittered and carrying a lot of baggage from their past that they haven't addressed. Such people have a tendency to be surrounded by dark moods and drama, themes that will inevitably be injected into your world and affect you. If you are a progressive, goal-oriented woman with a plan for her life, your friends should be mirrors of this. They don't have to have the same pursuits, just positive outlooks and aspirations. They should be self-starters who take responsibility for themselves and not blame the world for everything that doesn't go their way. Your friends should definitely be able to relate to your lifestyle; otherwise, you won't ever feel like you can truly be yourself around them without being judged. It's both comforting and encouraging to sit and talk about the same things with a woman who understands your positions on family, love, career, and life overall.

Vixen Tip

It's sad but true that over time we tend to outgrow our friends. This doesn't mean that we dump them by the wayside just because our lives begin to differ. What it does mean, however, is that you shouldn't be afraid or leery of making new friends with some of the same interests and ideas as you. You'll find people like this in different personal and professional groups like the PTA at your children's school or among the people you work with. Find a common interest in the women around you and build friendships from there. Hopefully, one of these will end up being a true friendship with a woman you can confide in during times of turmoil.

What you don't want as a friend is a woman who, every time you and your man have an issue, is quick to respond with "Fuck him, girl!" This is usually the instinctive advice of a bitter woman, one with no man of her own or with a no-good man. Your girlfriends should be the kind of people you admire, and they should admire you. You should uplift and motivate one another, knowing that every piece of advice given is given from a place of love and understanding. When you're happy, they are happy for you, and vice versa. When you're down, they feel your pain and help pick you up. There is a mutuality of regard and support between you. These are real girlfriends, the kind you want in your life for the long term.

My mother was right, though. Not everyone is your friend. Be aware of the people you allow into your personal realm. Choose carefully, because these are women you'll be entrusting with your intimate secrets and relationship woes, essentially your life; if you're lucky enough to find just one true, lifelong friend, that is a blessing. If you manage to find several, the heavens have surely smiled upon you. It means you're doing something right.

No matter what, even if your girlfriends are the best friends you could ever ask for, never let them make relationship decisions for you. It's nice to be able to get advice from a different perspective, but never let someone else's experiences shape your life. Friends are there to provide support, advise, and be sounding boards, not captains of what should be your ship. You are responsible for the path you navigate. Everyone's views are different. Your life is your own.

Recap

- As we get older, life and people disappoint us.
- We often make the mistake of referring to acquaintances—meaning someone we only know in passing or on a surface level—as friends.
- Real friends are people who know you on your most dynamic level, not just the surface.
- The best way to have a true friend is to be one.
- If you are a progressive, goal-oriented woman with a plan for her life, your friends should be mirrors of this.
- What you don't want as a friend is a woman who, every time you and your man have an issue, is quick to respond with "Fuck him, girl!"
- Not everyone is your friend.
- Never let your friends make relationship decisions for you.

Chapter Forty-one

The Mind Fuck

After all you and your man have been through—drama after drama, conflict after conflict, and lie after lie—you've decided you're ready to move on. We all know it sometimes takes us women a while to make up our minds to leave. We endure and debate, weigh the good versus the bad, get counsel from our friends. It's a slippery slope, and we want to be certain if we're going to take that step. Once we've made up our minds, however, that's it. We're out. And now you've finally made up yours. You promised yourself a short while ago that the next time he comes home in the wee hours of the morning, you were done. No explanations and excuses would make you change your mind.

And then it happens again. It's four in the morning and he's sauntering through the front door smelling like that drunk uncle at the family reunion that everyone avoids and makes sure no kids are around. Oh, and he's got yet another lame excuse, to boot! You go through the standard interrogation, asking where he's been. My mother's, he says, obviously backpedaling. But you were at his mother's earlier and he wasn't there, so you ask him again. "Where were you?" He stalls, stutters, sputters, then finally spits out, "Ralph and I were at Hooters watching the game." That might actually be plausible, if you hadn't been on the phone with Ralph's wife earlier and she was busy taking care of his fever since he was in bed with the flu. *Hmmm,* you say to yourself. You already know he's lying. Should you ask again? What the hell. Why not, if just for sport. So you try it again. "Where were you?" This time he's got nothing, and during the brief-but-quiet standoff that ensues, you finally feel vindicated and triumphant. But wait! What's happening? Suddenly he flips, turning the tables on you. You're bugging him, he declares with outrage. You're nagging him and causing him strife! He doesn't need this! Nobody needs this kind of stress! And before you can utter a word in reply, he heads out the door.

You stand there, perplexed. This was supposed to be *your* moment, after all, the one you'd been planning for. This was the proverbial straw that broke the camel's back. You were going to pronounce this as the very last time you were putting up with his nonsense. You'd made up your mind. He was the one in the wrong, not you…wasn't he? Wait a second. Could *you* be wrong? Maybe he *was* innocent for once, and your lashing out at him was unwarranted. Maybe…maybe…

Do you find yourself feeling confused? Welcome to the Matrix.

No, you realize after a moment. You *weren't* wrong. You were *right*. You're convinced of it. He's a lying bastard! And now you're livid, pacing around the house in absolute turmoil. You dial his mobile phone several times in rapid succession, but he doesn't answer—then he turns it off completely—and you grow even more furious. Wherever he is, he's got the leverage now. By the time the sun comes up, he'll be somewhere in a deep sleep. You, however, will be wide-awake, exhausted, stressed out, and feeling guilty for having come at him that way. You should have handled it better, should have let him explain. He didn't deserve to be attacked like that.

Stop it, girl. Stop it right now. You're falling for the mind fuck. This is a trick!

Ever heard of reverse psychology? What he's doing is straight out of a Psych 101 textbook, and you're walking right into his trap. When he's wrong, he's wrong. He knows it and you know it. How you proceed, once you're aware of this, is all about strategy—which you will need, because *this* is war.

A man who's on the verge of being thrown out knows it. His sixth sense has already kicked in, even though he's well aware that his bad behavior is what got him there in the first place. A smart manipulator knows how to play you, especially if he's been able to get this move over on you in the past. He knows that if he can make your attack against him seem like your fault, it buys him more time, more advantage, more power, more everything. The key is not to let this happen. When he comes home late or seems to be lying, if you can't get a straight answer from him that can be checked and double-checked, there's no need for you to blow up. Just give him silence and your ass to kiss. Silence and indifference are much more terrifying than an emotional outburst. He won't be able to read you and, as a result, will begin to panic. He can't turn the tables on what he can't read. Whatever you do, don't give him the leverage he'll need to turn the issue around onto you. Therein lies your ability to not get caught in the Mind Fuck Matrix.

Vixen Tip

Unlike the film *The Matrix*, there is no red or blue pill to take you away from the mind fuck, and no cool visual effects to help you dodge this relationship bullet. This tip is very basic and, though it should be common sense, is the most skipped-over solution of all time. Be alert and be decisive. Set your principles and stand by them. Mind games work only on the unvigilant. Don't let that be you. Something tells me, however, that this is not your first dog-and-pony show. You've been to the rodeo before, my dear. So let's not pretend you didn't know there are men out there who'll try to get you to fall for their bullshit. How you proceed when presented with the mind fuck will determine how you handle everything else in the relationship. If you go for it, you'll go for anything. If you don't, he'll know he can't pull any false moves because you'll always be on high alert. He'll be less likely to resort to these tactics. Why? Because he'll realize that you're capable of pulling a few mind fucks of your own! As the saying goes, "Game recognizes game."

But before we go all the way off about how he's messing with your head, make sure you're not the one who's fooling with his. We have a way of pushing a man's buttons when we have rendered him helpless against our feminine wiles. Ladies, you can't drive a man to the brink and not expect him to push back. We are emotional creatures who can run hot and cold, which can confuse the hell out of most men. When a woman is skilled enough to pull it off, her mind fuck can be way more potent than his. Between our housekeeping, cooking, and sexual skills, compounded by our supple, soft, and pleasantly fragranced bodies, men are often putty in our hands. When we apply ourselves, we can be just as adept as men, if not better, at whatever we choose—mind games included.

This is no way to carry on a relationship. When this sort of game comes into play, it's a good sign things aren't going well. It might be in both of your best interests to let the relationship go, no matter who initiated or continues the mind fuck. Neither of you will be happy in this scenario. It is an exhaustive cycle that can only breed anger and resentment.

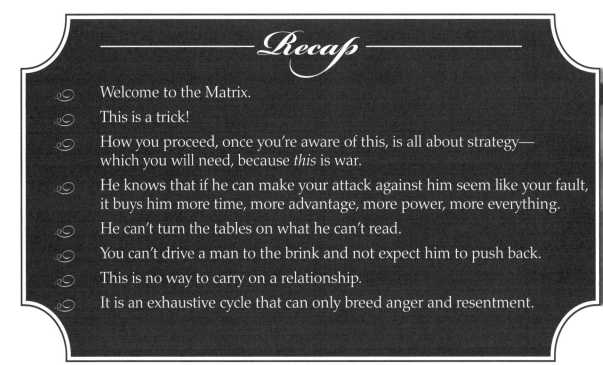

Recap

- Welcome to the Matrix.

- This is a trick!

- How you proceed, once you're aware of this, is all about strategy—which you will need, because *this* is war.

- He knows that if he can make your attack against him seem like your fault, it buys him more time, more advantage, more power, more everything.

- He can't turn the tables on what he can't read.

- You can't drive a man to the brink and not expect him to push back.

- This is no way to carry on a relationship.

- It is an exhaustive cycle that can only breed anger and resentment.

Chapter Forty-two

When It's Over, It's Over
(And Honey, It's Over!)

Once you realize that there are more cons than pros in your relationship and you make up your mind to end things and move on, it's imperative that you stick to your guns and not look back. Conversely, if your man has decided that he is through and has already left the relationship—either mentally, physically, or both—you must get out of the way. Let him go, no matter how much it hurts. We can get over the pain of a breakup, but to hang on to someone who doesn't want you can do much more damage to your psyche in the long run. Whatever the case, whether it's you wanting out or him, it's important to recognize the universal signs that the relationship has run its course and to respond accordingly.

The two of you have had your share of fights, maybe even broken up a few times and gotten back together, all with the intention of making the relationship work. He's lied to you and you've been lying to yourself. Too many things have happened for you to count, including the fact that you've had it with his flirting and/or cheating. Hell, maybe those are *your* issues and he's had enough of your shit! You're convinced that all men are dogs and have been tortured by thoughts of the other woman, whether she really exists or not. Whatever the scenario, you've reached your saturation point and can't stand any of it anymore. You've finally gathered your composure, vowing to never let him see you sweat, and have begun confiding in your real girlfriends. And even though he's been dishing out a good, old-fashioned mind fuck, you're determined to leave. Enough is enough. You're ready to take a good, hard look at yourself. This relationship is over. Dunzo! This man is out of your life. Doesn't it feel good? No? Well, don't worry. It will.

Your ability and willingness to move on is, in itself, very sexy. It takes a strong and confident woman to be able to step away, knowing better options will always lie ahead. If a part of you still wonders if there's some leftover love between you after all the two of you have been through, it's still important that you leave. The relationship as it stands now is undeniably unhealthy for you. Start a new life, one without him in it. Reunite with your girlfriends, if you haven't been spending quality time with them

Vixen Say What?
I don't want nobody that don't want me.

because of the relationship. Take some time to be with yourself and enjoy your own fabulousness. Get into a regimen that is completely different from the one you had when he was around. Go so far as changing your contact information. That's right; help him lose contact with you. It's the only way to allow yourself to move into a healthy space where you can find solid footing again, especially if the breakup was bad. It's very easy, and dangerous, to get caught up in the hope that a man who was bad for you will call again, reeling you back into the same negative relationship with its destructive patterns. Be strong. Cut the ties. If the split is an amicable and a friendly one, leave him a lifeline—an e-mail address or a voice mail number—but send a definite signal that things are changing, and changing fast.

Vixen Tip

Well, you've made it this far—too far to turn back now. However, it's okay to stop and regroup before moving forward. Now would be a good time to review all the previous Vixen Tips and start over again. Gather yourself and prepare for a relationship better suited to your needs, but first take a moment to reflect on what you've done right and what you've done wrong. Reconfigure your blueprint and rework your plan. Most important, learn, learn, learn. Every man has his season and every season has its reason. Find the purpose in your pain and make your mistakes make sense.

Take some time before dating again. Once you're ready to get out there, however, make sure you don't allow what went wrong in this relationship to scar you, thereby affecting your future relationships. During the time you spent alone, you should have examined all aspects of the relationship you just ended, using it as course training for the University of Life. Look at all the teachable moments. Every relationship is filled with them. There's something to be gained for your personal growth from every good and bad experience. It is only through encountering negatives and counterintentions that we can determine what our intentions are in terms of the things we do want in a relationship. It is good to have learned from your past courtships. Instead of being suspicious and untrusting in your new ones, choose to be alert and decisive, all the wiser for your rich emotional journey.

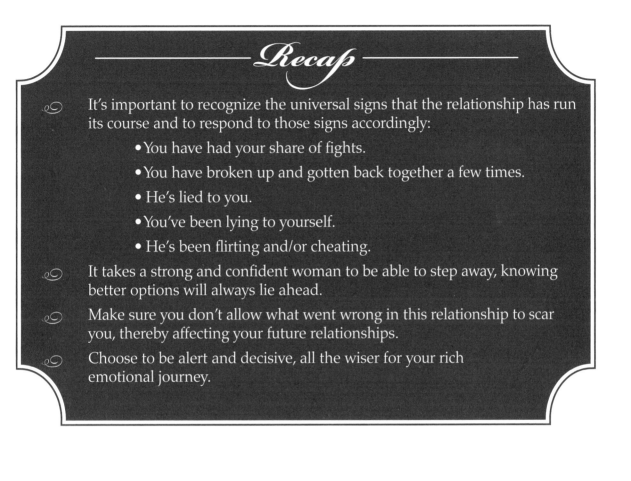

Recap

- It's important to recognize the universal signs that the relationship has run its course and to respond to those signs accordingly:

  - You have had your share of fights.
  - You have broken up and gotten back together a few times.
  - He's lied to you.
  - You've been lying to yourself.
  - He's been flirting and/or cheating.

- It takes a strong and confident woman to be able to step away, knowing better options will always lie ahead.

- Make sure you don't allow what went wrong in this relationship to scar you, thereby affecting your future relationships.

- Choose to be alert and decisive, all the wiser for your rich emotional journey.

Chapter Forty-three

Breaking Up

They say breaking up is hard to do, yet it's done every second of every day, all over the world. The truth is, breaking up isn't hard to do at all, not nearly as hard as it's made out to be. It's the getting through the aftermath of a breakup that can turn into rocket science. While there are amicable breakups, in most instances one partner walks away much more wounded than the other, surrounded by a fog of collateral hurt that seems as though it will never end. The key to the art of breaking up is to be able to deal with it and move on, hopefully with a friendship still intact. It's even possible to emerge with a newfound sense of independence, greater wisdom about what it takes to be in a relationship, and a more refined concept of what you want in a partner. Still, even as I write this, I know that breaking up is much easier said than done. In many cases, it feels downright impossible.

I've always been aware of my desire to be intensely in love. As a result, I love hard. I'm both capable of and willing to fall apart and completely lose all sense and reason when a relationship no longer works. It's not unusual after a breakup to find me on the bathroom floor with a bottle of Jack Daniel's and my mobile phone, drunk-dialing exes to see who would take me back, or, at the very least, patch the newly gaping wound in my heart.

What I know for sure is that when a woman has herself together—when she has met her own needs emotionally, physically, monetarily, and otherwise—she is better equipped to handle life's rough patches and unexpected losses, including the exits of boyfriends and husbands. Goals, principles, power, and all other subjects covered in previous and following chapters become essential to a woman's survival in times of peace and in times of emotional warfare. There is no way that a man who is worth anything will want a woman who is worthless to herself and cannot weather something as basic and common as a breakup.

> **Vixen Say What?**
> If you are not empowered enough to stand alone, how will you stand with a man?

Most of us are looking for the fairy tale, but what if the fairy tales have got it all wrong? What if we've been duped into believing that "happily ever after" and waking from eternal sleep can come only with the prince? After years of being fed such pap, it's no wonder so many of us have a hard time recovering, once the fairy-tale rug is yanked out from underneath us and we realize there's not going to be a "happily ever after" for our relationship. We end up growing bitter, carrying around baggage from one failed relationship to the next. Resurrecting whatever friendship the doomed romance was built on becomes an even more daunting task, if not impossible, as we can't bear the thought of being platonic with someone for whom we still carry a torch. How can you be his friend and hear him talk about other women, or (God forbid!) someone he becomes serious about, when you still have leftover love? Being unable to move forward in friendship with an ex is one of the most unfortunate aspects of a bad breakup. For one, we end up missing out on the opportunity to learn from the experience. Also, by discarding all the love we had in our heart for a person we once swore we would love forever, we end up throwing the proverbial baby out with the bathwater.

My philosophy has always been that the best revenge is success and happiness. It's also true that success and happiness are key components on the road to recovery when a breakup has shattered your faith and esteem. It may take you several months to get out of bed and back into the world again. Maybe you'll lie under the covers for days without showering. You might even go without showering for as long as a week. Your appetite may diminish and you find yourself crying every few minutes of every day for months. That crying, moping, and not eating then turns into severe depression, as you end up fighting with your psychologist over whether or not you should be given antidepressants and if it's really wise that you be left alone for large stretches of time. It feels as if you're in the middle of a never-ending catharsis, where the pain just seems to go on and on. We've all known this feeling at least once, even if you never went as far as seeing a shrink for your heartache. It's a horrible place to be emotionally but, as bad as it feels, there is still some good that can come from it. You learn a lot about yourself during these moments of intense, seemingly hopeless dejection. You learn your boundaries, your limits, and your thresholds for pain. You make decisions during these moments that determine whether you will ever visit such painful thresholds again. You examine your recently ended relationship and measure it against what you really want. Ideally, you grow a bit wiser, choosing to make positive steps forward instead of remaining stuck in the fog of failure.

You owe it to yourself to emerge from the ashes renewed, reinvigorated, determined to be even better than before. Experiencing the pain is a necessary part of growth, but it's just as important to take steps toward healing. The loss of a romantic relationship, in many ways, is comparable to a death. The grieving process takes place in stages, and an appropriate amount of time must be allotted for coping and healing. How much time is appropriate varies from one person to the next. Remaining stuck in a grieving state for too long can have a corrosive effect that's even harder to recover from. Fortunately, we are made of tough stuff. Women were built to be resilient, capable of weathering emotional storms and springing back stronger than ever. In my case, I don't always remember the first day I knew I was back on the road to wellness, but I do know the things that helped me get there. It may sound corny, but it was all the things your grandmother or junior high gym teacher told you to do when you were in grade school trying to recover from your first crush. Things like taking care of yourself and redirecting your attention to what really matters. Now that you're an adult, those same rules apply, with a more grown-up focus.

Vixen Tip

Here's how to start getting over him.

1. Pay very close attention to yourself. Focus on your physical and mental health and well-being. Now is the perfect time to be self-indulgent. Pamper yourself with spa treatments, if you can afford it, mani/pedis, and/or a wash-and-set (if not a whole new hairstyle). One of the best feelings in the world is having someone, even if it's just a masseuse or a stylist, take care of you when you are going through an emotional transition.

2. Focus on your needs and yours alone, with the exception of your child(ren).

3. Put your household on a regimen that ensures stability and keeps you focused. Get up at the same time every morning, if you can. Have breakfast according to schedule, get dressed in a consistent fashion, follow a constant pattern as you head out to work. Clean, vacuum, and pay bills on days that remain fixed. Attend classes at the gym that force you to arrive by a certain time. Take full baths nightly, even if you typically don't do so. The tranquility and soothing waters will help restore your peace of mind. By setting things in place that allow you to feel structured, you can, by degrees, begin to feel in control of your life again.

4. Take your life one hour at a time, knowing that if you think too much, too long, or too far in advance, you could lose concentration and fail.

5. Write your schedule down and follow it to the letter. No exceptions.

6. Keep busy with your housework and career.

7. Go out alone and enjoy being you—a single woman.

8. Go out with your friends and have fun. Laughter and a good time always help you remember the beautiful, vibrant person you really are.

It is crucial during the wake of a breakup to eat three square meals a day, even if you don't feel like it. Drink plenty of water. Sleep eight hours a night, if you can. Exercise for an hour each day.

Just taking a power walk through the neighborhood or the park will do. You must maintain your health, no matter what. Even though you're heartsick, if you can manage to keep your mind and body well, your heart will have no choice but to follow.

Eventually, once you adjust to being alone again, *single* will no longer be a dirty word. You shouldn't consider it a dirty word anyway, not if you have your own success by which to define yourself. Look at your life, taking the time to admire all the things you've done well. Find success in your children and all you have accomplished in your career up to this point. Give yourself credit for how far you've come. By focusing on the things you have, and not the losses you've incurred, you'll be able to shift your mind-set from negative to positive and continue on the path toward even more success.

Allow breakups to change you for the better. They should make you want more for yourself, if for no other reason than to show him that you can and will do better once he's gone! Be determined to not fall by the wayside, as if you actually needed him to be happy and successful. Fulfill all your dreams on your own and maybe, just maybe, one day you'll realize you no longer want or need a man around to validate who you are. Take some time out and revel in your oneness, realizing that, as long as you've got *you*, you'll never be alone.

Recap

- The key to the art of breaking up is to be able to deal with it and move on.
- When a woman has herself together, she is better equipped to handle life's rough patches and unexpected losses, including the exits of boyfriends and husbands.
- You learn a lot about yourself during these moments of intense, seemingly hopeless dejection.
- Remaining stuck in a grieving state for too long can have a corrosive effect that's even harder to recover from.
- Even though you're heartsick, if you can manage to keep your mind and body well, your heart will have no choice but to follow.
- Allow breakups to change you for the better.

Section 5

Maybe It's You

After serial failure you have to find the common denominator

in all your relationships which, of course, is you. So, here's a thought:

maybe it's not everyone else's fault or responsibility. Maybe the weight of

your relationship woes rests solely or mostly on you.

Chapter Forty-four

Getting Married vs. Being Married

You did everything right. You worked on you, pursued your dreams, and met many of your personal goals, becoming a strong, confident woman who knows her worth and place in the world. You mastered being single, but when you felt ready for a partner in life and love, you took all the appropriate steps to attract the right man for you. Once you found him, you fully engaged him. Things were wonderful. He was just as excited about you as you were about him. The relationship was established on solid footing where you both took the time to know each other, and it continued to positively evolve to the point where you both wanted it to continue to the next level, the big level—marriage. So you do it, and it's the happiest day of your life. His, too! This is all the bliss you've ever dreamed of and more.

Then, somehow, everything goes terribly wrong. The relationship unravels and the dreaded D-word—*Divorce*—has come into play. You're stricken. This was never supposed to be a part of the plan. So, what happened? Why are you suddenly faced with splitting up your lives, your property, and your children?

Looking back, most of us can remember when we got our first Barbie doll and how we couldn't take her home unless we had a Ken doll (or "action figure," for you men reading along) to go with her. Even if you bought Career Barbie, with her pink briefcase, pink business suit, and matching pumps, you still needed Ken. What's a Barbie without a Ken, after all? (Although Barbie famously split with Ken in 2004, only to reunite with him again. How very telling. Even doll couples have their ups and downs.) You never once imagined Barbie as a single, successful girl, happy to be single, even if just for a little while. There would be no alone time for her. Ken was coming home with Barbie whether he, or she, liked it or not! As if that wasn't sad enough, you played with them in your room for about twenty minutes, then married them off and moved the forced couple into their very first apartment, fashioned out of a shoe box. Better days were ahead for them, though. Thanks to your favorite aunt, they were able to move into their very own Malibu beach house and drive up in a pink convertible Corvette. By the end of this cute little charade, you were stuffing toilet paper down Barbie's dress, instantly impregnating her and, after a fifteen-minute gestation period, *whammo*—Ken Jr.! Ken and Barbie had it all, including a swinging marriage where all was apparently cool. They always stayed together, even after Barbie cheated on Ken with G.I. Joe and Ken got it on with Hawaiian Barbie, when your cousin brought her along during your sleepover.

Not very long after creating this soap opera, you stopped adding to it and started all over again. This time, you had them meet at a different place and changed their outfits. You even cut Barbie's hair. This was about the time you realized that your mother's curling iron wasn't as effective on plastic hair and that Barbie's new bangs would always stick straight up. With a marker, you changed the color of Ken's hair from blond to black, colored Barbie's lips with your red marker, and their courtship would start anew.

As children, we never saw the pretend marriage of our inanimate plastic dolls through anything beyond the birth of Ken Jr. and the swapping out of new clothes. All that mattered to us was the wedding, with its white flowing makeshift dress fashioned from toilet paper, and the immediate spoils thereafter. That's when the dolls had permission to dry-hump each other. Ken would mount Barbie and do the Malibu hustle. (Don't act like you didn't do this with your dolls. Every girl did.) Once the kids, the house, and the car came into play, we quickly grew bored and created a new scenario, a whole new life with different hair and clothes. We never once took the time to nurture the relationship between this anatomically absent pair of perfect people. That's what marriage meant to us. The rush-up to the wedding, a baby, and then…you got nothing. This stunted cycle has set millions of little girls everywhere on a pattern that has managed to replicate itself in their adult lives. We dream of getting our Ken, having the lovely wedding (and the dry-humping), and babies, but after that…we got nothing. We don't exactly know what to do.

For starters, here's an obvious difference between the two: your wedding lasts for just a few hours, but your marriage, if handled correctly, is meant to last a lifetime. There are all sorts of planning books for weddings you can buy at your neighborhood bookstore and Web sites dedicated to the preparing for your big day, but where are the books and Web sites dedicated to the arrangement of your entire marriage? Where's the big emphasis on keeping it alive? We've all heard of *Brides* magazine and *Modern Bride*. There's *Contemporary Bride* and *Southern Bride*, but where on earth is *Wife* magazine? How come no one bothers to focus on what it really takes and means to be a wife? Sure, there are things for wives and husbands—classes, courses, self-help books, an abundance of material. But that stuff gets nowhere near any of the attention as all things bride related. You usually have to hunt for the stuff about keeping a marriage together. There's nothing glamorous about it, so it's usually kept out of view until needed. Unfortunately, by then, it may be too late.

But, oh, the attention we give to the wedding! We imagine our gown and the flowers. We know who'll be sitting where, how tall the cake will be, and who's having the chicken versus who's having the beef. We plan our romantic getaway honeymoon, the lingerie, the room service. And once we return from that fabulous connubial inauguration…nothing. Crickets. You're looking at your man. Your man is looking at you. Now the actual being in the marriage, and all the reality that comes with it, has to begin. What to do, what to do?

Think about it. In all your imaginings of what it would be like to be married when you were that dreamy-eyed young girl, did you ever picture what it would be like to celebrate your fiftieth anniversary, and did the thought of it make you excited? No? What about the hard times that lie ahead? Did you ever daydream about those? What about mortgages, IRAs, life insurance, child-care costs, episiotomies, the inevitable moments of marital doldrums? Did you ever consider any of it? No? Then you should, because it's all very real, very common, and definitely not the stuff that fluffy, star-spangled fantasies are made of. It's a classic case of setting yourself up for failure. You know what you'll be wearing when you walk down the aisle, but what will you be wearing when your marriage is boggled by financial, family, and emotional woes? Who will have the beef and the chicken then? Who will be sitting where?

Marriage isn't about place settings and taffeta, exotic locales, and perfectly posed photographs. We plan for the fairy tale but not for the "happily ever after" and what it may or may not entail, because in those storybooks we read as little girls the last words were always just *happily ever after.* No explanation or plan was included. We didn't know *happily ever after* could mean "but sometimes really boring and not always liking each other." There was never any talk of the sacrifices and the pangs that might come in your marriage to Prince Charming. There was no solution offered to his death rattle of a snore or how to deal with his unbearable bitch of a mother, Queen Not-So-Charming. Nope, ladies, no one ever explained to us how in the hell we were supposed to be fucking happy for the rest of our goddamned lives!

As a result, you end up failing. You never stood a chance since all you were focused on was the dream.

So, you had a husband and now you don't. Or maybe you almost had a husband and now you're alone. All because we modeled our lives based on Barbies and Kens, Sleeping Beauties, Rapunzels, Cinderellas, and all the other absurd, fictitious characters who got fed potions, were shoved in ovens, kissed frogs, or had a man scale their five-hundred-foot-long hair to take them away to a life of implied-but-unexplained bliss. We bought the farm, girls. We fell for the okey-doke.

Guess what, though? We don't have to keep buying in to this silliness. Let's take this time together to journey back into your dating and marital past, through all those relationships that never were or almost made it, and let's find the one thing every single one of these relationships had in common—you. At some point, we have to stop blaming the men in our lives for our relationship failures and take a good, hard, excruciating look at our bad habits, our shortcomings, and the possible reasons for our being unable to ever stay on the road to "happily ever after," even if it somehow managed to find itself under our feet.

Vixen Tip

As a couple, take the time to conjure up a five-year plan. Whether before or after you are married, seek out books at your local bookstore about getting married like *1,001 Questions to Ask Before You Get Married* by Monica Mendez Leahy. These books pose pertinent questions for the both of you to answer and face about your relationship and future together. Make plans for your family's financial and educational goals. Don't forget about the emotional goals as well; decide what your household will be defined by and where you see yourselves and your family in the next five years. Facing the tough questions early in a relationship or marriage is the only way to know you two are ready for what lies ahead.

For married women, maybe the issue is that once you snagged your man and hauled his ass down the aisle, you gave up because your goal was realized. You, as Barbie, got your Ken. Mission accomplished. If you've always dreamed of *getting* married and not of *being* married once the honeymoon was over, perhaps you have no more substantial goals you've identified, outside of having a nice house and some children. You probably never considered how to keep your relationship fresh, exciting, and new. You got your man, after all, so why should you keep up appearances? You have no one to impress anymore, right? Wrong! Sorry to break it to you, honey, but marriage means that now you have a *legal obligation* to impress this man for the rest of your life, a *legal obligation* to have sex with him, a *legal obligation* to be a present and functioning partner. This is what you signed up for, and this is what he signed up for with you.

Some of us have let ourselves go after marriage and children, thinking the chase is over. As long as there is a man in your life, the chase will never be over. Just because you have captured a lion doesn't mean he's suddenly going to turn into a tabby. Your man is a hunter. He always has been and always will be. You have always been bait. Don't stop now. The same way you attracted him is the same way you'll have to engage him and keep him—forever. Sounds exhausting, doesn't it?—but whoever said marriage was going to be easy? It's not. It requires hard work, just like anything else that matters to you, like your education and career. Marriage is a long haul, so you'd better be up to the eternal chase, because that's how it goes, even once you've tied the knot. Chase, capture, release, and repeat—ad infinitum, or at least until death.

Change the way you think and speak about marriage. Instead of telling your man you want to *get* married, tell him you want to *be* married and *stay* married. Every day you wake up next to him, show him how badly you want to be married. Knock his socks off with your prowess and ability to please. Be that same sweet, understanding woman you were when you were dating. You know the one I'm talking about. The woman who didn't nag and push him away with major attitude because she was busy setting the stage for a wedding. The other woman, the one who's all hyped up about putting together a big bridal affair, she's scaring him to death, making him wonder if he may be getting hitched to someone who might turn out to be a total bitchy disaster. Calm down. Step away from the bridal magazines and www.theknot.com. Continue to enjoy dates with your man and wild nights of unbridled (yes, that pun is intended) passion. Be his whore, be his freak, his own personal slut, but most of all, be his wife. *Be* married.

Recap

- As children, we never saw the pretend marriage of our inanimate plastic dolls through anything beyond the birth of Ken Jr. and the swapping out of new clothes.

- This stunted cycle has set millions of little girls everywhere on a pattern that has managed to replicate itself in their adult lives.

- You usually have to hunt for the stuff about keeping a marriage together.

- We plan for the fairy tale, but not for the "happily ever after" and what it may or may not entail.

- You probably never considered how to keep your relationship fresh, exciting, and new.

- As long as there is a man in your life, the chase will never be over.

- Change the way you think and speak about marriage.

Chapter Forty-five

Relationship Stockholm

In August of 1973, a bank was robbed in Norrmalmstorg, Stockholm, Sweden. Gunmen held four people hostage for six days, from August 23 until August 28. During that intense six-day period, a very interesting thing happened: the hostages became emotionally attached to their captors. Despite the fact that they were being held against their will, in what could only be classified as a dangerous situation, when they were finally released, they defended and expressed loyalty to the robbers. It was a phenomenon that previously had never been given a name, but in the wake of the robbery, this kind of behavior came to be called Stockholm syndrome.

As it pertains to men, women, and romantic relationships, it is not uncommon for this same peculiar pattern of victims supporting victimizers to evolve. A woman whose esteem, confidence, and morale have been deeply eroded after years of being treated poorly in her relationships, may find herself sympathizing with, then overglorifying, unworthy suitors and mates. Let's say your man is a pig. He comes home after work and throws his things all over the place, letting them drop where they may. He then sits on his fat ass, dishing out orders with no concern as to how you're feeling or if you need any help around the house. You make excuses for him by saying, "He's tired. His job demands so much from him that there just isn't anything left for me. He loves me, though. I know it. I mean, at least he comes home instead of going to a bar to unwind." Was that an option? He's not *supposed* to go to a bar to unwind. You're in a relationship, after all. But I digress. Back to the pig. Let's say one day, he decides to put his clothes away instead of just letting them drop on the floor. Perhaps it's out of momentary guilt, or maybe his mother's coming to visit and he wants to make sure things are letter-perfect. Whatever the case, he picks up his boxers from the bathroom floor and helps with the dishes. All of sudden, according to you, he's the cat's meow. He helped around the house (once)! He's the best man ever!

That's classic Stockholm, ladies. Learn to spot it. Does it sound like you?

How about this scenario: after years of dating men who were obviously missing the chivalry gene, you've become supersmitten with the one guy who has ever opened a door for you or helped you in and out of your overcoat. After just one date, you've confidently declared this poor man a keeper; he might be "The One," when all he did was what any decent man should. You want to reward him with the abundance of your regard and affection because he did something that should be standard. Now comes your self-imposed pressure. You've put all your eggs into his basket because, the way you figure it, he must be the be-all and end-all, since he cared enough to treat you like a lady. Fast-forward to the one day he doesn't return your call exactly five minutes after you called him and you're jumping down his throat. He's mystified by your behavior and, like any bright man confronted with something so extreme, bolts. Bye-bye savior! He was "the good one," or so you thought. Back to the drawing board.

The reality is he may not have been the one. He might have just been a decent man who knew how to treat a woman. There are plenty of them out there, but because you've settled for substandard behavior for so long, you now see any act of kindness and consideration as a bonanza. Kindness and consideration from a man should be a given, not a rarity. It should be part of the standard equipment, like his mouth, face, and the brain inside his head.

Vixen Tip

Sometimes when a man meets a woman who knows how special and important she is, he calls her stuck-up. The type of man who does this is the type who knows he could never measure up to her expectations of any man, so he tries to tear her down and make her feel badly about herself. He, essentially, tries to bring her down to his level. The sad part is that after a while of hearing, "You're stuck-up," "You need to lower your standards," or "You think you're too good," you begin to fall into the trap and your self-esteem decreases as a result. Soon, you've lowered your standards and expectations and giving any ol' local joker the time of day and night. You begin to grow accustomed to your new, downtrodden way of being. Then when a guy comes along and treats you like the gem you once believed you were, you act as if you've been saved from death by sea. Here's the tip: always hold yourself in the highest esteem and never allow anyone to make you feel badly for it. Know that anyone who doesn't want you to put yourself on a pedestal is only projecting his or her insecurities onto you. Period.

It's important that you realize your value and expect to be treated like the treasure you are. If a man doesn't hold the door open for you as you enter and exit buildings together, make a mental note of it. If he snatches up the last slice of pizza without offering it to you first, take heed. If he never gives a compliment, beware. These are all cues to who he is. That doesn't mean that he's a good-for-nothing dog if he doesn't open your door, but it might indicate he's singularly focused…on himself. We let way too many things slide when it comes to how others, particularly potential mates, interact with us. Almost immediately, from the moment we meet them, men show us and tell us who they are. Are you paying attention?

Refuse to enable and support a man who doesn't deserve you. Don't accept a subpar relationship when there are so many good, encouraging, loving men out there seeking a worthy partner. Enough with the dating Stockholm, already. Aren't you tired of bad treatment? Good! The next time a date doesn't hold open the door for you, don't open the door to your heart, your mind, and your life. The next time the man you've claimed is The One throws his dirty clothes on the floor for you to pick up, take a good look at yourself in the mirror as you're bending down and ask yourself if this is truly a man who deserves all your love and care. If the answer is no—and it should be—demand satisfaction. If he can't give it, then you need to put him and his dirty clothes out the door.

It's time to send these disrespectful men on their way. A queen would never stand for this kind of behavior. You are queens, ladies. Act accordingly!

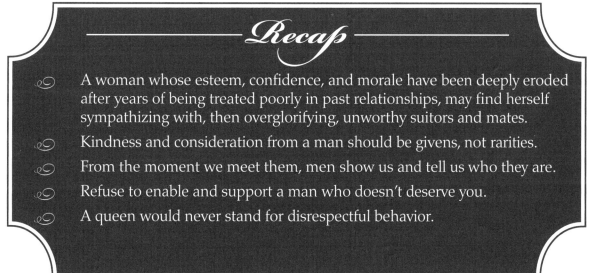

Recap

- A woman whose esteem, confidence, and morale have been deeply eroded after years of being treated poorly in past relationships, may find herself sympathizing with, then overglorifying, unworthy suitors and mates.
- Kindness and consideration from a man should be givens, not rarities.
- From the moment we meet them, men show us and tell us who they are.
- Refuse to enable and support a man who doesn't deserve you.
- A queen would never stand for disrespectful behavior.

Chapter Forty-six

Choosing the Wrong Man

Let's be brutally honest with ourselves. After all, that's what this book is about—brutal honesty. Most of us have done our fair share of dating and being in and out of relationships. Take the time to ponder the following for a moment: when you think of all the men you've dated, have you ever noticed a pattern? We often find ourselves striking out with men over and over because we are, essentially, dating the same man over and over. Most of us have a type, a certain sort of person we find most attractive. Some of us like them tall, dark, and handsome, and others are attracted to the short, bald, aging executive look. But types, like beauty, are much more than skin-deep.

There are plenty of psych courses and psychotherapists who can explain to you why you're attracted to what you're attracted to, just in case you're not sure. Perhaps it's the prototype of your very first love and you keep finding yourself mesmerized by men who remind you of him. Maybe men who smoke pipes are irresistibly sexy because you had a favorite uncle or grandfather who told you pleasant anecdotes when you were small and he smoked a pipe while doing so. Our attractions are often triggered by positive feelings and early impressions. Whatever the reason, when we're sparked by someone we find alluring, the instinctive response is to want to act upon it.

What we want, however, isn't necessarily what we need. How many times have we found ourselves with men who weren't good for us, but boy, did we love them! Like the stereotypical bad boy that no woman seems to be able to resist. He's rude; disobeys state, federal, and personal laws; pees in the potted plants at the finest hotels; and is always getting picked up by the cops for nonpayment of child support. Inevitably, when he's picked up, he's also got an unregistered weapon on his person somewhere. But damn it, he's so great in bed and really makes us feel alive!

Then there's the nomad. Like a snail, all he owns is on his back. He lives in his best friend's garage, and though he may work hard, he has very little to show for it. He lives in squalor, but he always has time and money to waste on romantic field trips to his favorite eatery on the beach or a Las Vegas casino. How can you not love this guy? He's such an adventurer!

And let's not forget Mr. Nice Guy. He's so nice, he's a pushover, not just for you but for everyone in his life. You're attracted to his kindness at first, until you realize he's got little or no fight in him. As your respect for him evaporates, you find yourself being rude to him and discounting him as a man.

These men aren't exactly what you need, yet you somehow keep finding yourself with one of them, time after time. The problem is that you're dating according to what's best for you in the short term and not according to what's best for you in the long run. When you take short-term gambles like this, the risk can be very, very high. There's the potential for you to lose it all. Even when that happens, when it all falls apart, you still tend to blame the man. He did *this*, you gripe, or he didn't do *that*. Perhaps he was never the problem. You can't blame someone for being themselves, but you can blame yourself for dating them. We've all heard that saying about the definition of *crazy* being someone who does the same thing over and over again but expects a different result each time. If you never had a name for what you were doing, now you know, which means that now it's time to stop acting crazy.

Go through your phone book and find the names of the men you have dated or have been interested in. Write a brief description of each next to his name, just a word or two, or the reason why you were attracted to them. From A to Z, be honest with yourself and look for a pattern. Whatever that pattern is, steer clear of it. That is the pattern of your past, empty, or failed relationships.

Let's start, ladies, by listening to these men when they tell us who they are and what they want. I can't emphasize that enough, which is why I've done so throughout this book. Men tell you what they want. A man who says "I can't stand kids" probably means it. You can't trick a man like this into fathering a child. You're only going to end up with a baby you're raising alone *and* a deadbeat dad. A man who says "I don't know if I'll ever get married" isn't jockeying for you to convince him of all the merits of matrimony. He just made a major statement: "I'm not interested in permanent commitment." Did you hear him? And if you did, and you know you want to be married, why are you still hanging around?

How many times have we dated men who were emotionally unavailable, then complained when they didn't show concern for the relationship? What about the times we dated men who were verbally abusive, then cried when they yelled obscenities at us? Yes, he's a jerk for yelling at you, but you signed up for this. Unless, that is, he's holding you hostage, in which case, you should see the prior chapter. If he's literally holding you hostage and has you locked in a basement, try to find a phone and call the police. No matter what, this man is not good for you. You know it. It's time we started acting with our heads and not from that visceral place where we remember sweet pipe tobacco and muscled limbs from the past that evoke wistful feelings. We should use practical thinking, planning, and assessment to determine who is and isn't suitable for us. Listen to your intuition. We always know when something's not right. You were given that intuition for a reason. Let it be your guide, a sort of internal GPS system, if you will. If something is telling you to not make that right turn and go out with that bad boy, don't do it. Go left. Get away from there. You'll thank yourself for it in the end.

Recap

- Most of us have a type, a certain sort of person we find most attractive.

- Our attractions are often triggered by positive feelings and early impressions.

- When you take short-term gambles, the risk can be very, very high.

- If something is telling you to not make that right turn and go out with that bad boy, don't do it.

Chapter Forty-seven

Prudishness

Somewhere along the way someone told you that men don't marry loose women. This often repeated refrain came from women and men alike, usually elders, as a warning to you lest you get sexually out of hand. So you believed them, and all your life you've been the good girl, the one who has never (or says she has never) given a guy head in a bathroom stall or tried your hand at a ménage à trois. You don't kiss on the first date and you most certainly won't have sex until marriage—so you say. You play this little game for as long as you can. Besides, it actually works in your favor at times, because men love the thrill of the chase. True to what the elders said, you were able to snag a fiancé because you chose not to be loose. You got your ring—a perfect 2.7-carat number from Tiffany—and you're so happy, thrilled beyond words. Your joy is so big, so uncontainable, you decide to break your own rule and let him put his hand, face, and throbbing manhood into the cookie jar, a reward to him for doing the right thing by taking steps to make you his bride.

Your good-girl attitude lives on, even in your secure relationship. You never stray from the basics: missionary, missionary, and more missionary, with fellatio saved for holidays and special occasions. That's the span of your repertoire. Doggie-style might get thrown in, but you don't care for it and don't hesitate to make your dislike known. You truly believe that certain sexual acts and uninhibited behavior are for those *other* girls, the strumpets and strippers of the world. In your mind, no self-respecting wife would ever take a good pounding in the ass or swallow a load of jizz, even if it *is* your husband's. (By the way, the dirty talk is just for you prudish girls reading along.) I'm sorry to be the one to tell you this, ladies, but everyone has fantasies, both men and women alike. When it comes down to a man's fantasies, very few of them include a woman who won't go down on him in a movie theater!

Sure, there are cute little fantasies where you're the prudish librarian with your hair pinned back, your shirt buttoned all the way to the collar, your glasses hanging off your nose, and a calf-length skirt rustling against your opaque panty hose. At first, you may come off as very shy, denying him your body, squirming and shrieking in resistance. At some point in this fantasy struggle, however, you have to give in, let your hair down, rip off that buttoned shirt, and fling off those glasses, discarding that librarian façade and giving your hunter what he's been stalking you for. Why? Because no one wants to fuck a librarian, honey, not even in a fantasy.

Vixen Tip

Gather your girlfriends for an impromptu "girl's night in," and without warning ask them what they think about anal sex or about putting a stripper pole in your bedroom. Hell, pull out your new sex toy and ask them if they've ever heard of the Masturbator 7000, then ask who's had the most orgasms during one session with their mates or by themselves. Go ahead, break the ice, and you'll see you're not alone and that for most women, prudishness is an act because we've been taught to be ashamed of our bodies and sexuality, to never discuss those sorts of things. If we can't talk about them, how are we to do them? Use your girlfriends as sounding boards and allow them to help you with their experiences, and vice versa. Even though prudes—I mean, birds of a feather—tend to flock together, you're bound to have one or two friends who are the adventurous type. Think of yourself as Charlotte from *Sex and the City* asking a Samantha-esque buddy for advice. What she suggests might alarm you at first, but we can all stand to broaden our horizons a little. You might even have fun doing it!

Men get tired hearing the words *no* and *I don't do that.* A man wants to be able to indulge in his fantasies with his woman. In the long run, it saves him lots of time, money, and secrecy if he can just get the goods at home. There would be no need to visit the local strip club if he has his very own stripper at home. He certainly won't need to sneak away with that younger, friskier woman if he's got a tigress waiting in bed for him at home. Put on some music, the kind they play at the strip club that encourages lots of bumping and grinding. Get decked out in provocative lingerie. Sit him down in a chair and do a striptease for him, complete with a lap dance and bending your ass over in his face, backing that thing up all the way to his mouth. Now is not the time to be shy. If these are things you can't imagine yourself doing, then you're in big trouble. A man wants and needs a woman who is willing to excite him. If you're not willing to do so, then perhaps you're not ready to be in a whole and healthy relationship.

So what's your point, Vixen? you ask. My point? You mean you still haven't gotten it yet? Okay, let me make it simpler: that good-girl shit can hold his attention for only a little while. It is, admittedly, cute in the beginning. A man loves feeling as though he's protecting someone sweet and innocent. Inevitably, however, his nature will rise, as the elders like to say, and whether your man is a kindergarten teacher or a preacher, you can bet there's a freak living inside of him. If that freak were being fed at home on a regular basis, there would be a lot less Jimmy Swaggarts, Bill Clintons, and Eliot Spitzers in the world and a lot more satisfied, faithful, and honest husbands.

> **Vixen Say What?**
> There are two types of men: Those who marry their ultimate lover and those who will cheat on their wives with their ultimate lover. Which would you prefer your man to be?

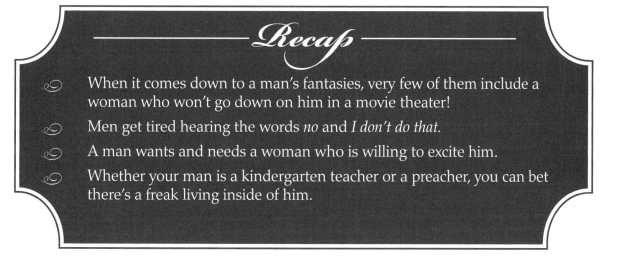

Recap

- When it comes down to a man's fantasies, very few of them include a woman who won't go down on him in a movie theater!

- Men get tired hearing the words *no* and *I don't do that.*

- A man wants and needs a woman who is willing to excite him.

- Whether your man is a kindergarten teacher or a preacher, you can bet there's a freak living inside of him.

Chapter Forty-eight

Insecurities

All right, ladies, how many of you have been guilty of being insecure? Raise your hand. Wow, that's a lot of hands I see raised! Of course, it's natural to be unsure of things, but what's not natural is to panic, accuse, freak out, and become downright hostile, all because you're afraid or don't know how to trust. If you're not sure of yourself, how is your man supposed to be sure about you? We all have insecurities, but for some of us these insecurities sometimes turn into man-eating beasts that can swallow up our lives and our men, and ruin any attempts we make at having healthy relationships.

A woman is least attractive when she is insecure. Ironically, insecurity has nothing to do with looks, as there are plenty of women out there whom you might not consider as attractive as you but are leaps and bounds ahead on the confidence scale. Confidence is a state of mind and affects the way you carry yourself, from your posture to the way you make eye contact and interact with others. How many times have you seen the scenario where a beautiful woman is abandoned by her man for someone others might call average? The abandoned, heartbroken woman can't figure it out. She's got it all, after all. Apparently, however, she doesn't. Her man was attracted to the strength and vivacity exuded by the other woman. She was sure of herself and he found that irresistible. Men always do. They may not even be aware of what's attracting them to you, but if you are filled with self-assurance, it's like flipping on a thousand-watt light switch when you enter a room. All eyes are on you.

Conversely, a lack of confidence in yourself or your mate is a surefire way to run him off. If you're constantly complaining about your back fat and the mole—sorry, the "beauty mark"—on the side of your neck, then all he's going to see when he looks at you is a giant mole with back fat! We all have things we believe are imperfections, but nothing in this world is imperfect if you believe in God. How can anything be ugly if He made it? If you don't believe in God, then the least you can do is believe in yourself. You are imperfect only if you say and believe you are. Words have power. There's no quicker way to bring something to pass than talking it up over and over again. As I've emphasized through this book, people treat you how you let them, and they also pay close attention to the way you treat yourself.

There are also those internal worries that, when given power, can grind your relationship into the dirt. If you've experienced infidelity in the past, odds are you're expecting to experience it again and will project that expectation onto your new relationship. Every time your man runs to the store for a loaf of bread and a gallon of milk, you'll swear he's off cavorting with your saucy next-door neighbor. Heaven help him if he's a few minutes late returning from work. He must be having an affair! Forget the fact that there was an accident on the freeway and he had to stop for gas on the way home. *Liar!* you insist, even though he can prove there was an accident because they're showing it on the news. *Bullshit!* you cry. That was just a convenient cover for his infidelity!

Vixen Tip

Ask the people closest to you what they would say your insecurities are. Take note and be aware of the times these insecurities surface. The most surefire way to not show your shortcomings is to learn to be silent and still at a time you feel like attacking your spouse. Give yourself a time-out, the same you would a child, then revisit the issues when you have calmed down and found your rationale. And, as always, venting with a girlfriend is superhelpful. Some issues actually exist and others are created in your head. Be sure to decipher the difference.

Your man just might be cheating. It's always possible. Chances are, however, he's not. We all have a tendency to allow leftover issues from bad relationships to spill into new ones. Do you have emotional insecurities in your current relationship based on the dirty deeds of past lovers? Perhaps your dad cheated on your mom before the big divorce, and you bore witness to it. Or—and how's this for a spin—maybe *you're* the one who's been unfaithful, either in this relationship or ones in the past, and your conscience is eating away at you. That's what happens with cheaters. The guilt tears at them, and they're constantly accusing others, all the while looking over their shoulders because they karmically expect to have dirt done to them as payback for them doing so much dirt.

If you find that you still haven't dealt with all the negative issues from your past, take the time to tackle them head-on before you jump into another relationship. Address why you fear being abandoned or cheated on, or have trust issues. More important, learn to trust yourself. Talk to a therapist, if need be. There's nothing wrong with seeking their help. If you're not comfortable with seeing a therapist, discuss your fears with close friends, ones who are encouraging and supportive, not those who will continue to feed your fears.

Whatever you do, don't let your insecurity fester. Left unchecked, it will only grow and, potentially, reach the point to where you become completely self-destructive in relationships, sabotaging all opportunities for finding happiness and love. Seek ways to build up your confidence. Start small, by congratulating yourself for what might seem like even the most insignificant accomplishments, like making it all the way through a workout at the gym, putting together your first dinner party for friends, or starting—and finishing—a celebrated book you've always wanted to read but felt intimidated by because of its size or lofty subject matter. Become strong in you and your knowledge of yourself. Then, and only then, can you move forward to a rich and fulfilling relationship.

Recap

- Insecurities sometimes turn into man-eating beasts that can swallow up our lives and our men, and ruin any attempts we make at having healthy relationships.

- If you are filled with self-assurance, it's like flipping on a thousand-watt light switch when you enter a room.

- A lack of confidence in yourself or your mate is a surefire way to run him off.

- Address why you fear being abandoned or cheated on, or have trust issues.

- Seek ways to build up your confidence.

Chapter Forty-nine

Misery Loves Company

Are you happy? Are you *ever* happy? Do you find yourself constantly running men off? When you do have a man, you nag him nonstop, to the point where he's constantly bolting out the door, away from you. You're an emotional wreck who never seems to be satisfied. You find fault in anything and everything. If man repellent came in a spray can, your face would be on it. What the hell is wrong with you?

No man wants to be bothered with us when we are like this, vexed and utterly unhappy, spewing and spreading venom through our accusations and actions. Being in that kind of environment can be toxic and debilitating. All the negativity becomes airborne, like a pathogenic disease, infecting everyone who enters your space, even those to whom your wrath is not directed. Everyone suffers, even the innocent. Still, you can't bear to be alone because you secretly can't stand yourself. You wish you could break out of your skin and be someone different, someone better, someone who doesn't complain at every turn. Instead, you remained trapped in this toxic state, afraid to change. Unable to escape your self-loathing, you choose instead to drag your mate into it. After all, misery loves company.

How long do you expect him to stay? How many men do you have to run off before you realize that you're not healthy relationship (or even healthy friendship) material? Sometimes it's difficult for us to see ourselves and even more difficult for us to believe the opinions of others as it pertains to our behavior. Stop. Take a moment before flying off the handle and simply listen. Do a ten count before you launch into your usual full-blown freak-out. Learn to master your emotions and don't let them master you.

If this is you, decide to try something different. The negative approach is obviously not working. Listen to the feedback your friends and loved ones give you about how miserable you are. Instead of taking offense to your man's observations, or those of your friends', use the criticism as an opportunity to evolve. When someone shows you who they are, you should believe them. It's also true that when you show someone who you are and they show it back to you, you should believe that, too!

Vixen Tip

Sometimes it's helpful to seek the assistance of a professional third party. People who are unhappy within themselves are constantly projecting their unhappiness onto others. If you are this sort of person, it will be increasingly difficult to find happiness or to keep a happy mate. Sometimes, girlfriends and writing your grievances in a letter just aren't enough. Sometimes, your issues are so deeply rooted that only a trained professional can help you. Consider all the options and roads to happiness if you wish to have a pleasant and productive relationship.

If you're the type of woman who can't get happy, be happy, and stay happy, there's only one result you can expect, and it's not going to be a good one. You're going to infect your man with your negative spirit and corrode your relationship. More than likely, he will become just as miserable as you and remain in the relationship because he doesn't know how to leave, and you will be two of the most miserable, lonely folks alive…together. You will be people repellents. Who would want to be in a space where such unhappiness exists? Who would want to invite the two of you over? If he doesn't stay, he will leave with a dust cloud behind him, so desperate will he be to get away from you before you destroy what's left of his once positive outlook. Either way, you'll be miserable. There's no reason to ever choose to live this way. There are options, including medical ones, if your anger, depression, and resentment are at levels that even you don't know how to manage.

Happiness is relative. What makes you happy may annoy the next person, or it may not even register on his or her radar. It is not something you can define or put in a can. It is a state of mind brought on by things that matter to the individual. Most importantly, happiness is a decision. If you're trying to find happiness by comparing your life to the lives of others, you're destined to be disappointed, for that kind of happiness is both elusive and fleeting. If you're basing it on the life you used to live or the life you wish you were living, you'll never be happy or satisfied. Until you find your square, that place in the world that defines who you are and what brings you peace and joy, you'll always feel displaced and misplaced. You'll always be off put and off-putting. And an off-putting woman, more times than not, will find herself without a quality man or friends.

Make the choice to be happy. That doesn't mean you have to explode with joy at every turn and never be angry. What it does mean is that you choose to see the good in life versus always hunting out the bad. When you shine your light on the world instead of aiming your laser beam of destruction, more light shines your way. Be happiness. Happiness, in turn, will surely be with you.

Recap

- No man wants to be bothered with us when we are utterly unhappy.

- Sometimes it's difficult for us to see ourselves and even more difficult for us to believe the opinions of others as it pertains to our behavior.

- Use criticism as an opportunity to evolve.

- There are options, including medical ones, if your anger, depression, and resentment are at levels which even you don't know how to manage.

- Choose to see the good in life versus always hunting out the bad.

Chapter Fifty

Settling

I hate to break this to you, ladies, but odds are you'll never find that perfect man who does everything right all the time and comes with absolutely no baggage. He just doesn't exist. Fortunately, or unfortunately, the same holds true when it comes to us women. We don't do everything right and we certainly don't come baggage free, so we have no right to demand that of a man. We've been convinced, however, that if we choose a mate who is not letter-perfect in every way, we are somehow *settling,* the implication of that word being that we are taking on something that is substandard or lacking in quality. The harsh truth is, we're *all* settling. Even when you find the right guy for you, you're settling in some way. The irony is that, once upon a time, *settle* wasn't a negative word, especially when paired with the word *down. Settle down,* per *Merriam-Webster's Dictionary,* means "to take up an ordered and stable life." That is a good thing. Somewhere along the way, however, *settling* took on a negative connotation and it doesn't have to be so. There's still a way for you to turn it into a positive, where it does, in fact, mean you are taking up "an ordered and stable life."

Let's say there are ten things on your list describing the perfect man. The chances of you finding a man embodying all ten items are extremely slim. There will be at least one request he cannot fulfill. He *is* human, after all. Would you throw this nearly perfect man away because he comes up short in one area? Do you hone in on that one missing thing, or do you focus on the nine areas where he hits a home run? I truly hope none of you chose the former. If you're smart, you're going to snatch this man up and make him yours, because since you started this dating thing, you've probably been mostly bumping into men who could barely meet one of your requirements, much less nine! If you choose Mr. Nine Out Of Ten, guess what? You have just settled! Does it feel like a bad thing? It shouldn't. Look at all the things you're getting versus the ones you're not. If you find you're still focusing on that one thing he doesn't have, go back to the previous chapter and read it again, because you're truly a miserable person and wouldn't know what to do with a good man, even if you found one who had all ten things from your list!

Now that you've accepted the fact that you will be settling one way or another, the next step is to decide just how much you are willing to settle for. No man is really better or worse than the next, just different. Everyone comes with baggage and shit that you'll have to put up with. It's your job to determine what kind of baggage and how much shit you're willing to handle.

Interestingly, we are more inclined to settle for fewer things on our list as we grow older. When we are young, in our twenties and thirties, we tend to feel immortal, as though we've got all the time in the world. We pass up perfectly good men—ones who meet eight or nine of the requirements on our list—because we insist on getting ten out of ten. As the years go by and no one hits the mark, not only do we find fewer men with eight or nine of our requirements, it becomes hard to find men with only three or four. Pretty soon, you find you're ecstatic to snag a guy who hits two out of ten. Now you're *really* settling, in the negative sense. Perhaps you shouldn't have been so unreasonably picky before.

Good men are always coming our way. Whether you notice them or not depends on whether you are a woman with a positive outlook or a negative one. A positive woman will see the good things a man has to offer. A negative woman will focus only on what is missing. Expect the best for yourself, but don't set the bar so high that no man could ever reach it.

Settling is a way of life and love that we should all embrace. When you find the man who you feel is right for you, rejoice in the fact that you are, indeed, ready to settle into a rich and fulfilling life with him. If he meets more than half the things on your list, you've done well. If you've got nine out of ten, then, girlfriend, you've truly found yourself a winner! Whatever the case, love your man and cherish him. You get what you give, and if you give your all to the man you've chosen to make your life with, you'll get even more in return. When someone asks if you feel like you've settled, you'll smile with pride and say, "Yes, and I'm so glad I did!"

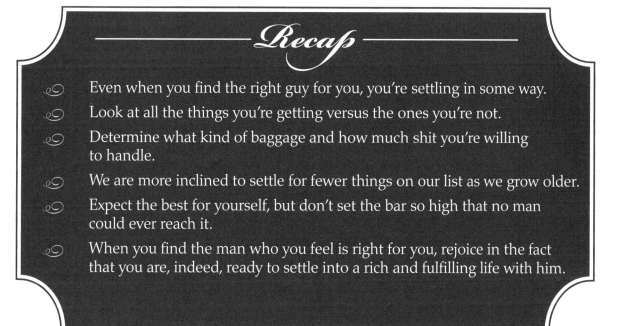

Recap

- Even when you find the right guy for you, you're settling in some way.

- Look at all the things you're getting versus the ones you're not.

- Determine what kind of baggage and how much shit you're willing to handle.

- We are more inclined to settle for fewer things on our list as we grow older.

- Expect the best for yourself, but don't set the bar so high that no man could ever reach it.

- When you find the man who you feel is right for you, rejoice in the fact that you are, indeed, ready to settle into a rich and fulfilling life with him.

Epilogue

Fuck! Shit! Motherfucker! Cunt! Dick!
(And Other Liberating Outbursts)

Ah, we made it! Thanks for hanging in there with me for all fifty chapters! It took four years, a change of publisher, several changes of heart, what seems to have been hundreds of failed relationships, and, finally, one amazing love to make this manual possible. No, it's not that my life has all of a sudden worked out perfectly because some guy waltzed into it and patched all my punctures. But what happened is that I have learned, I have lived, and now, finally, I have loved. The right way. The healthy way. All of this, as covered in my two previous books, before the age of thirty! One day I decided what I wanted for my life. Not just for the next five years, but forever. I decided what I wanted for my children and for theirs. I decided what my family would be defined by and, as its matriarch, what I wanted to pass on to this generation, those to follow, and even those who were here before me. And what's my message? What was it all for?

No person's life and ideals are completely concordant with another's. This, my friends, is the beauty of expression. I am sure there are a few things in *The Vixen Manual* that are not for you (as if!), just as I am sure there are a few things you'll take with you and cherish (or use to torture your husband in bed). In either case, I'm glad you've been with me from the beginning of this book to its end.

My sincere hope is that I've managed to make you laugh, examine your own life (and labia), promoted a bit of growth, made you say naughty words out loud (since I've already forced you to say them in your head because they're part of the book) and, hopefully, helped you find your inner temptress, or—dare I say it?—Vixen! Be spirited, be wisecracking, be incorrigible. Be insatiable. Dare to be different or dare to conform. It makes no difference. Be whatever you really want to be, but whatever you choose, be the best that you can. We women are multifaceted, and we deserve the space and opportunity to explore our personalities and sexuality without being made to feel ashamed of either. I intend *The Vixen Manual* to cause a flurry of conversations between your girlfriends, your lover, and you. Let's open our lives to others and talk about all those taboo subjects that outside influences have convinced us would make us grow hair on our chests or keep us from ever being respected, loved, or wanted—just a gaggle of cackling hens, old maids, and spinsters.

That is not to say that all old-fashioned notions are incorrect or ineffective. Many times they are quite to the contrary, and for this reason, I think it's important to seek advice and learn from women who have come before us. From Baby Boomers to Generation X, from the MTV Generation to what may now be described as Generation Disconnect, so much has changed. In our evolution as women, and as a culture, we have made enormous forward strides and then unfathomable leaps backward. For some of us, we stop and take a look around and realize our grandmothers were right and that there's a way to take a smidgen of that old-school conservatism and couple it with our new-school liberation to create a new and improved women's movement. The kind of movement where we actually move!

 In the end, no matter what you may say or think about me, know this—I live for movement, self-discovery, and advancement. I am roused by the opportunity to inspire change and by the vocalization of my needs and desires, fantasies and inhibitions. I trust *The Vixen Manual* has provided these in some aspect of your life; goodness knows it has in mine. Still, I don't have all the answers, and at no point in the manual have I professed to. Something tells me that as I get older, there'll be more than a few revisions made. Turning thirty has been good to me, but just you wait until I hit my prime and let it be no surprise when this book meets its match by way of its maker.

All the best of life and love,

Karrine